BALUTA

Daya Pawar

Translated from the Marathi by
Jerry Pinto

SPEAKING
TIGER

SPEAKING TIGER PUBLISHING PVT. LTD
4381/4, Ansari Road, Daryaganj
New Delhi 110002

Copyright © Pradnya Daya Pawar 2015
This translation copyright © Jerry Pinto 2015

First published in Marathi by Granthali Prakashan 1978
First published in English by Speaking Tiger 2015

ISBN: 978-93-85288-46-3
eISBN: 978-93-85288-21-0

10 9 8 7 6 5 4 3 2 1

The moral right of the author has been asserted.

Typeset in Adobe Garamond Pro by SÜRYA, New Delhi
Printed at Sanat Printers, Kundli

All rights reserved.
No part of this publication may be reproduced,
transmitted, or stored in a retrieval system, in any form or by any
means, electronic, mechanical, photocopying, recording or
otherwise, without the prior permission of the publisher.

This book is sold subject to the condition that it shall not,
by way of trade or otherwise, be lent, resold, hired out,
or otherwise circulated, without the publisher's prior consent,
in any form of binding or cover other than
that in which it is published.

Daya Pawar (Dagdu Maruti Pawar) was born in
Dhamangaon, Maharashtra in 1935. Primarily a poet,
he published his first poem in the Dalit literary journal
Asmitadarsh in 1967.
His first collection of poems, *Kondvada*, appeared in 1974
and won the Maharashtra Government Award for literature.
In 1979, he won the award for the second time for *Baluta*,
his most celebrated work, which had appeared the previous
year. Apart from these, his published works include *Chavdi*
and *Dalit Jaanivaa*—both collections of his essays on
Dalit literature, culture and politics—and *Vittal*,
a book of short stories. He also wrote the screenplay
for Jabbar Patel's film *Dr. Ambedkar*.

Daya Pawar received the Government of India's
Padma Shri Award in 1990.
He died in New Delhi in 1996.

Jerry Pinto is a writer and translator based in Mumbai.
He is the author of the novel *Em and the Big Hoom* (winner
of the Hindu Literary Prize and the Crossword Book
Award for Fiction) and the non-fiction book *Helen:
The Life and Times of an H-Bomb* (winner of the National
Award for the Best Book on Cinema). His other works
include a book of poems, *Asylum* and *Cobalt Blue*, the
English translation of Sachin Kundalkar's Marathi novel
of the same title, which was shortlisted for the
Crossword Book Award for
Indian Language Translation.

PREFACE

BALUTA WAS THE first Dalit autobiography to be published in Marathi. It was released on 25 December 1978. The publisher, Granthali, had just begun publishing important books that did not fit into the fixed profiles of other publishers. It was started by a group of like-minded people headed by Dinkar Gangal who gave up his job in *Maharashtra Times* to devote himself full time to this work. Granthali was not just a publisher, but a readers' movement. Thus it was in the fitness of things that they should have spearheaded the publication of Dalit autobiographies. Two years later, in 1980, again on 25 December, which they celebrated every year as Readers' Day, Laxman Mane's *Upara* was released. Other publishers then stepped into the space created by Granthali. Shrividya Prakashan published Laxman Gaekwad's *Uchlya* in 1987. Just before that, in 1984, Usha Wagh had published the first Dalit woman's autobiography, Shantabai Krushnaji Kamble's *Majya Jalmachi Chittarkatha* (My story in bits and pieces).

It is difficult to describe the shock with which the middle-class reader received *Baluta*. Speaking of it personally, this was the first time I had been exposed to a life of such squalor, deprivation and cruel discrimination. As a middle-class woman who had had a privileged upbringing, it was a rude awakening to the realities of our pernicious caste system.

I must digress here to relate an anecdote. We were at a place of holy pilgrimage where the priests were bugging us to pay for special prayers. 'What is your gotra?' asked one persistent priest. My father turned round and said, 'See, I'm a Mahar. Do Mahars have gotras?' I narrate this incident to underline the fact that we—as 'liberal' Brahmins—were brought up to deny caste. And yet there was deep ignorance. When my father called himself a Mahar, perhaps he knew what he was talking about. I didn't. I was ignorant of all the humiliating specificities of what being a Mahar meant. I didn't know that Mahars skinned dead cattle and ate their flesh. I didn't know that Mahar children were made to sit apart from the upper castes in village schools. I didn't know that their touch was supposed to pollute water, rendering it undrinkable for the upper castes. *Baluta* opened this other world to me without mincing words, in direct, simple language, making escape impossible. I had to look at Daya Pawar's world as part of the reality of being Indian. It filled me with shame. I felt complicit in the creation of these harrowing lives. I felt frustrated because there appeared to be nothing I could do about it.

Then I met and got to know Daya Pawar. He was a gentle man, a reticent man, one who listened more than he spoke. I knew from my reading of *Baluta*, from its extraordinary clarity and self-implication, that he carried a freight-load of anger and grief inside him. He seemed always to stand on the line that divided those who could claim privilege as their birth-right and those whose only birth-right was to submit to the location in which Hindu society had placed them. The most searing part of his story is the work he is appointed to do despite his school and college education.

Education is a double-edged sword. It leads you to expect equality with your fellow students. That equality is not granted to you; but having college education distances you from your own people. Again and again Daya Pawar refers to how reading books gave him a glimpse of life that was not his or his people's. And yet, when I met Daya Pawar as an established writer, I found a way out of the suffocating frustration I had been feeling from the time I read *Baluta*. It was reading that had given him a hold on the Marathi language, on the construction of sentences, on the creation of a narrative. Although he has confessed that the release of *Baluta* filled him with dread, because his own life, including his beloved mother's, was out there, for all to read, there was the other side to consider. Reading books brought him the dignity and fame that had been denied him as a member of the Mahar caste. He and others who heeded Dr Babasaheb Ambedkar's three-fold exhortation to his followers to educate, unite and agitate, was a partial way out of the trap that Hinduism had set for them. A complete escape was offered by Mahars abandoning Hinduism altogether and converting to Buddhism. I like to think that writing his life, however painful the process obviously was, released Daya Pawar to some extent from his past.

I do not know whether today's reader will feel the same sense of shock that I did on first reading *Baluta*. Atrocities against Dalits are reported every day in newspapers. Has that blunted our sensibilities? Daya Pawar felt the need to create an alter ego to whom he was going to relate his story. It was a defence mechanism. But already in 1980, 1984 and 1987, emboldened by the space he had opened up for them, the other Dalits who wrote their autobiographies told their stories directly, to our faces.

Two of the others, *Upara* and *Uchlya* were translated into English almost immediately after publication. For some reason *Baluta*, which was the first of them all, was not. It is with deep gratitude and admiration that I have read the present translation by Jerry Pinto. It cannot have been an easy task, but Pinto has done it with great meticulousness and close attention to Daya Pawar's voice. Daya Pawar died in December 1996. He would have been very happy to read this translation.

SHANTA GOKHALE
Mumbai
January 2015

TRANSLATOR'S INTRODUCTION
DAYA PAWAR AND ME

I NEVER MET Daya Pawar but we go back a long way in the manner of literary relationships. I remember the astonishment and excitement I felt when I was reading *Poisoned Bread: Modern Marathi Dalit Literature*, edited by Arjun Dangle (Orient Longman, 1992). It was an eye-opener in many ways and it has remained indispensable to my understanding of Indian society. I remember then reading a section of *Baluta*, translated by Priya Adarkar. It was called 'Son, Eat Your Fill' and it was about an area I should have known well. Nagpada was close to where my maternal grandmother lived and I had spent a fair amount of time in the area. And yet I knew nothing about Kawakhana. Our wanderings were restricted to the 'safe areas': Mazagaon and Matharpakady, Clare Road and Spence Lane, the grounds of the Christ Church school. Once in a while, we would walk down Sankley Street to visit Mother Teresa's Asha Daan with charity offerings but that was as far as we would go. Daya Pawar showed me how limited my notion of the city was and how many subcultures you could pass by without noticing they were there. When Naresh Fernandes and I were editing *Bombay Meri Jaan: Writings on Bombay* at the behest of Ravi Singh who was then at Penguin India, I remember asking if *Baluta* had been translated and was told that it was expected very soon. In the meantime, I thought, we could make do with that piece translated by Priya.

It was while I was editing Adil Jussawalla's prose for what would eventually become *Maps for a Mortal Moon: Essays and Entertainments*—again a project that Ravi was to guide, but now at Aleph Books—that Pawar and *Baluta* jumped back into focus. Jussawalla has an essay that describes Pawar in Paris and suddenly I wondered why I had never read *Baluta*. So I asked Shanta Gokhale, repository of all that you need to know about Marathi literature, whether it had been translated and was told that it hadn't.

So I went for a walk and bought myself a copy of *Baluta*; it was still very much in print and later I would discover that it was one of the Marathi books that has had the honour of being pirated and so it is available on the streets of the city too. I started reading and was immediately confused. This was an autobiography, surely? So why did there seem to be two Daya Pawars stalking the first few pages of the book? Why is one Daya Pawar talking about the other Daya Pawar's poetry? And why is this fiction dispensed with so suddenly and unceremoniously a few pages in? What was going on?

But I read on mainly because the story was so compelling

and so simply and honestly told. And I discovered that being split into two seemed to be a precondition of Pawar's life. He compares himself to Jarasandha, the man whom the Pandava, Bhima, tore into two in a brutal wrestling match. Pawar feels split between city and village, between the world of books and the world of reality, between the world that seems possible and the world as it presents itself to him. Perhaps this is why he found it necessary to split himself into two in order to write about himself.

When I discovered that *Baluta* was the first Dalit autobiography, another reason suggested itself. This comes from how we discover what makes a story and how to tell it. We all tell stories, whether we are writers or not. We tell jokes, we narrate anecdotes, we recount gossip. We tell what we know and we tell what we have been told. And in the process of telling and retelling, we discover what works and what does not, what is a successful story and what is not, what elicits a response from our auditors and what makes them turn away. So how do you know whether your own story is worth telling when you have never read about yourself in a book? How do you know someone will publish it? And even if it is published, how do you know you will have readers? How will you know what their responses will be like? I suspect this is why the beginning of *Baluta* reads like an interview, as if one half of Daya Pawar is still reluctant to tell his story and the other half knows that it needs to be told. Without history and without references, he must encourage himself, goad himself on to the sticking point.

But once that river has been crossed, the boats may be burned and there is no going back. As Pawar grows into his story, as he finds his pace and his tone (both of which are essential to the telling of a Life) he no longer needs the fictive, encouraging other. If after you have read the book, you read it again, watching now for process, you can see that it is like watching sedimentary rock being formed in some vastly speeded-up film: out of the shifting sand and silt, we see the firm platform from which this story may be told. And this is also why Pawar probably did not bother with reinserting that fictive self later. It had served his purpose. If its appearance and sudden disappearance disconcerted the reader, well then, the reader must deal with that. It seems very little to bear when you consider how much the Dalit community has suffered.

It is interesting that Pawar chose to name his book for a demeaning practice that kept the Mahar in something close to bonded labour to the village community at large. There were supposed to be baarah balutedars, twelve categories of labour which were to be offered free to the village by those who were born into certain castes. They would not be paid to perform these services but in return they were entitled to baluta, a share in all of the village's produce. In *The Mahar Folk: A Study of Untouchables in Maharashtra* (1938), Alexander Robertson records that there were more than fifty services that were expected of the Mahar. These included skinning and disposing of dead cattle, running in front of any important visitor's horse when such a one honoured the village, announcing deaths and births throughout the village, drawing the chariot of the folk goddess Mari-Aai when a pox broke out, playing music at the weddings of the upper castes, playing escort to a bridegroom, paying the village taxes, tending sick animals…the list is extensive and in many cases includes work that requires considerable local knowledge such as the verification of land ownership and use. By naming his autobiography for this practice, Pawar places his story in a social context that is wider than a boy's own story.

But he is not speaking for the Mahar. He is speaking for himself. His attitude to his own people is often mixed. He says in one place that they sometimes conjure up, for him, the image of primitive people sitting in caves. As he grows older, he finds himself repulsed by the food at a wedding to which he is invited and almost immediately deeply touched by the generosity of his hosts in sending his second wife a sari.

What prevents this from being a misery memoir is the way in which Pawar implicates himself. For a victim narrative, the central assumption is that the teller is blameless and the villain is someone else out there. In his relationships with women, Pawar presents himself with warts on. He presents a startling picture of a pretty Vadarin (a herding tribe) but he seems unable to save her from her brother-in-law's predatory instincts. He marries the beautiful Saee but maddened by jealousy, he rejects her on what seem to be fairly flimsy grounds. To recover from the heartbreak of a broken marriage and the loss of his daughter, he moves to another area of the city and begins a long-distance flirtation with Salma, a girl who he loses too. But each time, he lets you know that it was his lack of courage, his lack of conviction that ended each romance. It is as if he is deconstructing the entire concept of Mahar machismo which depends on the abuse of women. Look at the models he has around him as a boy. His father, he tells us, never hit his mother but had a series of affairs with other women. His uncle beats his first wife with a stick for simply showing up in his presence. Another uncle sells his wife into a brothel. When Pawar marries the second time, this happens offstage so that his constant references to his very educated wife are almost confusing.

This is not an easy book to read. Even when we think we know all about the horrors of caste—the practice of untouchability, the constant and extreme humiliation—the sheer pervasiveness of the cruelty shocks us. So much of the violence done to the Mahar seems gratuitous. Why would one ask Mahar children to sit at an angle to other children? How can you deny a boy a chance to act in a play because he is dark of skin? And then, here's something that everyone in charge of children or the young might learn from: At one point, the young Daya Pawar recites a poem he has learned up and it is assumed that he wrote it. He is unable to tell the gathering that it is someone else's poem but he confesses the next morning to his teacher. And that teacher, in an act of careless generosity, says: 'Arré, what's so special about that? You can be a poet too.' How many teachers might have turned this the other way round and said something damning.

And yet reading and writing are not unalloyed gifts for the young man. Here is what he says about reading:

> The poison of reading took the last few simple pleasures left to me. At that time, we lived like animals in the Maharwada, our lives based on an earthy philosophy. I was filled with revulsion against the life I was leading and wanted to get away. But those who seemed to be leading the kind of life I wanted for myself would have nothing to do with me. This was my conundrum.

It would be difficult to imagine any middle-class person talking about reading in this way. Our world makes reading a sacred enterprise. Daya Pawar's world turns that upside down.

And so it happens again and again. Take the Bombay Docks Explosion of 1944. The *SS Stikine* sailed into harbour carrying 1,395 tonnes of explosives and some gold bars and some cotton that she had picked up in Karachi. Now cotton has a high internal heat. You leave a hundred bales alone for a couple of days and the internal heat will start the cotton smouldering and very soon you have a fire. This is why someone has to keep spraying the bales with water from time to time. Someone didn't spray it—or didn't spray it enough—and so on 14 April 1944, the cotton caught fire, the explosives blew up and the shock waves were recorded as far away as Simla. The rest of the city ran away from the explosion. But the residents of Kawakhana, young Pawar's family and neighbours, many of them rag-pickers, ran *towards* the explosion because they knew that there would be some money to be made in salvaging things from the rubble.

There are ghost stories in *Baluta*, and childhood games; there are romances and rumours; there are songs and sayings, there are corpses to be photographed and the tale of how to use a dusting-rag to romance your new bride. And a cast of characters that is as colourful as my city: there are counterfeiters and hijras, sex workers and distillers, gamblers and con women, political leaders and opportunists, dancers and exorcists. You'd think this would get unbelievable and exotic; if it does, it is my translation that is to be blamed. In the original, it is told in a matter-of-fact manner that takes in the wandering Raiwand and the aghori who would lick up his own vomit and makes of both the stuff of life itself.

This is one of the finest autobiographies I have ever read, and I count it an honour that I was given the opportunity to translate it.

JERRY PINTO
Mumbai,
May 2015

BALUTA

PROLOGUE

EVEN NOW, WHEN I meet him, he is always alone. As I became self-aware, I got to know him better; I now know him as well as I know my own shadow. But as with shadows, when darkness falls, or it gets cloudy, he disappears.

Over the last few years, he seems to have developed a special liking for crowds. He's always with someone or at a public meeting. Today is no different. He is at a discussion of a social issue of the day. On the stage are the usual suspects. He's sitting among them, yet somewhat aloof. When it is his turn to speak, his words seem to come from his gut. Many people approve, going by the scattered applause.

The meeting ends. The faces around him begin to dissolve. He comes up to me and asks: 'How did my speech go?'

'You spoke well. But you never look happy. Your face seems stretched like a catapult, as if you're always annoyed.'

'Then maybe you haven't seen me in a while. Have I ever hidden anything from you?'

'One of your academic friends abuses you, says you're a Dalit Brahmin.'

'There might be some truth in that. If you look at me

from the point of view of the man on the street, I do seem to be wearing the shirt of the happy man. I earn seven to eight hundred rupees a month sitting in a government office, that too in an auditor's office. I have government accommodation, in the suburbs, even if it is on rent. I have a well-educated wife, two daughters in school. My son at five or six is still the age to climb onto my shoulders. He will carry on the family name. My elder daughter is married. Last year, she had a son. I became a grandfather before I was forty, but I don't think you'd be able to tell. My vine, it would seem, has blossomed and borne fruit.'

'And you're still unhappy.'

'Have you heard of the shepherd boy who lost his cap?'

I shook my head. He began:

'A shepherd boy lost his cap. It was just a cap but to him it was no ordinary loss. It plagued him day and night. Memories of it haunted him as he ate and drank. One day, he went, as usual, into the forest to graze the animals. A young couple from the city had come there to canoodle. The shepherd began to eavesdrop. The young man said, "Darling, in your eyes I see the moon, the sun, the flowers, the sea, the twilight—the whole of the forest." The shepherd could not contain himself. He burst out with, "Oh! Then can you please find my cap?"'

'Don't act like a philosopher, speaking in parables,' I tell him. 'Can't you simply tell me what has happened?'

'Can a story, told from beginning to end, ever be simple? And mine is not the story of a single day; it's a history that spans forty years. And then there's the problem that I sometimes can't remember what I had for dinner last night. Perhaps that's what's kept me alive: my ability to forget. Or else my head might have exploded. Come to think of it, I don't even remember my children's birthdays. My wife has to remind me.'

'But how can it be difficult to tell me what your youth was like, what circumstances moulded you, that kind of thing?'

'I'll tell you what I remember...I have always liked a poem from *In Prison*. You know the one in which sorrow is compared to an iceberg?

My sorrow: an iceberg,
Its tip alone breaking the waterline.
My memories: drops of acid
That leave me shivering in pain.
On my shoulders, the crucifix of life
On my forehead, the placard of my fate—
You who have washed the guilt off your hands,
You who have exfoliated your past,
How do you manage with these new-hewn faces?

'That poem mirrors my life in more ways than one. Most people see only the tip of the iceberg. And even this causes much discussion in society. My past is like the submerged part of the iceberg. But an iceberg is constantly being fed by the sea. My face seems frozen too.

'And yet, ever since I've become aware of this, oddly, the

past has begun to elude me. When I think I've got hold of it, my spirit trembles. For a long time, I think I've been seduced by surfaces. This shocks me.

'Then you come along and ask that I should take an axe to the iceberg. Will it break? Or would I reduce myself to the state of a Pothraj? You've seen them, haven't you? Those bare-chested men who whip themselves on the street, who wear anklets on their feet but have rather good biceps, which they pierce with needles till blood spurts…That's who I'd be, and then people would gather around and clap and sigh and say, "Poor chap." Do I want to become an object of people's pity?'

'How would you be to blame even if you do?'

'I know. If I'd been born in some frigid tundra, would my past have been different? There too I would have known sorrow. But it would have been a different kind of sorrow, not a result of calculated inhumanity.

'I cannot tell you if you will meet this "Me" in the story. The reflection of a man in a mirror does not know the whole story of the man it is reflecting. Consider this: My real name is Dagdu; you've forgotten that, right? So have I. But that's the name you'll see in the school register. No one in the city knows me as Dagdu. Who knows whether even my wife and children know the name. Since my childhood I've hated this name. Shakespeare may have said, "What's in a name?" but tell me, why should this name fall to my lot? It smacks of a clod on which a clod was born. Look at our nicknames—Kachrya, which conjures up dirt; Dhondya, which suggests stones. If by some chance someone were to name his child Gautam, it would be shortened to Gavtya. The *Manusmriti* has a list of names for Shudras; it requires that our names should reflect society's contempt for us. Brahmins' names signify learnedness—"Vidyadhar", for instance. Kshatriyas' names suggest valour—like "Balaram". Vaishyas can be named after the goddess of wealth, say "Laxmikant". And Shudras? For us, names like Shudrak or Maatang, names that declare our low-caste status. That was the order of things for centuries.'

WHEN I WAS a child, Aai would say, 'Child, I had ten or fifteen other children whom I stuffed into the earth. My babies just kept dying. I asked for a boon and when you were born someone advised me, "Just name him something like Dagad or Donda. He'll live."'

And so I was named. I began to go to school. Since I didn't like my name, my classmates began to call me DM. If one of them came home and asked for me, Aaji, my grandmother, would stand at the door and say, 'Dyaam is not at home.' Dyaam was her version of DM.

My childhood was divided between the village and the city. It would not be wrong to say that I had one foot in the city and one in the fields. Perhaps this is why I am never really at home in either place. Just as Krishna ripped Jarasandha's body into two and tossed them apart, my life has split my psyche into two.

My father worked at the dry docks in Mumbai. I called him 'Dada'. My son calls me 'Dada' too. I would not like it if he were to address me as 'Daddy' or 'Papa'. It feels like someone calling the humble cactus *Opuntia Dillenii*...

What was I saying? Yes. My childhood. At that time, we were living at Kawakhana. In a ten-by-twelve-foot room. A tap inside, common toilet outside. Aai, my paternal cousin's family, and later Aaji, all lived there.

You won't find Kawakahana on any map of Mumbai. In those days the tram from Khada Parsi turned into Foras Road on its way to Girgaon. Aaji says that she remembers horse-drawn trams. She would tell me her memories. As a child, I would dream of those horses, foaming at the mouth, struggling to get the trams up the bridge. Nagpada props itself up against this bridge and in the middle of Nagpada was Kawakhana. Today, it's all tall buildings, five or six storeys high. On one end was Chor Bazaar or the thieves' market. On the other side was Kamathipura, the red-light area. Golpitha was where the prostitutes lived. Kawakhana was squeezed between these two.

The Mahar community lived in little islands in the surrounding areas. All of us came from the Konkan plateau, from Sangamner, Akola, Junnar, Sinnar. And around us, there were communities of Christians and Muslims.

The Mahars lived in squalid homes, each the size of a henhouse, each henhouse having two or three sub-tenants. Wooden boxes acted as partitions. But they were more than that: we stuffed our lives into those boxes. At night, temporary walls would come up, made of rags hanging from ropes.

The Mahar men worked as hamaals or labourers. Some worked in the mills and factories. None of the women observed purdah. How could they? They worked harder than the men. They scavenged scraps of paper, rags, broken glass and iron from the streets, sorted them out and then sold them each morning. And however much their drunkard husbands beat them, they continued to serve them, hand and foot, and indulged their addictions.

Most women gathered discarded paper from the cloth shops of Mangaldas market. They had to bribe the shopkeepers' servants to be allowed to take this waste paper away. Each woman had a few shops marked out as her territory and border disputes were frequent and noisy. Other women washed the clothes of the ladies in the brothels. Some of the prostitutes, tired of keema pao, would also ask them to cook bajri bhakris and fiery meat dishes. Sometimes, sly customers would ask for these women instead of the prostitutes. Then the Mahar women would run for their lives, guarding their fragile honour.

Another special thing about Kawakhana: next to us was a club. This was a large hall with straw mat walls and a tarpaulin roof. This club was the 'Kawakhana' that gave the area its name. All day long, rich white men, Jews, well-built Arabs and sometimes even a Negro or two would gamble there. They played strange exciting games: flush, billiards. From the slits in the door, we watched the colourful balls bounce across the table, sped on their way by long sticks. The men in our colony did not play games such as these. They were not poor men's games.

We never saw these rich men going to work. They hung around there from morning to midnight. They drank tea, but without milk. And there was another beverage, made from cocoa pods. This, they called 'kaawa'. What pleasure the carrot-red Jews got drinking this black bitter stuff, we could not tell.

Speaking of the Jews, I remember their unique way of

killing chickens. Right near the community's most important synagogue, on the same road we took to school, was a maidan. The birds' throats would be split and then they would be flung into the maidan to die, flapping and gushing blood. It was impossible to watch.

At times, the club was a nuisance to those who lived around it. You could never tell when a riot would break out and tables and bottles would fly. All day long, there'd be talk about stock market speculation, horse racing, betting and suchlike. Thousands of rupees would change hands and at the end of a session, some would be bankrupt and others rich. Every morning, young boys would be asked about their dreams and their meaning and significance would be debated for a long time. If they featured fire, it would mean a certain number; if it were water, then it could be another number.

You only needed an anna for what was called Cheena Betting. So everyone in the family participated with a great deal of zest. Even the local madman, his body covered with the filth of ten, acquired a certain prestige. What he did could be treated as an omen, and if someone made money on such an assumption, he was treated as a yogi.

Next to the club was a tiled chawl in the shape of a horseshoe. That was where we lived. Next to us lived Aaji's elder sister's four children. One of my uncles was called Jaba; my cousins were Rhaba, Naba, Shiva and Kaba. I would call my uncles Tatya or Baba; some of them pulled handcarts; others were labourers. My father was the first in his family to begin work at the docks; he got the others in, one by one.

Aaji worked at a clinic for dogs. A sahib who knew her had done her this favour. She had to feed the dogs, clean their shit and wash them. I would sometimes go to the clinic with her. I loved the newborn puppies. I could spend hours just watching them. I specially enjoyed listening to them lapping milk from a porcelain dish. I wanted to pick them up and pet them. But the fear of what the sahibs would say stopped me.

They say a man draws his coat to himself more closely in a storm and nowhere could you see this more clearly than in the way the small island of Mahars in Kawakhana behaved. We loved each other intensely; we hated each other passionately. We supported each other. During a fight, it would seem to the outsider that the combatants would never speak to each other again; that afterwards we would go our separate ways; but nothing like that ever happened. If you try to uproot a bean-pod creeper, all the bean-pods will fall. The Mahars were no different.

When the Mahars first came to live here, the tall buildings around were mostly empty. They could have chosen to live in the buildings, but they didn't want to be bothered with climbing the stairs, they said, so they chose this single-storeyed chawl. It might have once been a stable for horses. Today their naivete seems laughable.

Of course, that wasn't the only reason. When you spent your life collecting the rubbish of the city, sorting it and selling it, who would let you live in a flat in a building? But what a hell they chose instead! I would spend many years of my childhood and youth in this dump. During the rains, every house leaked. All night we would place vessels and cans under the leaks. And when sleep came unbidden, it was to the music of this jaltarang.

As the only little boy in that row of houses, I was spoilt rotten. If I said I had a headache and lay down, immediately a bright yellow malpua from the Irani restaurant would be bought for me, and my headache would vanish. The family teased me about these convenient 'illnesses' but nobody scolded me.

My father and his brother, my uncle—my Tatya—would be paid on the same day. On one such pay day, I demanded a suit and shoes to match. I must have been about seven or eight, no age for a suit. But I wept up such a storm that in the end, they took me to Pila House and for the first time, I saw big shops that looked as if they were made of shiny glass. I chose a woollen coat and trousers and a fine pair of shoes. I couldn't wait to put them on. I changed right there in the shop. Dada looked at me and decided that we would all have our photographs taken. I had held on to those pictures for a long time but at some point in the next twenty or twenty-five years, in all the moves and shifts and turmoil, they vanished. Now I feel as if I have lost a great treasure: unique photographs of my Dada and Tatya. I can only hold on to the images in my head but even those seem to be fading.

I can still picture Dada's face. He was black as ebony, tall, slim. He dressed in high style. A brilliant white Mercerised expensive dhoti, a woollen coat. On his head, a black Bal Gandharva topi. A lovely smile. The glint of a gold stud in one tooth. He was an unlettered man but in the photograph from my childhood, he had a big fat tome in his hands and a pen stuck in his coat pocket.

He was a stylish man. His hair was brushed back from his forehead. In his youth, he had exercised regularly; with sticks and clubs. He could slice a sour lime while spinning his sword and staff doing the dandpatta. He had many black strings and a talisman around his neck.

Aaji, his mother, was a guileless woman, garrulous and full of stories. Her name was Devki. Her husband died when she was young and she had borne widowhood with great courage. She had brought up her two sons, making something out of nothing. If you asked her, 'Aaji, when did you come to Mumbai?' she'd look into the distance and reply:

'Boy, your grandfather died of drink. Your father was about knee-high. Tatya was an infant. There was so much oppression in the village. It was the time when the mamledaars* were no longer in power. Mahars took turns at doing the village jobs. I had no man in the house, no support from neighbours and relatives, but they expected me to take my turn too. They expected the widow to beg for

---

*The mamledars were officers of a special court appointed, first in 1876, to function as a rural civil court. There must have been considerable discontentment, for the courts were reconstituted under another act in 1906. But here there is a suggestion that they were very powerful in the countryside for a while and then their powers waned.

her food. They expected her to help clear away dead cattle. If someone died in the village, whatever the weather, off the widow would have to go, announcing it to all and sundry.

'One day, the Patil sent me off with an announcement. It was the day of the Holi festival. Smallpox had broken out and Mari-Aai's* chariot had to be pushed through the villages. The Mahars were expected to drag her chariot. Before that, I was told to announce in every home: "Talloo-golloo naka"; in other words, "No frying, no eating oily things." So there I was with my stick-and-bells. Young Kondiba was sitting on the wall of Vithoba's temple. Who knows what occurred to him but he decided to make fun of me. He blocked my way and began to say, "Catch that Mahar woman, tie her up in the village square, she's run mad. Why is she telling us 'Talloo-falloo naka'? Why tell us not to have children?" People began to gather. Some were laughing and some were mocking me. They surrounded me. I fell at their feet. I swore that I was only saying what I had been told to say by the Patil, that I had said "Talloo-golloo naka", not "Talloo-falloo naka". The villagers were in no mood to listen. Only when my brother-in-law decided to turn up did they let me go. He had some influence in the village. But I couldn't

---

*Mari-Aai is the folk goddess of fevers and poxes. When smallpox broke out in the villages, it was believed that it was a visitation of an enraged goddess who had to be placated by being taken in a chariot through the villages so affected so that she might be worshipped. It was, of course, the Mahars to whom the duty fell to draw her chariot.

sleep that night. I knew I could not stay. I came to Mumbai to my sister.'

Aaji could not remember the names of any of her husband's ancestors. I have seen the genealogies of many families in books. Some of these take the form of magnificent family trees and even find mention in history books. But even I do not know the names of anyone before my great grandfather. The priests, the Badves and Pandas, in the holy places, keep family trees carefully; but would my people have gone to these places? At the most, they might have gone to meet Khandoba* at Jejuri, but no further.

I remember Aaji for another reason. As soon as the earning member of the family sat down to eat, Aaji would sit by him till he finished. She would keep stroking his back and begin her refrain: 'Gobble, gobble, little one, gobble it up.' When Dada was the earning member, she would sit by him. Then it was Tatya's turn. One day, Tatya came home roaring drunk. When Aaji began, he lost his temper. In a fit of rage, he took the plate and all its contents and threw them into the courtyard.

---

*Khandoba is said to be a form of Shiva. He carries a 'khanda' or sword and some sources say that he was a warrior king. One of the most famous pilgrimage centres is Jejuri, Maharashtra, 38 kilometres from Pune and 60 kilometres from Sholapur. The Mahars have an intimate relationship with Khandoba and hence I have retained Pawar's formulation of 'going to visit Khandoba at Jejuri'. The town also gives its name to a brilliant sequence of poems by Arun Kolatkar, first published by Clearing House in 1976.

'Don't say that again. What am I, a child? Don't you dare say that ever again.'

For a few days, Aaji stopped. But she never lost the habit.

Later when I began to contribute my mite towards the family's finances, Aaji would sit next to me when I was eating. She would stroke my back and mumble in the same way: 'Gobble, gobble, little one, gobble it up.' I would feel my eyes go moist.

Although Aaji is no longer with us—she had been stuffed into the earth too—I remember her every time I sit down to a meal. Her words echo in my ears. If I think about it, I realize that she didn't have a matchstick worth of happiness in her life. And yet the sweetness of her temperament was never soured by her circumstances. That generation seems to have vanished. Now you only see people who are filled with bitterness and driven by material interests.

I remember the time when we had moved to the village and I was studying in the middle school in the district. When Aaji, who was in Mumbai at the time, heard that I had begun to sprout my first facial hair, she was delighted. Without letting her son or daughter-in-law know about it, she sent me a cut-throat razor with someone who was coming home to the village. I still shave with that razor. It's gone old and blunt now but I can't bring myself to toss it away.

—

Some people have memories of earlier lives. I can't tell supernatural tales as well as Rabindranath Tagore and his ilk. But if I screw up my eyes, I can bring into focus a scene from the time before I went to school, an event that has left a deep wound. Aai and I were living in the village for a while. My father would come to visit us from the city from time to time. That night, he came home very late. I had stayed up waiting for him and the gifts he brought: date-bread from Mumbai, a brand-new Krishna-style headgear resplendent with peacock feathers, crisp new clothes—enough to keep me happy all night. Despite this, I woke up earlier than usual. Dada was sitting on the wall in front of the house, cleaning his teeth with burnt tobacco. And then I saw two policemen in khaki, coming towards us. Before I could tell what was happening, they had clapped handcuffs on Dada. Aai began to wail. I was watching wide-eyed, dumbstruck. There was tumult in the Maharwada. My father had been arrested on charges of murder.

This was a time of hostility between two groups in our Maharwada, as the Mahar settlement in every village is called. The Pawars and the Rupavates were the two groups. If someone from the Pawar faction died, the Rupavate faction would make an effigy of the dead person and take it out in a procession with music. If someone from the Rupavate group died, the Pawars would do likewise. My father had become a victim of this feud.

A man called Uma-ajya lived in a dilapidated house in the Maharwada, with his wife who could not speak. He earned his living by tying talismans on people, telling their fortunes or reading the *Ramayana* and *Mahabharata* to them. Everyone called him Shakuni Mama after the evil uncle in the *Mahabharata*. He was a truly Machiavellian soul. He could not bear to see anyone doing well. This time, an issue arose over whose land was to be used to flay an animal that had died in the village. Near the village square lived a priest called Jagtap. Long ago, he had wandered into our village one day with his wife and children. At that time my great-grandfather was childless. Since he did not have any heirs, he had given Jagtap half of his farmland, some of the land near his house and two annas of his share of the Maharki, the Mahar's share in the village produce.* And then in his old age, my great-grandfather had a son. But one cannot lick up one's spittle. My great-grandfather did not try to take back his land. Jagtap put up a Shiv ling on this land. And so a dispute began between the Pawars and the Rupavates. The Pawars maintained that the land might still be used to flay carcasses as it had always been. The Rupavates maintained that it was now no longer Mahar land and had been consecrated to Shiva. Jagtap was on the Rupavate side.

The matter went to court and the Pawars won.** Uma-ajya took this badly. He saw it as a personal defeat and

---

*It is likely that Daya Pawar's ancestor donated so much of his land and his share in the baluta in the hope of attaining the merit that having a son might have brought him. Or he might simply have been motivated by a charitable impulse, made easier perhaps by the fact that he was getting on and had no heirs.

**The Pawars under British jurisprudence would have had an easement, a right of traditional use to the land.

wanted revenge and so he floated a rumour. When my father was in Mumbai, he had become friends with a man called Murhya, who was a neighbour of the Pawars back in the Maharwada; they lived together and were the best of friends, even sharing a saucer of tea. This Murhya had vanished into thin air one day. Uma-ajya said that Dada had killed his friend because of a fight over a woman they were sharing in the city. He instigated Murhya's mother, Dagdav, who killed a cockerel and splashed its blood all over her son's clothes and ran off, crying and weeping, to the tahsil office. The mastermind behind this was Uma-ajya. Dada was accused of murder.

When Dada was taken away, Aai and I followed. Dada was put in the lock-up. I wept to see him there. My mother's uncle, Tanaji, came as fast as he could from her birth village, two miles away, when he heard the news. There was no substance to the case, but it was a terrible thing to be accused of murder and so Tanaji's wife pawned all her jewellery and paid the faujdar a bribe.

Dada never forgot this incident. The disrespect also rankled with Tatya. Both the brothers would wander all over the countryside looking for Murhya. Then one day, Uma-ajya came to Mumbai to meet his daughter. She had married a man who lived in Kawakhana. That night Dada beat Uma-ajya black and blue. Uma-ajya screamed and shouted but no one went to his aid. This could have been the reason that Dada brought us all back to Mumbai. This time we stayed there until he stopped working.

—

The year 1944. All I remember of it is the explosion in the docks.

Aaji's sister, Taibai, lived in Bandra. Aaji and Taibai were milk sisters; they shared the same mother but had different fathers. Taibai had been dedicated to Khandoba in childhood.* But as soon as she grew up a little and became aware, she abandoned the profession. She would work like a man but her nature was very loving. There was general amazement that the glass bangles from Rajapur she had on her wrists had not broken right up to her death. She would help with her brother's family. When her brother died young, she looked after his young bride as if she were one of her own children. She brought up her brother's child too. Even though she lived in a predominantly Muslim and Christian area, none of the local boys thought to approach her. It was said that she had once slammed a Muslim boy's head on the ground when he had dared tease her young sister-in-law.

When Aaji left the village, she came to live with Taibai in Bandra. Near Mount Mary's Basilica, there was a Christian children's hostel. Aaji would buy and carry baskets of mutton

---

*For a variety of reasons, sometimes to do with poverty, sometimes to do with a promise, and often for something as inexplicable as a child's hair being found to be full of knots, girl children would be dedicated to a folk god or goddess. This meant that they would never marry and often end up doing sex work. Hence, when the young Taibai saw what her future might be, she simply walked away from it in an act of courage that one can only admire at this distance and across this time.

to the hostel. We loved going to Bandra, especially during the Mount Mary Fair.* Our whole family would arrive seven days in advance. There would be an abundance of food. We would get all kinds of meat and fish. We would get to wander about the fair. Since Taibai's home was right near the creek, we would get to swim too. From the house itself, we could see the sea at a distance. The air was thick with the smell of fish. On the beach, we'd make sand castles and decorate them with shells.

One evening, we were taking a dip in the sea. It was getting on; in no time at all, the sun would stumble off to bed. Suddenly, we saw flames leaping into the sky at the Colaba end of the city. It was as if someone had set alight a sea of petrol. Deafening explosions followed. We ran home. We took the train back to Kawakhana, taking Aaji with us; the only talk was about what must have happened. We got down at Bombay Central. There, everyone seemed to be trying to leave the city in whatever vehicle and by whatever mode they could. The air was filled with fear and rumour. No one knew what had really happened.

---

*The Mount Mary Fair starts on the Sunday that follows September 8—the day taken to be the birth of the Blessed Virgin Mary, the mother of Jesus Christ—each year. It runs for eight days and Mumbaikars of every religion and community come to pray and to seek darshan. After all, it was a Parsi, Lady Jamshedji, who prayed for a child who would survive and promised to make the Basilica more accessible to the faithful. When she was so blessed, she built the Mahim Causeway that linked the island city to Bandra. Before that, people used a ferry to get across.

When we reached Kawakhana, we heard that there had been an explosion at the docks. All of us were very worried; both Dada and Tatya worked there. When they returned, they brought good news. 'There's a lot of waste metal at the docks. It's a windfall for us.' All of Kawakhana was abuzz with all sorts of rumours. Gold bricks had torn through the roof of someone's house; someone else had found a treasure trove in the ashes. By the early morning, everyone had picked up whatever tools came to hand and rushed off to the site of the explosion. For the next seven or eight days, this became routine: scavenging for the re-saleable in the debris. No one found the smallest speck of gold but other treasures surfaced. One day someone brought back some huge rolls of white paper on a handcart. His face was aglow with the joy of an Ali Baba. What if the rolls were wet? Our walls, our courtyard were soon swathed in paper hung out to dry. Our homes were filled with the strange smell of paper. When it was dry, it was sold at a handsome rate to a nearby godown. I could have had no idea then that my life would be enjoined with paper.

—

I was enrolled in the Nagpada Municipal School. I think I studied there until the second standard. I remember we had a teacher from the Chambhar or cobbler caste. His fingers were covered in gold rings. The birth-date recorded at the time of my admission to school? I could not believe it was the correct date. How could it be? My parents were illiterate.

They put down a date related to some family event around the time I was born. So we never celebrated my birthday. A couple of years were spent in shuttling between Mumbai and the village. But when we left the city, it was for strange reasons.

Dada was by this time an alcoholic. I can't remember when he started drinking. Perhaps it was even before I was born. That was the custom of our people. No one thought ill of drinking. Dada did not pay much attention to his home. For a couple of days or weeks after pay day, he would not show his face at home. Aai, poor thing, would keep us going with her scavenging. Sometimes she would get angry but she never expressed her rage when Dada was around. Sometimes we would wait outside the docks for him for hours. But there are many gates to the docks. Which one he used to slip away would always be a mystery.

I can't tell what work he did at the docks or how much he was paid. But I have clear memories of going with someone to deliver his lunch. From the outside, you couldn't tell the sheer size and sprawl of the docks. Just the restless deep blue sea stretching to infinity. And the ships, tall as buildings, rocking on it. White men boarding and descending from ships—what arrogance they showed in those days! The Indian workers were as dirt to them.

At that time, an incident sparked off much discontentment among the workers. During the lunch break, a labourer was eating his bhakri. One of the white sahibs kicked the man's meal out of his way. He swore at the worker too. The dock erupted with outrage. With great courage, a young worker named Rokade raised his voice against such injustice. He threatened to fast unto death unless the sahib apologized. The outcome was as expected. The workers became aware of their strength. After this, Rokade acquired no little fame as a leader of the workers. I was rather proud that this very man came often to Kawakhana to chat with my father and uncle.

What was I saying? Yes, my father's job. I saw him sitting next to a huge furnace. He was probably in charge of feeding the flames with the waste from the docks. Now it occurs to me, had this dock swallowed up his skills, his creativity? For Dada was a man of many parts. He played the shehnai beautifully. In the village, he would be asked to the dholki, darkening the skin at its centre so as to deepen the sound. Before he came to the docks, he had worked on a yearly contract at a Brahmin house. He was an expert at the sowing of seeds. Once, he caught a snake by its tail, slammed its head on a rock and broke its back. That kind of man. And here at the docks, he was the man who burned the rubbish. Was that it? Did *that* make him an alcoholic?

After work, Dada would head straight to the country liquor bar. In those days, there was one at every corner, all run by Parsis. I think during the Prohibition imposed by Morarji Desai these bars vanished.* It was difficult to find

---

*When Morarji Desai (1896-1995), was chief minister of Maharashtra he introduced Prohibition which resulted in the
(contd...)

alcohol on open sale. But Dada was unable to stop. He was like an animal that has tasted blood. He began to drink industrial alcohol. He would send me to buy it with a small German silver vessel. 'Empty it if anyone catches you,' he said. He needed about eight or twelve annas worth to keep him going. He would dilute it with water so that it became white as milk. If you brought it to your nose, an acrid stench rose. I can still remember the smell of spirit; it settled in my nose as a child. This was truly a poison. Dada would present a comic sight, screwing up his face into different shapes as he forced it down as quickly as possible. Why drink it if it tastes so horrible, I would wonder. It would have been a miracle if it hadn't corroded his intestines in a year or so. And on top of that, he ate whatever we could get hold of, just enough to fill his stomach. No wonder his body grew feeble.

Aai suffered in silence. Dada was black as coal but his skin had a shine to it, like ebony. By comparison, Aai was much lighter-skinned, what is called a 'wheatish complexion'. He was tall, she was short and slight of build. Even after ten or twelve children, her body hadn't changed much. She

---

(contd...)

Parsi-owned bars closing down. However, many speakeasies, called 'Aunty bars' or 'Maushis', opened all over the city where illicit liquor was served. Dom Moraes gives a glorious account of this period in his autobiography, of how he had to acquire a permit to drink as an incurable drunkard at the age of fourteen, and how the ground squelched queasily under his Oxford-returned feet when he went to find some alcohol.

would wear the nine-yard sari and since she was a married woman, a huge koonkoo mark on her forehead. Always, around her neck, a black string. Sometimes, a mangalsutra with a pendant and some gold beads. Jewellery? Silver bangles, but these would often be pawned for spirit.

When Dada was drunk, he was no longer my father but the devil incarnate. Aai would avoid him in these moments. I never understood the secret of their love. She did not seem to feel a matchstick worth of revulsion for Dada. Without a protest, she would pour out what little she had in front of him. When he was sober again, he would swear that he would never touch the stuff. Those promises did not last the day.

Dada was a womanizer too. One instance of this is etched in my memory. It must have been payday. He comes home and says the usual: 'I'll just go to the corner and be back' and starts to get ready. I pester him to take me with him and he gives in. We go to one of the 'family rooms' in the Irani restaurant. A woman, dark-skinned, sharp-featured, is waiting for us. I may be young but I know what is going on. 'If this is what you wanted to do, why bring me along?' I ask him savagely. He smiles to himself, as if proud of me. This only angers me further. The woman tries to make up to me, tries to draw me into her arms. I push her away. 'My mother is so much better looking,' I think. 'Why does Dada have to do this?' Seeing that I won't stay, Dada brings me home and goes back. I tell Aai everything. She smiles sadly. Perhaps she knows already. To womanize is a badge of honour, a sign of masculinity, or so it is believed around here. People look at such a man with admiration.

Dada's women were very ordinary. Some were housemaids, others carried loads on their heads to the lorries. How many came and went? There was no counting.

I do not remember, however, a single time when Dada laid a hand on Aai. No, I do remember one instance, but for other reasons entirely. It was as if this shed light on a dark corner of my father's mind. That day, he drove everyone out of the house, shut the windows and locked the doors. The chawl women were saying that Sakhu was in for it now. I was weeping hysterically. Aai's terrible scream. The sound of Dada's cane. The Jews from the club came running. Dada paid no heed to the hammering on the door. Now there was the very real fear that he might kill her. The Jews broke down the door. Inside, Dada was hammering the mattress with his cane and Aai was weeping quietly in another corner.

Aai wanted a daughter. After me, a girl was born but she died young. Aai would make all sorts of promises and vows to get a daughter. She would go to Sion to propitiate Satvai. A girl was duly born but then my aunt Kaku's sickly daughter died. The blame was put on Aai. My aunt was sure that Aai had used black magic to kill her niece in order to fill her own womb—and she never relinquished this idea, right up to the time of my mother's death. This started a life-long feud between the two sisters-in-law. Even today, my aunt clings to this belief. Both my wife and I tried to persuade her otherwise but she remains adamant. She did visit us on a couple of occasions but she refused to drink a drop of water, let alone eat anything. Perhaps she feared we might poison her or work some more black magic.

And yet one or two years ago, when someone in the family spread the story that I had fallen under a train and died, Kaku and her family came running, weeping. Love can also be like this.

But what was I saying? Yes, my sister. A new baby in the family was a distraction. I was very fond of her. One of the nurses at the maternity home where my sister was born had given her the name Indu. She had my mother's round face, her complexion, her build, her expressive eyes.

My father's behaviour in those days shamed me. His pay was meagre. And then there were his women, his alcohol habit. These addictions meant that money was always scarce. And so, he began to steal things from the docks, items made of copper or brass. Security at the gates was strict. It was impossible to hide things in one's pockets so Dada concealed his stolen goods in his loincloth. Had he been caught, I would have found it difficult to show my face in society even today.

Even if all of this seemed to be distasteful, I could not express my opinion. It was unlikely that I would have had the courage of my convictions at that age. But *were* they my convictions? Here, in school, I was being taught 'Always speak the truth' and there, I was taking Dada's loot to sell at

Chor Bazaar. The world I learned about at school seemed fraudulent compared to the world I lived in.

The things that went on in our neighbourhood! Our local forger could turn out a ten-rupee note every day. He would hang it to dry on the terrace. He would send one of the children out to spend it for him. He did not believe in printing too many notes; he stopped when he had enough for his daily needs. He knew that if he grew greedy, he risked a jail sentence. If I had grown up in that atmosphere, I don't think I would have become what I am today. Who knows, I might have joined their ranks.

Meanwhile, Dada's addictions were growing. Almost all his pay would go to satisfy his creditors. And then we borrowed from a Pathan. All this got too much for him one day and on an impulse, he resigned. He used his Provident Fund to clear his debts and announced that he was going back to the village.

Dada's philosophy was a strange one. 'Naked, I came, naked I shall return,' he would babble when he was drunk. He had never tried to save any money. He stole from the docks, it is true, but even in this there was a method in his madness. He would not rob anything too valuable. Dada had a good relationship with an old Jew, a dealer in diamonds, who came to gamble at the club. This fair-skinned gentleman, dressed to the nines, would come to our house. He would doff his hat and sit down on the bedding and eat mutton barbaat. The fiery spices would turn his cheeks red and his nose would run. He would bubble and blow to cool his mouth.

Once he had to go to Palestine for some time. He trusted Dada so much that he left his trunk at our home. He did not return for a long time. We thought he might have popped it. But Dada never felt any desire to sell the old man's jewels. After two years, the old man came back. His box was returned to him, intact. That kind of man, my father.

—

Leaving Mumbai was not easy. I had no great love for the village. Mumbai was the city of glittering lights, a precious stone set in a ring. After we moved to the village, I would often have a dream: from a high wall, I would leap…and land in Mumbai. Mumbai was where you got bread and butter with your tea. Or even a buttered bun. We went to see films regularly—but only action movies. Once Dada made a special effort and took Aai to see *Sant Sakhu*. Aai wept through it, moved by the saint's sufferings. Did she see her life mirrored there? Perhaps Dada took her for the film because she shared the saint's name. I didn't like that kind of weepie at all. I liked the films that starred Nadia and John Cavas. You could watch these at Pila House for four annas.

What else did children my age do, what games did they play? I could not play marbles or cards. There were chikoti and handjyup, among others. If someone said 'Handjyup,' you had to raise your arms and he was allowed to clear out your pockets. Chikoti meant you had to cover your bum with your hands. If your buttocks were not so protected, you risked a resounding thwack. The Christian settlement was right in front of us, with its swings, a slide and a see-saw. We sat on the wall facing it and gambled endlessly on the licence plate numbers of the cars that passed. It was also a big thrill to dangle from the back of a Victoria, and risk a flick of the driver's whip. We would tie tattered bed-sheets on ourselves and wander about in the gardens and play Tarzan, yodelling like him. I would miss all this in the village.

Back then, we had to get down at the Ghoti Railway Station. We were from the Ghats. The Sahyadris ran an arm through our district, and from the highest peak, Mount Kalsubai, you could see the island of Mumbai clearly—at least that's what the old folks used to say. The Pravara Amritavahini flowed close to my birth village which was in the lee of a hill. We were known to the rest of the country because of the Bhandardara dam. Its waters fed Kopargaon, Shrirampur and other talukas. As for our own taluka, perhaps the epithet 'Land of stones', as the poet Ram Ganesh Gadkari uses it in his poem, arose from here. Our Taluka also had many aboriginal residents: Thakars, Kolis, whom we would call loincloth wearers. My village, however, had a majority of Marathas.

Up to Ghoti, I travelled ticketless because my parents did not believe in buying tickets for the little ones. I'm sure the tension of travelling 'without', as we call it, showed on my face. Under cover of darkness, as the station neared, I would have to slip out of the train, evading the eyes of the ticket collector. My parents would get down at the station and come looking for me at the gate. Standing at a distance, I would wave to attract their attention. They were all praise for my 'skill'.

From Ghoti to Sangamner, we used the road. There were no State Transport buses then. A rich Marwari had a car that ferried people up and down. We would be crammed in like sheep or goats, with some passengers even on the roof of the car. If some notable or rich person were in the car, it would stop right in front of his house. The seat next to the driver would be reserved for him.

There's a story I remember from our trips between Mumbai and our village. Once, when we got to the village, we discovered that a large bundle had been left behind on the train. We figured it must have gone on to Sangamner station. Aai said she would wait at the bus-stand; Dada and I went off to look for the bundle. We traced it to the unclaimed luggage office, but the man in charge would not hand it over. 'How can you prove it's yours?' he asked. Although I was quite young, I rattled off a list of its contents. The thing was, as always, when people heard that we were going back to the village they had given us small parcels to carry for their relatives, and as always, they had stitched their names on each package. I remembered the names. When the official saw that I could tell the names on the packages without looking at them, he was persuaded to release the bundle. The items inside had no great value—some people had sent spices, others dry Bombay duck or date-bread—but if we had not delivered them, it would have been assumed that we had swallowed it all. There would have been talk all over the Maharwada—that was what had been worrying Dada. He was very proud that his son had recovered the bundle using his intelligence. He told every villager we met of my wit. It would have been odd if I had not walked tall that day.

Taluka: Akola. Three or four miles away was my village, Dhamangaon. The name was not unique, nor had it any trace of historical significance. The road to it was muddy, deeply rutted by bullock carts. In the monsoon, it turned to sludge. Even today, I can tell you more about the Maharwada than about the village. Between the main village and the Maharwada, stands an invisible wall. Between village and Maharwada, a road well-travelled: it acts as the border.

On a mound, the Maharwada; the rest of the village on the other side. This is how it has been from antiquity, so that the higher-caste folks can get clean water and fresh air; so that they are not polluted. Every Mahar house faces away from the village.

The Maharwada of my childhood was a bustling place. There was an imposing community hall, with a tiled roof supported by wooden beams. It had no doors, just an empty space inside it like a public hall. In the night, all the young men came there to sleep and argued about who was going to sleep where. From our home, we could see this community hall, the courtyard in front of it and any goings on there. Ours was an ordinary house otherwise. On either side were sturdily built wooden houses. Our home looked a little dilapidated in comparison, a gnarled tree trunk—mud walls, clay tiles on the top and under the tiles, a supporting beam, all soot-darkened. The house was naturally divided into two by a central pillar. When we came home from Mumbai, there was always a thorny jungle outside to greet us. All signs of human habitation would have been erased. After a few days of Aai's cleaning, the house would begin to look like a home. Even if it were only from a gasoline-powered petromax, light would begin to flicker inside

Aai would say, 'Boy, this is where you were born.' She would tell me stories about my birth again and again. Just as other castes have Brahmins to preside over their rituals, we had Bhaats. A Bhaat generally lives in the village. He performs your naming ceremony, your marriage. These Bhaats were also Mahars. But the community treated them with little respect. When a Bhaat came to the door, he would call out, 'Raosaheb, punya Maharaj' or 'Lord and Master, king of goodness'. I remember Sitaram Bhaat, who came to us. He was a man of sweet disposition. His manner of speaking was sweet too, a river of nectar. Everyone loved him.

Dada's generosity brought him much esteem in the village. When I was born, he presented the Bhaat with a young heifer and five vessels. Later, whenever I met him in the village, Sitaram Bhaat would say: 'You're nothing before your father in terms of generosity.' That was what I kept hearing. I don't think Dada's generosity was motivated by any fear of god. From what I can remember of him, he had a militant streak in his nature. He neither visited temples nor did he fast. When we were in the village and Aai would order him to bathe the Khandoba in our family shrine, 'on Sunday, at least', he would delegate the duty to me. When I was born, he was tasked with preparing a ritually pure meal for the Bhaats. Instead, he slaughtered a goat, over the priest's protests, and served mutton barbaat to the entire Maharwada.

I could tell you many stories about this militant streak. Once Dada went with his friend Satva to a wedding. They were well known in the area as exorcists. One of the women in the wedding party was possessed. Her hair lashed her koonkoo-smeared forehead as she spun round and round. A circle was drawn around her and various ritual items such as sour limes, pins and coconuts were put into it. Who knows what came over Dada. He broke through the circle, kicking people out of the way. He began to abuse the woman, besmirching the fair name of her mother. The woman began to act even more wildly. Whirling, she snarled, 'He called me a mother-fucker.' Satva replied in the same tone: 'Tell him to go back. This is a spirit from your own home'. This grand performance went on for quite a while. The wedding party was laughing uproariously. When Dada began to belabour the woman's buttocks with a thorny branch, the possession ceased. This story was told and retold for many years in the community.

Dada's nature was an intriguing mixture of the good and the bad. When he saw that the Mahar boys were not allowed to exercise in the village akhara, he opened up a space for them in our home. We began living on the front verandah. The interior of the house was dug up and red mud was put in. Sometimes he would get into the pit himself, teaching the younger boys the basic wrestling holds. Again, when the mrudang or the dholki had to be inked, he would be sent for. I have no idea where he acquired these skills.

When Dada returned to the village, the shine soon wore off. Now he had to find work to fill his belly. His job at the docks had not required much physical effort. In the village, the only work available was cutting the branches of neem and acacia trees. You had to buy the rights to the trees. With an axe on his shoulder, Dada would set out every day, accompanied by a couple of friends. His health began to improve because of the hard physical labour, the clean air. I remember him descending into a dry well to cut wood. Aai too began to work in the fields of the Maratha families, weeding, cutting grass, driving away the birds.

At that time, Prohibition was strictly enforced in the village. From time to time, Dada would feel like a drink. His solution? A distillery at home.

Dada's had a friend, Satva, a colourful chap who never bored you. He could make you laugh for hours. He would remind you proudly that he had got the woman who was in Patthe Bapurao's tamasha to dance for him. (In other words, he had slept with her.) He would describe her beauty in great detail. She was from our district. She had been dedicated to Khandoba in her youth. It was said that she was so fair that when she was eating paan, you could see drops of red running down her throat. Or so Satva said. He lived in a neighbouring village, Vashere, about two miles away. He was the lord and master of two women. Both of them slogged day and night to keep their husband. He lived off their earnings, a crane who stood still in the water and had its meals swim up to it. He would get up in the morning and go off to the taluka or come to our village. I had often seen his wives fighting, hurling filthy abuse at each other. It would seem that they were about to go for each other's throats when of its own, a truce would be declared. Tobacco and chuna would change hands. Then they would start again.

Perhaps it was Satva who introduced Dada to the art of distilling. Whenever he came home, he talked of little else. Rotten jaggery, ammonium chloride (or Navsagar, as it was called), the bark of whatever tree was to hand—he'd try anything to bump up the kick of the brew. For seven or eight days, the tin would be buried in a compost heap to brew. From time to time, Satva would go and sniff at it. Then he would get the wood ready to filter the alcohol. If the wood proved insufficient, Dada would pretend to be wandering about the village while actually scavenging for fallen twigs and branches. When the first drops began to flow, Satva would light a matchstick and test it. If the flame flared up, they would rejoice; it meant the brew was good.

But it was Aai who had to do the hard work to keep this enterprise going. She had to fetch water from a well two furlongs away.

Even though we had a still at home, Dada did not turn it into a business. Special friends or villagers would often be invited over to try his brew. At such times, a chicken from someone's henhouse would be stolen. Once Uma-ajya told me that I should kill a neighbour's chicken. I didn't like the idea and refused. When he complained to Dada, I was slapped soundly across the face. Dada had a skill at chicken-stealing that was all his own: 'Throw a wet cloth over a hen and it won't squawk when you're abducting it.' Sometimes an entire goat would be done away with. How does one keep a goat quiet? A pat of cow dung on the nose.

Dada was constantly tinkering with his brew. Once he bought a basket of sweet limes from the market. They were left to rot but that time everything turned sour. He spent sleepless nights wondering where he had failed.

Satva and Dada, the best of friends, would talk of everything, sometimes about their womanizing. Because I was young, they must have thought: 'What can he understand of these stories?' I heard that before coming to Mumbai, Dada worked at a Brahmin landowner's house on a yearly contract. Women would come to cut the grass. He would hide the scythe a woman was using and say to her, 'If you let me have sex with you, I'll return your scythe.' But sex was always a matter of mutual consent. If he had forced someone, the villagers would have beaten him up. In these matters, the atmosphere was quite free. The common saying, 'Before you choose your sheep, with me you'll have to sleep,' must have arisen here.

Satva and Dada would also talk about the tamasha. Both were connoisseurs of the form. Every tamasgir who visited the area had to stop at our home. One of them was Dashrath of Devthaan, a famous performer, who would visit with his company. Dashrath had a royal air about him; he could look every inch the heir to the throne when he was dressed up to play a royal. He composed laavnis too. Even in private, he spoke chaste Marathi. He was the female impersonator in Haribhau Wadgaonkar's tamashas. After that, he set up his own company. Haribhau was Patthe Bapurao's disciple. Haribhai Wadgaonkar had great respect, therefore, for Patthe Bapurao. The skit *Gaadvacha Lagna* ('The Wedding of the Ass') that is still hugely popular, was Wadgaonkar's. As a child I saw the same play as *Saawlya Kumbhar*.

When Dashrath grew old, he organized a brilliant company in the Maharwada at Devthaan, composed of sixteen- and seventeen-year-old youths. If you had no money for a ticket, a measure of bajri or jowar would do. For a long time, I nursed the ambition of becoming a tamasgir because of Dashrath. I still remember bits and pieces of the laavnis I had memorized: 'Raaya, dooroon mashi bola, shaalu maazha nireet laal zhaala' ('Your lordship, speak to me from a distance, the pleats of my fine sari have turned red') and 'Kunya howsyaana hows keli' ('That dandy slaked his lust') and 'Naar companyla geli, aan khaate oos, oos…Oosachi hote saakhar, naarila chaalana bhaakar/Hya goshticha yeta malaa radoo/Valya vaafyaat kashi mi padoo/Athhra shaal, shaal, khaate oos oos' ('A young lady went to the Company/ There she began to nibble sugarcane/Sugarcane turns to sugar, now simple food won't do for her/Oh, it makes me weep/How can I work in the muddy fields? Spread out a shawl for me and I'll nibble some cane.') That some of these could be obscene did not occur to any of us. Women, for instance, came in great numbers to see the tamasha.

Another famous personage I remember was Tatyaba Shinde. He was a real celebrity and sang well too. He had two or three bullock carts and at least ten or twelve dancers in his troupe, of whom Chandra was truly beautiful. His vagh—the farce that came after the laavnis—*Paathardicha Raja* ('The King of Pathardi') was always a big hit. The play maintained that where the king was a eunuch the court would be filled with eunuchs too. So how did Tatyaba's story end in tragedy? How did this man, so accustomed to playing royalty on the stage, end up on the streets with not even a beedi to call his own? When I went to the taluka to school, I saw him selling firewood. I can even remember a poem written about him in the old days. Later I saw this very Shinde doing physical labour—in the chorus of a production of *Gaadvacha Lagna* at a theatre in Lalbaug. Seeing him like that broke my heart.

I called Satva 'Mama', making him an honorary uncle. This had one benefit. He had a band in which he played the kaanda. Its sound resembled the shehnai but its pitch was higher. Dada also played the kaanda. Satva would begin a song, Dada would pick it up. The band had four players. Two played the kaanda, one played the soorkari and one the sambal. The soorkari player's single function was to go 'Bho…Bho' at intervals, holding the note. Playing the soorkari was exhausting work. It seemed as if the player might die one day, holding his breath. His cheeks would expand, blowing up as if he had a sour lime in each one. These breathing techniques would be taught in the Maharwada when boys were still young. Those who played the kaanda also had to learn specialized breath techniques. Young boys were taught how to blow through a hollow stalk of bajri into a basin full of water. Since I was going to school, I felt this was beneath me. Today I can play neither percussion nor wind, even though these skills were all around me.

I loved the sambal. In the left hand, a slender wooden stick; in the right, a hook, also of wood—both these were used to play the sambal, which was also covered with the kind of brocade used to adorn oxen. This was called a gajmukh, the head of an elephant. It was decorated with bits of glass. A circle of men would surround the musicians, dancing with the lejhim, an idiophone constructed of a wooden stick to which metal cymbals had been attached. I can see it still: the ends of the colourful turbans fluttering as the men danced to the rhythm of the sambal.

Sometimes, I went along with the band. I would say to Satva Mama, 'How well you play the kaanda. But look, your dinner plate has been set on the shitpot.'

He would answer with his patent abuses. 'I've danced at their mother's wedding processions,' he would say. 'Shall we curse these idiots with the kaanda?'

And then he would begin to heap abuse on the wedding party with his kaanda. The guests understood none of this; only we knew what was going on. I would roar with laughter.

Wedding season in the village meant good times for us. Money would flow into Dada's hands. We'd all have new clothes. The year's misery and poverty would be erased for a while. All the leftover food—the lhapsi porridge, the malpuas, the crisp puris—would come to us. At the weddings of the Thakars,* we would get only rice and bran and red masala. That was the extent of their wedding feast. Their wedding songs were always fun: 'Kaa re navrya, evdi raat re/Aata khaasheel shila bhaat re' ('Hey bridegroom, how late it's getting; now you'll be fed yesterday's food.') The groom would be carried in the crook of someone's arms or on someone's shoulders. No carriages or white horses for him. The wedding party would come from far and wide, taking the heat and the cold in their stride.

What if the Thakars were poor? They would treat the Mahars in the same way as the Marathas would. They would seat us at a distance from the rest of the wedding party. Our

---

*The Thakars are an Adivasi tribe who live in the forests of Maharashtra. They are Scheduled Tribes under the Constitution of India. The Marathi film *Jait re Jait* (Jabbar Patel, 1977) is based on the lives and beliefs of the Thakars.

water was slopped into glasses from a suitable height. Our leaf-plates were set out at a distance from the other guests'. The Mahar musicians were constantly spurned and rejected by the arrogant Maratha folk. Today I can see that the band gets respect. But at the time, they were slaves for those four days. Any child could come and order them to play. There was no schedule, no time table. 'Play because they're mixing delicacies from both sides and feeding the party.' 'Play because they're smearing the young couple with turmeric.' 'The wedding ceremony is on, play.' 'Play for the celebrations that will follow.' 'The wedding guests are washing their hands, come on, play.' 'Food is being taken to the groom's house. It's only three in the morning, why aren't you playing?' They wanted to extract value for every single paisa. But when it was all over and it was time to pay, they would begin to haggle. And there was no question of tips.

At times like these, Satva would come up with some outrageous solutions. If a particularly stubborn client refused to pay, he would set the soorkari after him. Each time the man left home, he would be followed everywhere by that 'Bho…Bho' sound. He would pay just to be rid of the nuisance.

We had a Thursday market. We would set out for it as if for a festival. Aai raised hens and would take their eggs to sell. It was an anna an egg. We enjoyed the market. We got bhel and jilebis to eat. The villagers sat in groups, according to caste, under the trees of the marketplace. The Mahar community sat near the Mari-Aai temple. This too was dictated by custom. Everyone could get to their designated spot with their eyes closed. The restaurants had different cups for different castes; there were Mahar cups and Chambhar cups, Mang cups and so on. Our cups were very often without handles and ant-infested. We had to rinse them ourselves before ordering tea. We sat separately; either on the verandah or on a bench behind the restaurant.

On market day, Dada would set off for the taluka as soon as he had had his tea. Even if he had no work, he would always make a quick round of the taluka. All the Mahars did this because they liked to wear clean clothes every day. Our village had no river close to it and water had to be drawn from a deep well. So the men went to the river in the taluka and washed their clothes there. While these dried, they made do with their loin cloths. On their way back, clean as cranes, they dazzled the eye. When I went with Dada to the river, there was a dilapidated old house that would always scare me. Aaji had told me a story about it. A Muslim mamledaar used to live in it. He had built extensions for his wives. During the British times, he had been a tin-pot tyrant. His hobby was fishing in the river; he would conduct official business there as well. It was said that he stuffed fish into the mouths of many ascetics and priests. This caused great unrest in the area. One day, one market day, in fact, the villagers rose in revolt. Everyone brought whatever weapons they had: spears, bows and arrows. They surrounded the house. The mamledaar hid in the basement. The beseigers poured gasoline into the house and sacks full of red chilli powder and set it on fire. They had brought the man's wives and children out to safety. In a while, he was turned to coal. Whenever I walked past it, I remembered Aaji's story. And wondered: Would I see the mamledaar's ghost?

—

The local board had built our school. Perhaps that was why we were not made to sit outside. In this matter, however, Tatya's experiences had been quite the opposite. In his day, the school was conducted in the Maruti temple. The Mahar children had to sit outside, on the steps. One day a Brahmin teacher had thrown a foot-rule at Tatya. Tatya had thrown it right back. It hit the teacher and drew blood. Terrified, Tatya fled to the Maharwada. He never went back.

There was a stony area behind the Maharwada, littered with huge black boulders. Around this was a cactus forest, which was useful in times of starvation. Our school building was also built on such a stony, dry area. It was well-constructed; it could be seen from a distance. My name was entered into the school's rolls in the third standard. Our teacher was also a Brahmin. He was lame in one leg and always wore white clothes that looked bleached. On his head, a Gandhi topi. If you went close to him, you could smell milk and butter.

The school had classes up to the fourth standard but from first to fourth, we all sat in one large hall. We would take a piece of sacking to sit on, along with our slates and schoolbags. I remember the early times well. We were not allowed to sit with the Maratha children from the village. They faced the teacher and we sat at right angles to them, facing in a different direction. If we were thirsty, there was no water for us at school; we had to go back to the Maharwada to drink. The Chambharwada was close by but they too would not give us water. Once a week, we would have to plaster the school with cow dung. There were teams of children who did this, in turn. But this was really the job of the older students. The Brahmin teacher would treat himself to a good nap in the afternoon, his legs up on the table in front of him. From time to time, he would tell us to steal sour limes or sweet limes from the orchard near the school for his use. When he was in school, we did not get the feeling that he discriminated on the basis of caste. But when we went to his house, he underwent a radical transformation. He became 'pure', in the ritual sense of the word. He had a small grocery store. If you had no money, you could take whatever bits and pieces of produce you had and exchange them for goods. But if we went to his house, we could not cross the threshold; we had to stand on the steps. The goods would be given in such a way that not even a finger touched us. The master we knew at school did not resemble the master in his lair. It was as if he had his caste consciousness hanging on a peg near the door and he could slip into or out of it, at will.

I was the city boy. I had brought some city words with me. For instance, while playing hu tu tu, I would use the word saboor,* when asking for a time out. The village boys would say thaamb or wait. The Maratha boys would not understand the word I used. They thought it was coarse. In reality, I spoke better Marathi than they. For this, I was mocked. Slowly, I stopped playing with them.

On the subject of language, then, some more memories. In the taluka school, we were mocked for using 'Mahardya' language. This cut to the bone. I would lash out in anger at the boys who insulted us. To prove how chaste my use of the language was, I would invariably use words like 'nahin' for 'no' or 'bazaar'. Both are words from Urdu but what of it? There are many words with Urdu roots that are now common currency in Marathi. I would invite them to explain why they didn't take exception to my use of these words. I could not say the nasal 'na' in a Marathi word like 'paani'. I was mocked for that too.

I began to escape from the Maharwada, not just physically but mentally too, into the world of books. I was becoming a little more sensitive with education. All sorts of questions formed a raucous tirade inside my head. In *Kondvaadyaat* ('In Prison'), there's a poem:

> Why did I ever discover the world of books?
> I could have been a stone in a stream,
> Grazed cattle in a meadow.
> No need then to bear the scorpion's sting.

---

*Presumably from 'Sabar karo', be patient, in Urdu.

These lines described my life. The poison of reading took the last few simple pleasures left to me. At that time, we lived like animals in the Maharwada, our lives based on an earthy philosophy. I was filled with revulsion against the life I was leading and wanted to get away. But those who seemed to be leading the kind of life I wanted for myself would have nothing to do with me. This was my conundrum.

And so I found myself growing increasingly isolated. Joining in the village children's play meant dealing with their contempt; but the Maharwada games held no interest for me either. Reading was my only pleasure.

Dhagya Hill was right in front of the school. In those days, it was rich in greenery; not bare and denuded as it is today. Aai would go there to gather firewood. What lay beyond, I would wonder. Over the crest of the hill, a postman would come every afternoon and return every evening. He had a rattle stick in his hand. Khaki uniform, a red turban on his head. He was the school's clock. The rattle of his stick signalled the end of the school day. Why did he cross the hill?

Eventually, I did find out. Over the hill was Kotul, a market town, whose mail he collected. He would be met halfway by the postman from Kotul. They would exchange letters. I marvelled that they seemed unafraid of the wild animals in the jungle.

At school, perhaps the number of students increased, because at some point we went from being a one-teacher school to being a two-teacher one. The new teacher was a

Mahar. He was dark-skinned, with smallpox scars on his face—the marks of the Devi. He wore a Nehru shirt and white pyjamas. He went bare-headed and combed his hair carefully. Of course, he wasn't going to get a place to stay in the main village. He came to stay in our verandah. He was a bachelor and wrote poetry. But his poems were really songs—and they dealt with Dr Ambedkar's revolution. It was from him that we got to hear about the movement that Dr Ambedkar had started in the city. He was nice to me at home but he snapped at me in school. I was bad at mathematics. I remember a couple of fine beatings he gave me. His village was on the far side of Dhagya Hill. At one point in time, his father decided to bring him a nanny goat, specially purchased so that he might drink fresh milk. I went with him to fetch the goat. Climbing the rough paths with him was terrifying but from up there, the village became an illustration out of a picture book: the trees, the people, reduced to miniatures. It was my first time in the terra incognita beyond Dhagya Hill. Masterji said, 'Can you see that peak over there? That's Mount Kalsubai.' Beneath us, the Mula River was a ribbon of silver. We didn't have to descend. His father brought the goat halfway.

Masterji was also a womanizer. My Tatya was his friend, their friendship was a deep, abiding one. Two women from the villages on the other side of Dhagya would bring baskets of eggs to sell. As the egg-sellers went by, Tatya and Masterji would shout teasing remarks at them. I didn't think they should behave like that, but it is only now, after all these years, that I'm saying this.

Masterji had some kind of arrangement with those women. They would generally take a break on the school verandah. The school keys were in his keeping. One morning when I went to school early, I found paper, string and crumbs of laddoos all over the floor. All kinds of suspicions flooded my mind. But such goings on were no novelty in the Maharwada. Some leftover bhakri was enough to buy the favours of a destitute woman.

The fourth standard. There was a well-built girl in my class. When she began to menstruate and her skirt was stained with blood, I was the first to notice.

Back in Mumbai, hanging around with loafers and dropouts at Kawakhana, I had peeked into closed rooms through the cracks in doors and windows. As a child I had seen many people having sex. One of these incidents is clear in my mind. I had an uncle whose name was Shiva. He had lost his wife and later took a mistress, a dark-skinned, voluptuous woman, a street acrobat. She would raise large stones with her hair and sling her body through iron hoops. She was a high-spirited woman. She wore male clothes—shirt and trousers—and did her long hair up in a bun. She would come to see Shiva-tatya, riding on a cycle. When all the men and women were at work, Shiva-tatya would bring her to the room in the chawl. He would give the old ladies who were still around some money for tea and snacks and they would absent themselves, often just going out to sit on the pavement. We boys found it rather amazing that this

Amazon turned all feminine and modest when she was with Shiva-tatya. We decided to spy on them with a mirror placed at the right angle to give us a look into the room. We saw them naked together, drenched in perspiration. I remember the wonder I felt, for a long time afterwards, at the discovery I had made: that women have hair between their thighs.

The rest of Shiva-tatya's life was tragedy. The street performer vanished one day, leaving him shattered. The happy-go-lucky fellow fell silent. Finding a place to sleep at home was always a problem so I would often sleep out in the street. And Shiva-tatya would be lying next to me. One night I felt his limbs threshing restlessly under the covers. I thought he'd had a drop too much. When the sweeper came along in the morning, Shiva-tatya would not stir. When they took off his bedding, I realized that he was dead. There was froth at his lips. The panchnama stated that he had taken an overdose of opium to kill himself.

Another memory: There was a three-storey building in front of our home. Vithabai, a white-skinned, pale-haired woman lived there. Bleached by vitiligo, her body seemed innocent of colour. Even her eyelashes were pale and her eyes were blue. Down her back snaked an orange-gold river of hair. She was full in the body and people would stop and gawp as she passed. Even though Vithabai had been born into the Mahar community, her speech and lifestyle were of a woman from the upper castes. If she stepped out into the sun, she went as red as a carrot. In comparison, her husband was truly ugly. He was as dark as night, blind in one eye, his face cratered with the marks of the Devi. He might have been nothing much to look at but he earned well. He was a motor mechanic who spent most of his time on his back under a car.

Their house was better decorated than anyone else's. Curtains hung at the door. Inside, a bed, a couch, furniture, cupboards with mirrors on them. I loved this house as a child for good reason. Amid all her splendour, Vithabai did not have any children. So she made much of me. Generally, childless women have a streak of restlessness. So Vithabai decided to pretend to be pregnant. She tied on a 'bulge' made of cloth. When the truth got out, all the women mocked her.

I was the love of her life. She would give me good things to eat, take me to the cinema and the theatre. I still remember that we went to see *Khajanchi* at the Roxy. If there was no one at home, she would hold me against her body. She would lie on the bed and ask me to press her thighs. At those times, she would hoist up her sari. While pressing those thighs that resembled the pith of the banana plant, smooth and pallid, something wild began to stir inside me. I was very young but the tumult inside me was intense, and that's the truth.

—

Dada's health began to degenerate. Staying in the village had brought some improvement for the first few years but this was only the flaring of the flame before the candle finally goes out. The spirit he had been drinking in Mumbai had burned deep into him. And his alcohol addiction had not subsided. No one in the village could diagnose what his illness was. Some said he had been possessed by an evil spirit; some said black magic had been used against him. He must have known what ailed him. He insisted on meeting his family and went to Mumbai. Almost a fortnight later, we got a telegram that he was seriously ill. When we got there, Dada was a shadow of his former self. He was moaning in pain, babbling as if demented. They kept smearing him with holy ash from the family graveyard. No one had thought to take him to hospital. But still death would not come. In his delirium, he kept trying to pile his clothes up and build some kind of house. The clothes would fall over again and again.

He died, threshing and flailing, like a lamb being slaughtered. I was watching a man dying for the first time at such close quarters. But before he died, Dada did not forget to extract a promise from his brother, my Tatya, that he would look after us.

Commotion broke out at home. I remember clearly that I did not cry. I watched it all with dry eyes. 'Arré, make the boy cry or grief will suffocate him,' someone said. A photographer was brought. It was the custom at Kawakhana for the family to be photographed around the corpse. It seems odd today but even in that time of grief, the bereaved would push and shove to get into the frame as the cameraman took cover under a black cloth that he draped over his huge camera.

The women of the area broke the thread of black beads that Aai had around her neck, the symbol of her status as a married woman. The one gold bead left on it was placed in Dada's mouth in a roll of betel leaf. The koonkoo on her forehead was wiped off; her glass bangles broken. The corpse had to be bathed on a plank taken from the door, according to custom. A shiny silver rupee was placed on his forehead. A floral bed-sheet, new and crisp, covered the bamboo sticks that were tied up to make a bier. Over the corpse, some loose coins, urad dal, puffed rice. The dal was to prevent him from returning as a ghost.

Tatya poured water into his mouth. The Mahars had their own separate burial grounds at Worli. In those days, we buried our bodies. A grave had been dug, its depth the height of a man. All those present dropped a handful of earth on the body. After thirteen days, we served the ritual meal. I refused to let anyone shave my head. 'Never mind, he's only a boy,' they said and did not insist. Getting the crows to eat the food that was laid out was the next excitement. Some beedis and alcohol were laid out with the food. I touched the food. And then the crows swooped.

In truth, we had nothing now. With all his stealing and petty theft, Dada had managed to provide for us. With our world in ruins, we turned away from the city and returned to our home. Aai's birth home was about two miles away from our village. Her family had fields there. My mother's grandfather came running up with the suggestion that Aai remarry. A prospective husband had been found for her, a widower, who had seen Aai and knew that two young children came with her. I was a baby then; my sister seven or eight. The Maharwada would not have pissed on our fingers if we had cut them, they were so callous. If you challenged their decisions, they would lay waste to your honour. And my grandfather was very careful about his honour. But Aai fell upon him like a lightning bolt. She resented his suggestion that she should remarry immediately.

'I am no beggar at your door. I will work and bring up my little ones,' she told him to his face.

When Aai was born her father died. Hardly had her father been shoved into the earth, when the family began to torment my grandmother. That she had not produced a son was counted against her. They starved the young mother. They made her work like an animal. They fed her bhakri made of chaff and husk. Finally, she tired of this persecution and returned to her father's house. My mother was at the breast but she was snatched from her mother. Aai would say: 'Once your grandmother went home, she never returned. She married again.'

And so my mother grew up without a mother. She had never known maternal warmth. Until she got married, Aai and her mother had not met. But my father, demonstrating an instinctive understanding of the bond between mother and child, took it upon himself to bring them together. After that, my maternal grandmother would come to our house often. She was now blind. I would lead her from her village, holding her stick. Her second marriage had produced no sons. She had not one but three daughters. But I felt a great respect for this grandmother of mine and her daughters, my aunts. They had spent their lives in poverty but they were very loving and did what they could for us. We felt much closer to them than to my mother's birth family.

Aai now became the man of the house. All her life she worked hard. I was deeply moved to see her strength. She gave us more love and care than our father could have. She nursed us with the tenderness you might show to a blister on the palm of your hand. I sometimes wonder: If Dada had lived, would I have become the person I am? Who knows whether I would have studied or not? Where are all those children who studied with me in the Maharwada? Aai's sacrifices gave me the impetus to push myself out of the abyss. Dada's ways were not ours. There was an unspoken agreement that we would never do any of the things he had done.

I remember asking Aai casually, 'What did you see in him?'

With tears in her eyes, she told me the story of her life. She could not even remember when she had married him for she had been in the cradle. When she was old enough to wear the long skirt and blouse that adolescent girls wore, she could not believe that she had been married as a child. The black beads around her neck seemed fake to her. When any bridegroom showed up, she would demand of her grandparents, 'Marry me to him.'

To explain what being married meant, the elders of her family would seat her behind the bridegroom. She would be given the role of the bride's maid, dressed in a nine-yard sari that would balloon around her slender frame, and with a coconut in a copper vessel on her head. And Aai would feel, 'This is *my* wedding.'

This is how she came to be married: Aai came from the same village as my paternal grandmother. They shared the same surname too: Kasbe. Aaji was then in Mumbai. When it was time for Dada to be married, Aaji swore that her daughter-in-law would come from her own village, Aurangapur. But there was no one of a suitable age to be found. So Aaji asked for little Aai as her daughter-in-law. Aai's father refused the match. He had no high opinion of Aaji's in-laws' village, Dhamangaon.

Our village did not have a good reputation then. 'Hoodlum's Dhamangaon' is how it was known. Almost everyone from Dhamnagaon's Maharwada was in Mumbai. No one had any farm land. Those who had some land did not cultivate it. Almost everyone drank to excess and gambled. When any one of them came from Mumbai, they would be kitted out in the latest styles but they would return bankrupt. They would be forced to pawn some household goods to the Marathas for the bus fare to the city. The Marathas lay in wait: the coat off your back, your umbrella, all these could be pawned. It was not likely that one would want to marry one's child into such a village.

But Aaji was not to be dissuaded. She got up from

Aurangapur's Maharwada and marched off to the main village and sat down in front of the patil and announced: 'I am a daughter of this village. I have my rights.' My maternal grandparents were summoned and told that their daughter was to be given in marriage to this woman's son. In those days, people did not have the guts to oppose the decision of the village. That is how Aai came to marry Dada.

When Dada was alive and not at home, Aai would curse him lavishly. 'My accursed destiny,' she would say. But his death seemed to bring about a gradual change in her nature. Now she could spend hours weeping in his memory. 'Your father never laid a hand on me in anger,' she would say between sobs. 'When your father sat down to eat, he would make sure there was bhakri for me to eat, some curry to help it down. He cared about these things.'

There were many in the community to praise my father's generosity. Whenever I went to the village with some money in my pocket, the old folks would say, 'What a miser you are, boy. Look at your father. What a man he was. Such a generous spirit. When he came back from Mamai, the whole Maharwada would have parties with mutton and liquor and toddy flowing. And you can't even stand us a cup of tea?' What could I say to this? I could remember instances of his generosity too. Anyone who got down at the village square was welcome to eat at our house. Once, a distant relative turned up. That was a bad day. We were going to eat bhakri, given to us for guarding the village border. But how could we offer a guest that? A secret signal passed between Dada and Aai. She took her last big copper vessel and left the house. The guest must have thought she was going to fetch water. When she returned, she had provisions—wheat, daal, jaggery—in the crook of her arm. That night our guest dined off puran polis. When the guest had departed, Aai wept over the loss of her hundi. 'Forget it, woman!', Dada said. 'Daane daane pe likha hai khaanewaale ka naam. (Every grain arrives with its eater's name inscribed on it).'

Blame it on this habit or on his growing addictions, but we lived hand-to-mouth. Though, even if he had lived a thrifty life, what could have remained? What did we have by way of household goods? Two huge vessels for storage which had probably been saved because they were so firmly embedded in the ground. A wooden handmill, a clay oven. A few German silver vessels. A few brass vessels. A wooden trunk. A couple of quilts against the cold winds of winter. I was rather proud of these quilts. No one in the Maharwada had such beauties. Aai stitched these quilts really well. She would design them in concentric circles. I still have one of them, carefully stored at home. Like her love, it does not wear out.

In our crowded room in Mumbai, the wooden trunk came in handy. Our entire world was stored in it: masalas, whatever we had to buy and sell, grains from the ration shop. Aai could tell, by feel, what each bundle contained. The trunk would also be used as a partition. 'This is the border. Up to the trunk is ours.' Even the little ones dared not trespass. One felt that it was strange, this way in which blood relatives lived.

After Dada died, I methodically and carefully smashed his still and all the paraphernalia that went with distilling. I had no use for such an inheritance. In later life, I never became addicted to alcohol. I faced many trials, I was often deeply disturbed. On more than one occasion, I contemplated suicide. They say that someone who comes to this stage often turns to alcohol, he 'drowns his sorrows', as the phrase goes. But to me, even the word evokes a series of family tragedies. My grandfather, my uncle, my father—all victims of alcohol. These days my cousin carries on the tradition. He is an incorrigible alcoholic. I have failed in every attempt to reform him.

That doesn't mean I became a complete teetotaler. I often hobnob with important people. In their company, I sometimes drink a peg or two. But I am always more interested in the food that accompanies the drinks. I am already intoxicated with life, a natural internal intoxication that makes the high of alcohol seem pale in comparison.

I did not hate the other things in the house or any of Dada's other effects. For instance, I loved the kaanda that he would play. For a long time, it used to hang on a peg. When I am alone, I often hear him play it, but I had never learned how. That his skill should have passed away with him is a matter of deep regret for me. But I was moving away from the Maharwada, seeking refuge in the world of books.

—

I can't say which year these things happened. But I do remember that I was in the fourth standard when we ate the jilebis of Independence. We also got shiny new badges with Bharat Mata on them. We wore these on our chests proudly. But what did it really mean? I don't remember my life changing in any significant way. Village leaders made speeches in our school; they made no sense to me.

I was quite smart. I had drunk of the forbidden waters of the city. When a supervisor came to the school, I was the first to jump up and answer his questions, recite a poem or sing it in the right tune. I was no good at mathematics, though. I just couldn't get those work-time-speed problems right or how many taps it would take to fill a tank. I sailed through language and history. There were just five of us in the fourth standard. I was the only thin one, the rest were cheerfully chubby. Bhagwant Awari was big and strapping. He could have eaten me alive, books and all, in a single bite. But he was affectionate in his behaviour towards me.

I failed at mathematics in the annual examination. But perhaps the teacher was feeling benevolent and thought to himself: 'The rest will go to the taluka school; what's the point of keeping him back?' He gave me some grace marks and pushed me up into the next class. Now the question before Aai was whether I should be allowed to study further or not. Uma-ajya said to her: 'Sakhu, what's the point of sending the lad to school? Are we Brahmins? Baniyas? Let him loaf around and eat scraps. Or take the animals to graze.

You'll get some money that way.' But Aai paid no heed to this. She decided to educate her son, make him a big sahib. I wonder: who could have inspired such aspirations in her in those times?

Babasaheb Ambedkar used to say: 'What dreams do the women of Maharwada have for their children? That their sons should become peons or sepoys? A Brahmin mother's ambitions are different: My son should become a District Collector, she says. Why do Mahar women not harbour such longings?'

Did this speech have some unconscious effect on my mother? Either way, I started trudging to the taluka school, three miles there and back again.

When I thought of Uma-ajya just now, I began to see that he was a malign presence in our family. We were not obliged to him in any way but some people just have a nasty nature. He could not bear hearing about anyone else's successes; his stomach would hurt. He would tell us ghost stories. He would tell us about the *Nilavanti*: 'If you read the *Nilavanti*, you will be able to understand the language of the birds and the beasts. You can also kill a man with your spit.' We would sit under a neem tree, a suitable place for such stories, and he would tell us again and again, never tiring of the story, of how as a young man he had gone to read the *Nilavanti* in a thorny and desolate forest and a five-hooded cobra had manifested and hissed warnings at him. There were yellow-paper-covered editions of the *Ramayana* and *Mahabharata* in his family shrine. I yearned to read them but he would not let me so much as touch them.

Once, this Uma-ajya made a remark in passing that caused a terrible storm in me. How could anyone be so cruel? Did Aai ever forget the hurt of having her child harbour doubts about her character? And was I even old enough to understand what it meant to destroy someone's character?

One day, I had returned from school and was chatting with Uma-ajya, under a tree. With a single remark, the cunning old man threw a matchstick into a dry haystack. This is how he put it: 'So tell me, boy. Your father's dead and gone but your mother's pregnant. How did that happen?'

The match caught fire. A storm of questions roared through my head. I had no answers. In Kawakhana, I had heard many stories about widows. Once I had seen a newborn infant in a dustbin… Now I felt suffocated at home.

One day I come home to find that my mother has taken to her bed. I do not feel like looking at her face. The old woman from next door is heating water on the fire.

'Hey boy, your mother miscarried,' she says.

I lose my head. I say what no child should ever, *ever* say to his mother. 'How come you're pregnant when my father's dead?' I ask straight out. My mother does not know whether to laugh or cry. She stares at me as if she's an imbecile.

Aai and I did not speak to each other for days. I ate what was set before me and went to school. In the end, the floodgates burst somewhere inside my mother and she fell upon my neck and wept. She explained exactly how it happened. She had already been a couple of months pregnant when Dada died. I felt like someone who had been released from hell. How much pain I had inflicted on her! I promised myself I would try not to cause her any further pain. Aai did not forget either. When she was sitting with the other village women, she would recount this incident and they would laugh themselves sick at my expense.

If you had asked me about this terrible moment even a couple of years ago, I would not have been able to talk about it. But Aai made me promise to tell the whole truth to at least one person in my life. It was she who gave me the strength.

—

I have tried my best to forget my past. But the past is stubborn, it will not be erased so easily. Many Dalits may see what I am doing here as someone picking through a pile of garbage. A scavenger's account of his life. But he who does not know his past cannot direct his future.

The Maharwada I knew in my childhood has been destroyed over the last thirty or forty years. But how can I erase those vivid images? They haunt me still.

It was not in the Mahar's nature to beg. The Mahar did not see baluta—his share of the produce of the land—as charity. It was his by right and it was one of the fifty-two rights that the Mahars had been granted by deed of gift. Everyone was proud of this tradition. By this tradition too, they had received land that had been granted with only a nominal tax attached. This is something you see especially in Western Maharashtra. The small piece of land that adjoined a Mahar house was called the haadki, the bone yard, perhaps because the bones—the 'haad' in Marathi—of the dead animals we stripped ended up there. The land that was some distance away was called 'hadavla'. I don't remember ever seeing the Mahars from my village at work on the land. I was told that they had once tilled the soil but that was in the time before my birth. But since it was very far away, everyone used the hadavla as the village commons. In return, we were given some nominal payment.

A disturbing story is told in the Mahar community about the fifty-two rights. The Muslim king of Paithan-Bedar is said to have given us these rights. Vitthal Ramji Shinde wrote in his book, *The Question of Untouchability in India*, that he had seen the copper plate recording the grant. It said: 'A bastion of the Purandhar Fort was being built but would not stand. The Padshah had a dream that if the eldest son and eldest daughter of a family were to be buried there alive, the work would be completed. When the king awoke, he told Yesaji Naik Chibe, [who was a Mahar], about his dream. Naik did not hesitate. "I offer you my son and daughter-in-law," he said. And so Nathnak and Devkai were buried alive on the eighth day of the bright half of the lunar month of Ashwin. And the bastion was completed.'

Another legend of the origin of these rights concerned the honesty of the Mahars. A beautiful young daughter of the Padshah had to be escorted to Delhi. On the way, she had to cross a dense jungle. This was the time when there were no vehicles and so a trusted Mahar was sent with her. He was a young man, virile and tough. When he returned to the court after completing his task, someone suggested that all was not as it should be. It was suggested that he might have raped the princess. The Mahar reminded the Padshah that before he left he had entrusted a small wooden box to the ruler's care. 'This contains something of value to me,' he had said. 'Please keep it until I return.' Now he asked the Padshah to open the box. Inside was his penis. He had had it cut off in advance.

The king was pleased by this display of honesty. He said: 'Ask what you want.'

'I want nothing for myself,' said the young man. 'But give my community something that will last for generations.'

The king granted the Mahars the fifty-two rights. These are the glorious traditions that gave rise to the Maharki, the entitlements of the Mahars.

What I saw of this Maharki as a child has left its scars. This history will not be erased. Perhaps it will only go when I die. This stain of helplessness on my face? It dates back to that time. However much I scour my face, even to the point of bleeding, it will not be wiped away.

There was no timetable for the Mahar's work. It was slavery, for he was bound to whatever work had to be done for all twenty-four hours of the day. This was called bigar labour. Most of these jobs needed neither study nor skill. Some of the jobs fell into disuse. But others remained, millstones around our necks. We still had to take the village taxes into town. We were supposed to run in front of the horse of any important person who came into the village, tend to his animals, feed and water them and give them medicines. We made the proclamations announcing funerals from village to village. We dragged away the carcasses of dead animals. We chopped firewood. We played music day and night at festivals and welcomed new bridegrooms at the village borders on their wedding days. For all this, what did we get? Baluta, our share of the village harvest. As a child, I would always go with my mother to claim our share. Each house had its own bounden Mahar and once the grain had been stacked in the threshing floors, someone from each Mahar family would be on his or her way, shorn widows included. Each Mahar would carry a coarse blanket. The farmers grumbled as they handed over the grain: 'Low-born scum, you do no work. Motherfuckers, always first in line to get your share. Do you think this is your father's grain?' The Mahars of those days were no pushovers. They were glossy black and well built. They gave the Marathas as good as they got. The Marathas would try to fob us off with grain from the top of the heap, where it is at its thinnest. We wanted grain from the bottom, where the ripe grain would settle. Finally, the Mahars would spread their blankets on the grain and the Marathas would give them whatever was beneath. This came with a stream of abuse. The Mahars would ignore them completely as they tied up their bundles.

Speaking of the duties of the Mahars, another story comes to mind. Once all the taxes of the village were collected, it fell to the Mahars to deliver the money to the authorities in the taluka. When the money had been deposited, the clerk would hand over a receipt.

In much the same way, an old widow goes to pay the tax. The poor thing deposits the money but forgets to take the receipt. The next day, when the old lady comes running to the courthouse for the receipt, the Brahmin clerk, cunning as a fox, shows no humanity. He pretends not to remember. Slapping herself across the face with both hands, the old woman comes back to the village. She is accused of stealing the money. She begs and pleads. She swears her innocence at the feet of the goddess. But no one has any pity on her. All the villagers spit their scorn at her. She is handcuffed and taken to the taluka headquarters, deemed guilty of theft. The clerk walks out scot free. The old lady serves a jail sentence of two or three months and returns.

Once, there was a great quarrel between the villagers and the Mahars at the time of the sharing of the harvest. Tradition had it that as soon as the grain was harvested, the Mahars should get their share. The villagers did not calculate exactly how much the Mahars were entitled to. As cats and dogs make do, so do Mahars; or so the villagers thought. Besides, it was good karma to feed the orphan and the Mahar. The Mahar community was also seen as an asset to the village. In a certain village, the Mahar community, tired of ill-treatment, decided to leave en masse. When the villagers heard of this, they rushed to stop them. They mollified them and brought them back with due honour. Perhaps they felt that some calamity might be visited upon them if there were no Mahars in the village. After that, the Mahars and villagers never let the tensions get to the point of no return.

One year the Mahars decided not to divide the share among the families. They decided instead to throw a feast to which the forty villages in the area would be invited. Of course, it would only be Mahars at the feast. A huge pile of food was stored in the bone yard. Not even the village headman had ever had so much. This pile of food caused the villagers to throw a fit. People began to say: 'See how they wax fat on our labour!' That was it. The next year, the Mahars got nothing. On one side of this war were the twenty or thirty Mahar families; on the other, the two thousand-odd villagers. The village also had a Chambar household, but the Chambars did not bother with the Mahars' quarrels. Their business—the making of leather thongs for the water-wheel—depended on the village.

Comparatively, some Mahar families were well off. Some had bullock carts, others had a surplus of milk and butter. They worked as drovers in the Konkan area and they bought and sold the stallions and local bull breeds there. The Mahars I saw as a child were tall and well built, a glossy black. The village went in fear of them. This was because of a poison they had developed, Soma Mahar. I saw some that Uma-ajya had. It was pure white. Once the Mahars deployed this weapon, the cattle in the village would begin to die off, one by one. It was a horrible thing to do but it was only used when some money-maddened tyrant tried to oppress the Mahars. The poison would be mixed with some millet or worked into a bhakri. In the dead of night, when no one could see, this would be fed to the animal. Any stripling, even a child the size of a fist, could do this. The Mahars thus killed two birds with one stone. They landed a blow at the enemy; and they got the meat and hide of the animal. Once in a while, though, the villagers would retaliate by burying the carcass in the fields. But it isn't as if the village was always at one over this issue.

The village had its factions as the Maharwada did—the feud between the Avari and Papal families, especially, was particularly strong. There were many Avaris in the village, fewer Papals. One of the Avaris always became the village patil. They took pride of place at the Pola festival or on other religious occasions. The Papals had migrated to the village, so the Avaris treated them as migrants. When the Papals came to the village, they had brought a Mahar household with them. These were the Rupavates of the Maharwada. We Pawars were watchmen for the Avaris. We got our share of the harvest from them; the Rupavates from the Papals. But if an animal of either family died, all the Mahars butchered it together.

If the villagers turned nasty or complained more than usual, the Mahars forgot their differences and became one. Gleaming choppers would be displayed on the village square. The Mahars would swear: 'We'll rip your arses open.' The village would ban the Mahars and forbid them entry. The road would be closed. No one would give the Mahars any work. Finally, some sensible villager would broker a truce.

I remember one such negotiation: village versus Maharwada. There were heaps of stones and rocks on the boundary of the Maharwada. A woman from each household stood guard, arms akimbo, on each heap. It seems as if this time blood would be shed. The Mahars were summoned to the temple. They filled the temple square, bare-chested men in their ragged clothes, their knives gleaming at their shoulders.

The patil, the kulkarni, and other important citizens were seated there. It began.

'Who do you think you are?'

Kashaba, strapping, youthful, black as night, replied: 'We are kings.'

'Of whom are you kings?'

'We are kings of ourselves.'

That day no compromise was possible.

But it was the quarrel over water that continued at a low boil. The Mahar well was to the west of the village. To fetch water, we had to cross the village, and walk past the Maruti temple too. The villagers' well was below the village. The local Board had a notice there: 'This well is open to people of all castes and creeds.' Be that as it may, no Mahar was ever seen there; the dark deep waters of the Mahar well were abundant, and delicious. In the summer it was as cool as if it had been stored in earthenware. As a child, I would wonder why the villagers were so stupid. Our well was at a height; theirs lower down. Water from our well would seep into theirs. But they could not see what I had understood even as a child. The Chambars did not drink from our well. To do so would mean they would lose caste. That the Chambar women sat, hour after hour, by the Maratha well, to beg for a pot of water rather than draw water from the Mahar well, made me very angry.

The village well was paved and had a water-wheel whose rumble I can still hear. Our well had no such facilities. One had to stand on the wall and draw water by letting down a pot. The children would spend the long summer afternoons drawing this cold water and dousing themselves in it.

One day the village woke up to the fact that the Mahar women were polluting the Maruti temple when their shadows fell on it as they passed up and down to fetch water. So they closed the road. The other route to our well went past the lake, a mile-long struggle against sludge and slime. The Mahars fought back; they took recourse to the law. 'We won't give up our right of way. You can install Maruti somewhere else,' the Mahars announced combatively.

Then a miracle occurred. A new mamledar, a Christian, was transferred to the taluka. He was a former Mahar and understood what it meant to be one. He took it as his mission to bring justice to the Mahars. Once a Mahar converted to Christianity, he could no longer be considered someone who could pollute the village. And if the Christian were also an official, he had nothing at all to worry about. The entire village would be at his beck and call. The Mahar community met the mamledaar and asked him to come to Dhamangaon and sort out the issue. Today, the mamledaar of a taluka is not an important person but those were the days of the British. The mamledaar agreed to come. 'I will not enter the village,' the Christian mamledaar announced. Instead, he called a meeting in the Maharwada.

This was the first time in living memory that a mamledaar was coming to the Maharwada. The Mahars were delighted. They decorated the area with garlands and gudis—bamboos to which colourful cloth was tied. The square was painted. They welcomed him with music. They tied an expensive turban on his head, one bordered with gold zari. The patil and the talati were looking to come to the Maharwada to supervise the arrangements. They wanted a meeting of the local dignitaries at the village square. That the mamledaar should choose the Maharwada over the village was an insult. But when the powers that be are against you, to whom can you appeal? They turned up, abject in their humiliation. Five or six of the village leaders had cases filed against them. All of them were made to sign apologies. They promised not to trouble the Mahars again, not to try and close off the right of way. For a long time, Javji Buwa—a village elder—kept this written statement in a cylindrical tin and guarded it with his life. When I had acquired an education, Javji Buwa would take out these papers and make me read them aloud to him. He would call it a 'mushalka', a word that means 'covenant' or something like that. His chest would swell with pride as I read. When he died, he left them as a legacy for his son, as if they were a cache of gold, added to over the generations.

—

'So have you eaten the meat of dead cattle? Tell me honestly, how does it taste?' I was asked recently by an intellectual at Sahitya Sahvas, a writers' colony in Mumbai. The question took my breath away. I answered in some confusion:

'When I ate it, I was not at the age at which one remembers tastes. I only knew how to assuage my hunger, by filling the hole in my belly. During a famine, Vishwamitra ate the leg of a dog. During the great war, the Maratha platoons ate the meat of horses. So I won't talk about the dead cattle that I may have eaten.'

But it is true that the death of cattle brought great excitement to the Maharwada. It is also true that if the animal had died falling off a cliff, the excitement was even more acute. Such an animal's flesh would be fresh. News that an animal had died in the wilds did not take long to get to the Maharwada. It would pass along faster than the telexes of today. When the vultures and kite began to circle, like aeroplanes, the Mahars would locate the fallen animal. They would rush to get there before the birds picked the carcass clean.

How many vultures? Fifty or so. Their wings flapping, they would make strange sounds, 'Machaak machaak.'

Annabhau Sathe has compared vultures to the velvet-jacketed sons of money-lenders. If you threw a stone at them, they'd flap and move away a little but their greed drew them back to the body. They probably hated the Mahars. After all, we were snatching food from their claws. Their cruel eyes, their sharp beaks! Were they considering me as a possible snack? I would wonder.

'It's been a while since we've had a good cut of meat in the Maharwada,' many an aged person would be heard saying. 'I've forgotten what it tastes like.' Taking whatever was to hand, pots, pans, dishes, ghamelas, the Mahars would run. Until the last strip of skin had been cleared, no one took a break. The women would chatter excitedly with each other. Children our age would be delighted for an entirely different reason. Just under the hide was a membrane that could be used to make musical instruments like the dafli and the dholak. A piece the size of a lota or an empty rolling board was enough. Stretched out and left to dry in the sun, it would thrum like a percussion instrument in a day or two.

Carrying a dead cow is killing. Its dead weight is enormous but only two men would carry it. All four of its hooves would be tied and a bamboo would be inserted between them, a huge needle threadled through the gap between its legs. It looked as if a palanquin were being carried. When it was a cow, the sight of those pathetic eyes turned sightlessly towards the sky would chill me. Those eyes haunt me still. My mother's eyes and a cow's eyes showed remarkable similarities, it seemed to me. When it was our family's turn to carry the carcass, my mother would have to do it. I could not bear to see her struggle for breath. I wished I were a little older, so I might be able to lessen her burden.

The carcass was distributed among the entire community. It was divided according to annas in the rupee, so that one Maharwada meant one rupee. Each family had a different share. One family might be entitled to half—or eight annas, as a rupee then had sixteen annas; another might get just one-and-a-half anna. These divisions and entitlements reflected our social structure. If a family was large, it got a smaller share. Within a family, the male siblings were entitled to portions of the share. If you had a larger share, you were worthy of respect. Those who got large shares were seen as our elders and betters. Our share was two annas in the rupee, one-eighth of whatever the Mahars were given. The suffering of those whose share was one or two paise (one-hundredth or one-fiftieth of the whole) was inhuman. Into some houses, half the carcass would go; into others, it would only be the intestines, the cartilage, the offal.

The animal was divided according to the gudsa. This word appears in Laxmibai Tilak's autobiography. Who knows whether the Marathi litterateurs have heard of it or not? Laxmibai had heard of it. After all, she knew some Mahar Christians. Unless you know something about that caste, you wouldn't know.

What was I saying? I was talking about the gudsa, a name for the animal's bones. I remember some of those names even today. The one near the back, we called 'dhharya'. The one above the fetlock, we called 'chaaklya' and the one above the knees, 'metya'. The Mahars would fight over these bones. Sometimes blows were exchanged. The women would pull each other's hair, and abuse each other's mothers. Even today, the struggle for the bones continues. It's a struggle over who should get the cut of meat with the gudsa. And everyone curses and swears, so much abuse flowing that it covers the whole carcass, from the tip of the horn to the end of the tail. I remember one of the scenes of this division. There was a huge boulder in the Maharwada. There were hollows in it, which looked like vessels of different shapes carved into the stone as if it were wood. Some old ladies would recount their childhood memories: 'We would sit and eat on this boulder. You could break the gudsa easily on the edge of the boulder. The gudsas of those days! How thick the blood that oozed out of them.' Who knows why but this would bring back my school history text books. Illustrations of primitive men sitting at the mouth of their caves. A fire in the middle. The carcass of an animal on the spit. Teeth tearing into the meat. I could see a relationship somewhere, or so I would think.

The Mahars worshipped Bhaadhava, whose origin was recounted in folktales that were full of magic and miracles. Balls of flour would be boiled and then worshipped. The story goes that at some time in the distant past, a Mahar had killed the patil's buffalo. It was in the month of Bhadrapad (around August-September), a time of hunger for the Mahars.

The villagers suspected the Mahars and came to the Maharwada to check. The aroma of meat came to their noses. How could it not? It was being cooked in every Mahar home. The Marathas were jubilant. Now they had the Mahars where they wanted them; they would beat them to within an inch of their lives. At that very moment, the Mahars were praying for Bhaadhava's intercession. 'We will never forget you,' they promised. And that was it! Every vessel, every plate was filled with snow-white balls of dough where once the meat was. And since he saved us from this difficulty, we began to worship Bhaadhava.

But consider this. If half a carcass were to be brought into a Mahar home, it would not be consumed in one sitting. And where did they have fridges? So what did they do with so much meat? They would dry it. They would cut it into thin strips called chaanya. These would be dried by the fireplace. The smoke would turn them bright red. I don't know how the Mahars learned to do this but when I read that they smoke pork in the West in the same way, I felt proud of the Mahars. When the chaanya were dry, they would be cut into pieces which were called todkya. These were held in reserve for the bad months of Shravan and Ashadh. Sometimes, a beautiful white fungus would grow over the todkya, or maggots would sprout on them. The young ones were given the job of drying them again in the courtyard, guarding them with sticks.

Not one part of the animal would be wasted. The fat was reduced and burned in lamps in the houses and the bones were sold to the Muslim who came to the village. You've probably read of the way the yak is used in the tundra. 'Chaanya', 'todkya', these must sound like new words to you. This brings back a joke about these words from childhood. Dhondu Bapu's tamasha group from Kothul was famous in those days. Bapu was a colourful character. His face bore the marks of the goddess and was as black as the bottom of a frying pan. His eyes were squint. He played the songadya, the clown. When the king sentenced him to death by hanging (phaansi), he would say, 'Oh I'll take faashi with pleasure.' The audience would roar with laughter. The Mahars got the in-joke. Faashi was one of the tastiest bits of an animal. The higher castes, of course, didn't get it.

While they might not have known these words, some of the Marathas had developed a taste for the meat. A Maratha youth would drop by our house. I won't use his name, for these revelations might hurt him. He would eat beef on the quiet and then threaten us with dire consequences if we told on him in the village.

One day, I filled my pockets with crisply roasted chaanya and went to school. I was going to sneak off to the back of the school in the break and have myself a feast. All went as planned but a Brahmin friend turned up and asked, 'What's this? Eating alone?' I flushed with embarrassment and mumbled, 'Oh nothing, just some crunchies' for want of a better answer. 'How do they taste?' he asked. 'Come on, give us a taste.' I didn't know what to do. Here I was, about to pollute a Brahmin. What if the village found out? Now he began to plead for some. I gave in, gave him some 'crunchies'. He loved the taste. He spread the word to his friends. They were also Sonar-Shimpis, upper-caste boys, and they wanted the 'crunchies', too.

When the examinations were close, all of us would sleep in the school. The teacher would conduct night classes. He would rouse us at dawn. When Aai came to sell fodder, she would bring my lunch with her. She would grind mutton on the grinding stone and place the cooked mince on a bhakri. One day, who knows how, a couple of my friends got hold of my bhakri and wolfed it down. They grew to enjoy the taste. So that I might not starve, they would bring me their poli-bhaji in exchange.

It was easy to tell the difference between the taluka and the village. The upper-caste boys treated me as an equal in the taluka school. I had the run of their homes, except for the kitchens. Mhase and Shahane were special friends.

It wasn't that I had some agenda; that I wanted to pollute my high-born friends. It was all innocent, childish fun. And later I would realize that my friends had known what they were eating all along but did it all the same.

—

I used to feel that going to ask for food that was our share, according to the terms of baluta, was like begging. But this was the time when the slaves were not even aware that this was a sign of slavery. It was our right, we thought.

Every week the guard duty would change. Just as there

were two factions in the Maharwada, there were two in the village. Each village faction corresponded to a Mahar faction; the Mahars would be given their rights by a certain village faction. At the time of the Holi festival, there was always a fight over whose bonfire the Mahars would ignite first.

When it came to asking for bhakri, it was generally the women who went. Where there were no women of appropriate age, an old man would take his bag and set out. They would always carry a stick with bells attached. This stick was also part of our tradition, our history. Some say it was once a flag. We were once rulers of our land until we lost a war. 'Had those Mahars remained united, they would have been powerful even today. But the enemy's plan was simple. Split them up the way you would split wood. Exile them from every village. Take the symbols of their might and turn them into signs of their slavery.' And from then, these sticks found their way into Mahar hands. It was much later, when I had acquired an education and read Babasaheb's book *Who Were the Shudras?* that I found these missing links in our story. It is difficult to say whether those who carried those sticks knew of this history or not; but the sticks did come in handy when the dogs began to bark. Once the Mahar women entered the village, some dog or the other would always begin to bark up a storm in a walled wadi.

When it was our turn to collect the Mahars' share of food, I would go with Aai. The Marathas were particularly proud of their generosity in giving their buttermilk to the Mahars. Although I knew of the saying, 'When you're going to beg why hide your bowl?' I was always ashamed of going. I took care not to be seen by my upper-caste school friends.

I remember seeing Gautam Buddha's son Rahul in an illustration in a book. He is holding a begging bowl. His mother says: 'Your famous father is in the city. Go ask for your inheritance.' If his father was alive, what could he have put in the boy's begging bowl? You're going to laugh but I was wondering then what *my* father would have put in my bowl, had he been alive…

What was I saying? Yes, the Marathas. They would also carefully set aside leftover bhakris to give to the Mahar women. We were never given fresh bhakris. They were always stale or hard; sometimes they were even covered in fungus. Sometimes a generous woman might drop some pickle on them; that would always make my mouth water. At the regulation distance from the door, Aai would call out piteously, 'Give the Maharin some bhakri.' On festival days, we would get puran poli. Even if we got papads and crunchies, we would rejoice. When it was time to go and get this food, not a single cooking fire would be lit in the Maharwada. Once I remember getting kheer made out of bajri but in return we had to spread a basket of gravel in the benefactor's courtyard.

Speaking about festivals, something else comes back to me. During the Padva festival the village was vibrant with gudis and torans—garlands of flowers at the doors. In the evening, the Marathas would have a 'procession of heroes'. A ten- or twelve-year-old boy from each house would be dressed up as a warrior and would be carried on the shoulders of the adults. Everyone would gather in the courtyard of the Maruti temple. In front, the Mahars would play their instruments—free, of course, that was part of the tradition. A ring of young men would dance with the lejhim. The 'heroes', would make peculiar sounds.

Mahar boys were not allowed to participate. They could only watch the show from a distance.

It was considered a sin to put a lejhim into a Mahar boy's hands. The Maharwada boys would watch, crestfallen.

Wrestling matches were also held at the time of the village festival, to the accompaniment of the Mangs playing the halgi and the dafli. Wrestlers would come from far and wide to participate. The little boys would be rewarded with sweets and savouries. The other prizes were money, zari-decorated turbans, silver bracelets—there was a hierarchy of matches. However accomplished, Mahar wrestlers were not allowed to challenge the upper castes. If one of them wrestled and was found out, he would be beaten mercilessly. And so the Mahars did not take part. They had wrestling matches, but within their own caste.

Seeing all this, my interest in sport died young and I withdrew into my shell. My sense of self began to seep out of me, as water out of an earthen jug. I did not want to play with the Mahar boys. I began to turn into a bookworm. But I was also completely fascinated by the tamasha. The tamasgirs would present their shows in the early morning in front of the patils. These were either Mahar or Thakar tamashas. The troupe that showed its skills in the shortest time would get the higher reward.

I remember one village festival when even the Mahar children were invited to a feast. Two miles away, the urs of a pir was also held, near the border of the village. In the hope that we'd get some barbaat, a throng of Mahars scrambled off. We were served on small earthenware plates. Bajri ghugris were served instead of bhakri. Under no condition could the Mahars be served until the high castes had eaten. It was a fiery barbaat! It started your mouth watering, then your nose began to leak. We'd crush the ghugris into the barbaat while blowing—'Ssssss...ssssss'—to cool our mouths, but we would not stop eating. To find a piece of meat was like finding the cosmic egg and generated as much joy. We scraped up whatever was left over after the feast and brought it home.

It was our duty to celebrate the feasts of Mari-Aai and Mhasoba.* Mhasoba was treated just as the Mahars were. Out in the open, he bore the brunt of every kind of weather. Who he was nobody could figure out.

There was one regret that the village had: that the Raiwands would perform only in the Mahar settlement. They would turn up once a year on their camels. They would not stop in the main village nor would they perform for the upper

---

*Mhasoba is a horned buffalo deity of the pastoral tribes. His consort is Jogubai.

castes. They would only entertain the Mahars. Even today, I find that intriguing.

But then, those who entertain the rich and famous of the villages should have someone to entertain them as well. The complexity and oddness of India's social structures sometimes leaves me dumbfounded. The whole system is designed to gratify every ego, even those of the insignificant, like us.

The Raiwands would alight at the square. On their camels, they carried their world: children, trestle beds, hookahs, dholki, ektaara, everything. The children from the village would flock to see the camels. We Mahar kids suddenly acquired some standing in the world. Sometimes, the Raiwands would even take us for rides. I see them now as I saw them as a child. They had colourful turbans, the ends of which trailed down their backs. Their jackets, bedizened with silver medallions, covered sinewy bodies. Their moustaches were turned up. Their voices had an extraordinary Mahari twang. They had our names off by heart; and this mesmerized everyone. The show would start in the morning, in the square. The elders of the Mahars would be sitting right up front. They were our judges and so they had the community's respect. The Raiwands would have coconut shells with cowries inside. They would dance to the rhythm they tapped out and would sing with devotion, 'Who will fill the bowl of the mendicant, Bajirao or Nana?' They would touch the heads of each of the elders with the coconut shells. They would also sing paeans of praise to them. Their words had a unique sweetness; they revelled in the richness of the language.

Everyone would set aside some provisions for the Raiwands. When they left, the Mahars would tie new turbans on their head and give them some money. Later, the Mahars turned to Buddhism. They began to abandon the old ways. I still wonder what happened to the Raiwands who at one time entertained the Mahars? I don't think I'd find them, no matter where I search in our villages.

—

Whatever I say about the Maharwada feels inadequate. Even though I lived there as a child, I always felt an alien. The apathy and the depression I felt in the village evaporated when I came to the taluka.

Every day, I had a three-mile trudge to the school and back. There were three or four Maratha boys who accompanied me. We were the first generation to go to the taluka school. I was the only one from the Maharwada. The Maratha boys were solidly built. One of them seemed a full-grown man, complete with facial hair. In front of him, I looked like a lamb. I was always careful in the way I behaved with him. Being aware of my status in society seemed to come naturally; it was bred in the blood. These village boys did not treat me as an equal. They were swollen with the pride of being born in a high caste. When I was insulted on the basis of my caste, I would feel as if the fuse of an explosive device had begun to sputter inside me. I didn't have the guts to say anything. I simply did not walk with them, either dropping behind or walking ahead.

But once I was in school, I was free as a bird. In comparison to the one-room village school, this school seemed rather posh. It looked like something out of a Balbharati text book. It had a tiled roof. In front, a big maidan dappled by the deep shade of banyan and neem trees. I had just entered the fifth standard. A Brahmin teacher called Samudra presided over us in a black topi and immaculately laundered white clothes. He was very fair and had a lovely smile. I loved looking at the gold ring he sported.

While I had been seen as a duffer in the village school, I began to excel in the taluka school. I'd rank among the first five in my class. If I lost marks, it was because I was often late. However much I tried, however hard I ran, I often missed the bell and then marks were deducted. Samudra Master was happy with my progress. He would present me to the class saying, 'Look at him, a Mahar boy! How clean he keeps himself. How clear his language is. And he studies hard too.' Naturally, after this, all day I'd be floating around like a feather. I did not feel like returning to my village when school got over; it seemed like hell. I felt that it could not possibly be my world. At every step, at every corner, I was confronted with contempt, treated with disrespect. It suffocated me.

I believe that I discovered my true identity at the taluka school. I realized that the flaw was not in me but in my stars; I knew now that my only way out of the prison of the village was to study. That I might be able to do better than the sons of the Brahmins and Baniyas became apparent. I was better than the other boys in my class at hu tu tu or kabaddi. I would break through the ring of boys, slipping like a fish through a net. 'He must be smearing himself with pig fat,' the boys would say.

At this time, I also fancied a career in the theatre. 'What do you see in this empty glass?', a monologue from *Just One Glass* by Ram Ganesh Gadkari was one of the set texts in school. When we had anti-alcoholism drives in the villages, I would recite this piece again and again, at street corners and village meetings. Once, I even recited it at an Independence Day elocution competition. Among the faces in the crowd was Grandfather Javji Buwa. When I came down from the stage, he couldn't contain himself. He hugged me proudly, his eyes wet with tears. 'Your mother's widowhood has been assuaged,' said the old man. 'Your father should have been here…' He sang my praise through the village and the Maharwada. This label, of being the benighted son of a widow, began to fade. The other Mahar children began to look at me with some respect.

At that time, I was dressed rather oddly. On my head, a white topi. On my feet, chappals. A white Nehru shirt, often creased and crumpled. But where in the village was there a pressing iron? We would put some twigs of the khair tree into a copper vessel and set them alight and then use the vessel as an iron. We didn't have many clothes. We had to wash what we had and put them on again. In order to keep them uncreased, we'd put them under the pillow and sleep on them.

In those days, the school would conduct many prabhat pheris, morning processions with the singing of bhajans and patriotic songs that Gandhiji had suggested. I was always at the head of these, shouting slogans, my chest swollen with pride, my body vibrant with energy. The Maratha boys from the village, who would be lazing about in the school, hated me for this. In the lunch break, we'd go to eat by the river. I had to sit at a distance from them. In their eyes I was still the outcaste. From time to time, they might spare me some of their chutney or pickle; but they would not share my bhakri. In time, I began to avoid them altogether. But I did become friendly with the high-caste boys of the taluka.

—

You have to wear a mask in society. But if I am to tell the truth here, then the whole idea of coming of age gave me gooseflesh. My childhood was slipping away but I felt no sense of loss. I would go and bathe with the boys of my age at the village stream. I was the first to attain puberty. Demonstrating this to them, my chest would swell up with pride. And according to the dicates of nature, I began to feel the pangs of desire. I had seen men and women having sex but it had always seemed like I was watching plastic puppets. It left me unmoved. Now I began to be attracted to the girls of the village.

Once while we were sleeping in the school, an incident occurred that, even today, has the power to make me feel as if a lizard has run over my body. A fair Maratha boy from the village would sleep next to me. One night I woke up and found that he was stroking my organ. Needless to say, I wet my underwear that night. I must have enjoyed it but later I felt repulsed. All day I felt as if I had done something unsavoury. The next night, I slept in another place.

I told a strapping boy about this. He took charge of the Maratha boy, who, the other boys were convinced, was impotent. He would not meet my eye after that. Many years later, he married a beautiful woman. Today his marriage has borne fruit: he has children to his account. But when I go to the village, he still does not look me in the eye.

I felt no attraction to the Mahar girls. For one, they did not bathe every day. Their hair was matted, their clothes dirty. I could not bear their company.

A man called Rupvate Mama lived in front of us. He had a daughter, fourteen years old, fair and pretty. She was always at our house, helping Aai with the housework. Many people would tease me about her, saying she was my fiancée. I would avoid her in the way one avoids a cockroach. She was not very clean. Her nose would often be running. She would blow it, phurr phurr, and wipe it on her own arm. I felt a terrible disgust for her. Once she came to sleep at our place and she settled down next to me. Aai and my aunt began to tease me about this. Enraged, I picked up my bedding and went to sleep somewhere else.

This does not mean I felt no desire for girls. But there is a difference between man and other animals. Some people behave as if they have just come through a drought and will take whatever they get, but I was not like that. At this time, I found myself drawn to a girl from the taluka. What *was* her name? Oh right, Banu. Today, I'd be hard-pressed to say whether I was attracted to her or to her caste. She was a Maratha, fair as a ketaki. A walk in the sun left her flushed and red. I began to dream only of her.

Our relationship began because of a prosaic set of circumstances. I had a Sonar friend in the taluka. Sometimes I would go to his house to study and sleep there if it got late. From his gallery, I would catch glimpses of Banu. If she saw me, she would giggle shyly. It was I who was drawn to her but it was she who made the first moves. I was in the sixth standard at the boys' school; she was in the same class in the girls' school. When we had exams, ours were held in the morning, theirs in the afternoon. Both schools answered the same question papers in the examinations. As soon as our examination ended, I would race to the riverbank where Banu would be waiting under a tree. I would solve the paper for her and she would go off and write out the answers I had given her. I would spend the day in a romantic ferment. The scenes of films that I had once seen in Mumbai would fill my daydreams. I would be racing across desert sands on a horse only to meet my beloved. Actually ours was a case of calf love. Although I knew all about the physical aspects of lovemaking, I lacked the courage to put any of it into practice. When Aai came to the taluka with firewood to sell, Banu would stop her in front of her house. She would bring her water to drink. And she would spin some yarn to get her mother to buy something from mine. I had never told her about my mother selling firewood. Who knows where she had managed to dig out the information?

It was with Banu that I went for the first time to a temple. (Later, she took me to the Agasti Temple* too.) To get there we had to cross a river. The temple was set in a grove of mango trees that cast deep shadows. I saw my first ramphal there too. In front of the temple was a holy pool of cool water. Ram had used an arrow to call forth this water to assuage Sita's thirst, or so the locals said. I didn't believe this story even as a boy. I was terrified as I set foot in this temple with Banu. The inflamed eyes of Agastya seemed to be following me. Banu settled down to a nice long pooja. I did not pray nor did I feel like praying but I enjoyed the pedha she stuffed into my mouth.

Once we had gone, as a group, to her family's sweet-lime orchard. She herself had invited us. There we began a game of hide-and-seek. She would come and seek me out where I was hiding and I would only go in search of her. This annoyed everyone else. Coyly, she put my name into a couplet with hers, as a newly-wed bride does just after the wedding ceremony. The upper-caste boys who weren't precisely my friends were outraged. How dare a Mahar boy think to whisk away their pretty princess? It was an insult to all of them. They picked a fight on some trifling matter and

---

*A temple on the Pravara River which is supposed to have been the abode of the Sage Agastya.

began to heap filthy abuse on us. I couldn't understand how these boys, my friends who ate from the same plate, suddenly turned against me. That night I was supposed to sleep at the house of one of these friends. All night, he said not a word. When I woke up, I found that my name and Banu's had been scribbled all over the town, in chalk, in coal, on walls, on the empty iron pans of the sugarcane refinery. I was terrified. Banu's father was the taluka's Congress leader, swathed in khadi, his Gandhi topi as sharp-edged as a parrot's beak. That this was only camouflage that concealed a crude aggression was revealed by his gaze. I went home saying I was ill. I didn't show my face in the taluka. After a week, I sneaked back into school. I feared the worst. I was going to be tied to a tree, lashed with whips. I chased those words through the taluka, erasing them where I found them.

This incident rubbed my nose in my social reality. Banu seemed like a fruit hanging in the sky; a reward that would forever be out of reach. I stopped my pursuit of her. She tried for a long time to talk to me. Once or twice, she called out to me on the road but I walked on, a slab of ice.

I saw her again thirty years later. I was returning to Mumbai in a State Transport bus, all of us stuffed in like sheep in a fold. I was busy trying to keep my footing when my attention was drawn to a corner of the bus. Banu was sitting there, looking tired, dark circles under her eyes. We were the same age but now she looked older. I made my way towards her. In a soft voice, I asked, 'Isn't your name Banu?'

She was taken aback. For a while she did not recognize

me. I recounted some anecdotes to help her place me and suddenly she seemed to shed the burden of the past. Her eyes took on a new shine. No one knew her as Banu now. Her face told of her predicament. Her husband had abandoned her. Now she was rolling beedis in a workshop for a living. For a moment, I was torn in two, at a loss for words. She kept insisting I go home with her. Her mother would still recognize me, she said. I used my job as an excuse and got down at the next stop. As the bus drew away, I could feel her eyes on me.

—

While on the way to the Agasti Temple with Banu, I remember seeing a procession of about four to five hundred men on their way to a meeting in a nearby maidan. Some had blue caps on. Their leader was carrying a blue flag. Some were shouting Dr Ambedkar's name in praise. I remember seeing Babasaheb Ambedkar at Kawakhana: fair face, high forehead, a long sherwani and surwaar, a stick in his hand. He was giving a speech at the neighbourhood community house. I was too young then to remember what he said. Even his face is vague in my memory. At this time, when I should have been attending his meeting, I was flirting. This is one of my intense regrets. I don't even remember what the subject of the meeting was but I did see Dadasaheb exercising his authority over everyone. Sturdy, fair, young, in a double-breasted coat, he looked as noble as a character in a play. But I did not repeat the mistake I made that day. I began attending meetings of the Republican Party of India

I remember that at the time of the Agasti Temple fair, there would be a meeting at the Mahar kund. The one in front of the temple was the Ram kund. I did not know why the other was called Mahar kund. Later, I learned that when the Mahars came for the fair, they were not allowed to drink from the Ram kund. It is said that they fought the temple trust and got a kund assigned to them. The land around this had been usurped by farmers who were ploughing it illegally. This was an issue that caused much heated debate.

Babasaheb had come to Kotul, a village beyond ours, and left again. His radical views were beginning to have an effect on the hinterland too. In village after village, the Mahar community stopped stripping carcasses and eating the flesh of dead cattle. Revolutionary songs were driving social change. The community was shedding its old ways, as a snake moults.

One of Babasaheb's stories, the tale of the drumstick tree,* had reached every Mahar home. There were once four brothers who felt ashamed to do any work. Outside their door grew a drumstick tree. In the night, they would sneak out and break off its fruit and manage somehow. One day a relative arrived and cut down the tree. Only then did the

---

*The drumstick tree is rather good as a metaphor here. *Moringa oleifera* grows everywhere, in poor soil, sandy soil, depleted soil. It needs little maintenance and fruits regularly. Its leaves can also be eaten, being high in protein.

brothers set to work. This story illuminated what our share—our baluta—had done to us. Refusing to do the traditional work that was expected of us began a revolution in the villages.

If I was attracted to revolutionary movements at a young age, the credit must go to Javji Buwa. He was an old man but made of stern stuff. His body was as hard as an iron rod. He was like a grandfather to me. His one-storeyed house towered over ours. And in just such a manner, Laxman towered over the movement in the Maharwada. He had been elected to the local board. This duo—Laxman and Javji Buwa—travelled tirelessly to spread the word in the taluka. They would go from village to village, urging the Mahars, in the language of the unlettered, to refuse demeaning labour, to live with self-respect. They had gathered some young men and divided them into groups that went into each village. Those who still did the old jobs went in fear of them. Those who stripped dead cattle or ate its flesh were called to the village square. Kerosene would be poured over the dead animal so no one could eat it. If the offenders listened to reason, well and good. If they did not, their faces would be blackened. Then they would be made to look at their faces in the water in a clay shard, since there were no mirrors.

Sometimes, the weapon of social ostracism would be used against them. They would be refused a turn at the hookah, which was seen as a stern punishment. This was the movement that Dadasaheb Gaekwad, the politician and social worker, would be asked to lead. He had earned his LLB, a law degree, in Mumbai. When we learned that Babasaheb knew Dadasaheb personally and had specially sent him to the village, our respect began to border on fear. We approached him with caution. He spoke eloquently at the meetings. He would offer examples from daily life and from tamashas. You could hurt yourself laughing, listening to him. Although he was a lawyer, there was no pomposity in him. He would play viti-daanda with the children in the Mahaarwada. Or he would spend hours swimming in the river. And in the evening, the dholki would come out and revolutionary songs would be sung. No wonder he was something of a hero to the youth.

At one such meeting, the old guard brought up an unpleasant matter. They pointed out that Dadasaheb's own father was doing the old Mahar work. He was going to the weekly village market and asking for 'shev'. Two Mahars would spread a dhotar between them and go from shop to shop asking for whatever was being sold within. Either the shopkeeper or the farmers who had come to sell their produce would throw something on to the cloth. Everything would get mixed up—in other words, it would become a microcosm of Indian society. When they got home in the evening, they would divide it up. Even though he was a leader of the movement, Dadasaheb had failed, in his own village, to end this practice that reeked of slavery. The activists accused him of trying to change the country, while his own village remained mired in these practices. At a meeting, while he was speaking of the need for social change, someone interrupted, 'You're sitting on shit and teaching others. First talk to your own father.' That was it. There was only one subject to be discussed that day. Dadasaheb did not lose his temper but he saw that this was a conflict waiting to happen on several levels. He roared: 'If one of you brings me a pistol, I will kill my father.' That meeting was talked about for a long while afterwards. This was another feather in his cap.

The movement came to the village when the jalsa from Sinnar arrived in the Maharwada. The Marathas, eager to discover what a jalsa was, turned out in their numbers. The programme began in the light of torches. One of the tropes of the jalsa is that the milkmaids of Mathura set out to the bazaar. Krishna stops them on the way. But in this one, the milkmaids are on their way to the Kalaram satyagraha, a temple to which the Mahars had demanded entry. This was a new twist. The Marathas began to get angry. These Mahar milkmaids were on their way to a temple? To defile the deity? They felt so strongly about the movement for access that they couldn't even bear to see it on stage. They demanded that it be stopped. Chaos ensued. 'This is our settlement,' said Javji Buwa in his forthright manner. 'We will dance naked here if we want. Watch it with us or leave.' The Marathas left in a huff. This trifling incident caused another breach between village and Maharwada.

The Mahars stopped doing the work that was theirs by tradition. Bridegrooms were no longer greeted on arrival.

The Mahars did not play at the village festivals. They did not take Mari-Aai from one village to the next on her chariot. An acrimonious argument broke out when the Mahars refused to light the Holi bonfires. One or two heads were broken, as if there were no matchboxes in the village. But no one could look beyond custom. Some terrible calamity would be visited upon the village now that the Mahars were playing hard to get and would not light the bonfire, or so the villagers thought.

These social movements had their effect on our families; some old traditions were being erased. By tradition, at home, we worshipped Khandoba, the deity who sits on a horse, a sword in hand, Bahiroba at his side. Aai had some new silver Khandoba coins made. After the death of my father, she was always fearful. She would tell me to bathe Khandoba on Sundays. Bathing him meant taking a plate full of water and washing the images. Any rust would be scrubbed off with a piece of brick. When he was sparkling, it was done. The water so used had to be thrown onto the roof tiles. In the evening, we prayed and remembered god. We collected bel leaves and bhandaar powder was thrown into the air. Pieces of coconut were distributed and more bhandaar powder smeared on the forehead. Just as there was a day set aside for the pooja, Thursday was set aside to offer worship and water to our ancestors; it was also a day of fasting. As a child, I was curious about these ancestors. At that time, the hills to the east of the Maharwada were covered with dense forests of cactus. Here, there was a memorial to some ancestor in a thorny clearing: a pitch-black square of stone on which padukas had been carved.

I would look at the stone with the carving of a mendicant's footwear and ask Aai: 'Whose memorial is this? Why do we worship him?'

She didn't like to talk about the memorial. She would shudder in fear and fold her hands in that direction and say: 'Arré, he's an ancestor. They say he renounced the world. They say he went on pilgrimage to all the holy places. When it was time to die, he came back to Paai Paandhari. That's his tomb. He has spread his wings over our home. If he gets even a little angry, we will be destroyed.'

Then she would tell me a story from my childhood: 'When you were young, you would walk in your sleep. You'd go out into the courtyard and babble aloud in some language no one could understand. When I lit a lamp to him, you would recover.'

I didn't believe any of it but to keep her happy I would make an oblation. While offering him the ritual fruit and flowers, I would notice that the dogs had sprayed him, the crows had spattered him. Such a great man, I would think, and neither dogs nor crows fear him. What kind of god was he? In those thorn-ridden cactus jungles, I would always think of the *Nilavanti* that Uma-ajya had told me about. I felt that if you dug under the tomb, you would find the *Nilavanti* and then learn the language of the birds and the beasts.

But at that age, I did not dare try. And later, as I was

drawn to the Ambedkar movement, this ancestral spirit, we called him Samadhya, seemed like a fake. I began to wonder: in what way was he better than we were? We now knew so much more than he ever could. My interest in him waned. I stopped giving Khandoba his ritual bath and put the coins away. Aai did not insist either. But my aunt from Mumbai continued to live in awe of Samadhya's powers. She promised to build a shelter over him if he freed her son from addiction to alcohol.

—

I wasn't the only one changing. The Maharwada was changing too.

In the upper reaches of the Maharwada appeared a lunatic named Shankar. He was black as night, with an overgrown head of matted locks. No clothes, just a loincloth sometimes. No relatives. I saw his home once. It was a pigsty: a layer of dirt as thick as the mud of an akhara over everything. And lolling there, in the nude, Shankar. Perhaps the dirt kept him warm. Outside his home, he took on the air of a nocturnal beast. He didn't speak to anyone nor did he trouble anyone. He lived on what people gave him to eat. Or he would dig up roots in the forest and boil them. Everyone was wary of his enormous strength.

When he got up in the morning, he would take a pot to the well. He'd spit there: thhooo, thooo. Then he would have a bath, a bath so long that most other people would have tired but in which he luxuriated. With his vessel on his shoulders, he would then make his way through the main village and stop for a moment outside the Maruti temple. He would kick the steps, the same number of times every day. What this meant, only he knew. Until he died, he did not fail to perform this personal ritual. The villagers could only dismiss him as a madman. 'God fears the naked', as the saying goes. There was another Mother Goddess temple with the deity painted red. He would visit her too and scream at her in a language no one understood. He would belabour her with old shoes and sandals.

Talking about Shankar brings another madman to mind, but this one was well-educated. The question was whether one could actually call him a madman. Shirsat Master would come to our village on a bicycle. He would be talking all the time, as if he were delivering a lecture at a public meeting. His father-in-law lived in Ganora Taluka where he presided over the festival of the Mother Goddess every year. Shirsat waged war to get his father-in-law to give up this role. But its perks were considerable; he could live for the rest of the year on his earnings in those few days. Besides there were the gifts: hens, goats, pieces of cloth, coconuts and the days' cash offerings to the deity were all his by right. The goddess's priest a Mahar? It was a question many people asked. But, apparently, in some unspecified period in the past, there lived a poor woman who was harassed by her in-laws. For instance, they would make her fetch water in unbaked pots which melted even before she got home. She killed herself eventually and became the incarnation of the

Mother Goddess. All the lower castes began to worship her and her festival was therefore an important event on the calendar.

Only a child or an idiot would ask a man to abandon an active godhead. Since his father-in-law would pay him no heed, Shirsat left his wife. He gave up all pretence of coherence and began to jabber away like a madman. He began to tour the taluka on a cycle, a long bag dangling behind him. He would go to each Maharwada, collect minium pebbles and immerse them ceremoniously in the river. Collecting them with him became a kind of thrill for us.

They say he was suspended from the school in which he had taught. The supervisor gave him a severe dressing down in front of all the other teachers. As soon as school was out, Shirsat went to the crossroads, industriously chewing betel leaf. Along came the supervisor in a freshly-laundered, immaculate white shirt. Without stopping to think, Shirsat Master spewed a stream of red paan juice at him. This caused a sensation. That kind of master, Shirsat.

I don't think our movement had much impact on the trader class in general. On the contrary, they began to grow increasingly materialistic. The change here was that their homes now had Mangalore-tile roofs, they planted cash crops like sugarcane or grapes. Motorcycles appeared. They began to take part in zilla parishad politics. But in their heads, it seemed, their attitudes to us were unchanged. They had an odd method of recognizing another Mahar:

look for the cleanest person around, that would be the Mahar.

When I went to the village temple a Maratha would say, 'You motherfucker, whose son are you? How dare you lean on me?' Once, in a rage, I replied. 'Motherfucker yourself. I'm Maruti's son.' This was a first for me. I'd taken his words, his style and thrown them back at him. It would have been truly odd if he had not got angry. I thought: damn it, I've studied, I've improved myself, but in the village, the same accusation: 'Hey you, Maruti the Mahar's son!' My Mahar identity was a leech that would not let go. I was ashamed to be called Maruti's son, specially since there were two men called Maruti in the village. I would say hurriedly, 'I'm Lower Maruti's son, not Upper Maruti's son.' Upper Maruti, so known because he lived in the upper regions of the village and was afflicted with leprosy. I did not want to be known as the son of a leper so I was keen to clear all doubts on that score. I laugh at myself now. But what did Hari think of me?

Hari was Upper Maruti's son and about my age. He did not go to school. He was cowherd to the villagers. On holidays, I would go with him to the forest. He would catch crabs in the streams. I was afraid of their claws but not Hari. He could make a living garland out of scorpions. Catching them was child's play to him. Aai didn't let me play with him but I could not do without him. Sometimes, when I went to Hari's home, his father would be sunning himself in the courtyard. His fingers were reduced to stumps, his nose had sunk into his face. He was pale, his body covered with a fine network of lines. It looked like a watermelon cracked open. Later, his condition worsened. His family began to be revulsed. The Maharwada began to talk about having him shifted out. And in the end, they got their way: he was exiled.

Hari served his father until the old man died. Far from the fields in a patch of barren scrub, Maruti now lived in a hut built of hay. Hari would take him meals and I would sometimes go with him. He would not let me approach too close. One could not bear the old man's sufferings. He spoke to no one. It is said that he was seen sticking his hand into a snake hole. But the snake did not bite him. His limbs began to rot as days passed. Sometimes one would see him picking black worms from the sores on his legs. He died there, in his hut in the scrub. His body was not brought back to the Maharwada. He was wrapped in a sack and dumped in the stony earth. Nothing marks the spot: no lamp, no headstone.

Not so long ago, I was travelling from Victoria Terminus to Byculla in a local train. A great number of people were sitting in the passage. Among them, a face drew my attention. Hari. It was a shock seeing him. His limbs seemed as scarred as his father's had been. His face was turning leonine, patches of red skin were beginning to spread over it. Hari had leprosy...and for a few moments I felt the dreaded disease as if it were in my body. I remembered the poem 'Tree' from *Kondvada*.

Somewhere I see a tree, shivering in pain.
Like the banyan, its roots go deep.
Unlike the banyan, it never flowers.
This tree is bare whatever the season
In each vein, pain seeks release.
Its leaves slough, a leper's fingers.
Each branch bears strange fruit:
Corpses that dangle.
But the end will not come
And the tree must bear death pangs
In each living moment.
Somewhere I see a tree, moaning its pain.

I did not want Hari to see me. Scenes from our childhood appeared before me: Hari and me chatting; Hari and me swinging from the banyan's aerial roots; Hari and me catching fish in the streams.

Without stopping to think I call out to him. He is startled, embarrassed. He stares at me, sees me as a sahib, says nothing. His energy, his enthusiasm seem to have been drained from him. At the next station, he gets down hurriedly. I can see from his hobble that his legs hurt, the soles make walking difficult. I watch his figure recede as the train hurtles out of the station. That night sleep eludes me. His ravaged face keeps coming back.

Hari had two brothers: the elder was Damu and the younger Bhaukya. Of the three, how Hari alone was infected with leprosy was a question that plagued me for a long time.

If I remembered Damu, it was for another reason altogether. In the area, he and his brothers were known as the sons of a leper. This became a problem when it was time for them to marry. No one dared marry a child into that house. I cannot remember anyone ever calling Damu by his given name; it was always 'Damya'. He was a well-built man and as he came of age, the needs of the flesh must have begun to torment him. He was never very clean. One of his habits, disgusting to onlookers, was to spit on his palms and rub them together. Hari would take the cattle to graze. Damya looked after the village's horses. The rich people of the village were fond of breeding horses; mares were preferred. In my childhood the Brahmin's mare was very famous. She was black as coal and would not let a fly sit on her. The Brahmin fed her liquor, eggs and other delicacies, or so it was rumoured. On the road, she would shiver in fright. The fair Brahmin would ride her, fast as the wind, whipping her as he went. To compete with the Brahmin, the Patils also bred horses. Damya would take these three or four horses out to exercise and graze. In my youth, I tried to ride one of these mares. Damu taught me to let go of her mane and use the reins instead. But once a mare lashed out with her hind legs and I was thrown a considerable distance.

One day, there was sensational news about Damu. It was said that he had thrown a mare to the ground as one does when shoeing a horse, lashed her legs together and mounted her. How he could use such a huge animal as one might use a woman startled us as children. Some boys said, 'Arré, he takes the mare home, then he drives his poor aged mother out of the house and gets down to his filthy fucking.' Others said that he climbed onto a boulder and mounted the horse. Whatever the truth of the matter, his name was now 'Horsefucker Damya'. When someone called him that, he only smiled without a trace of shame. I could discern the pain behind that smile. After this, the Patils did take one step. They put chastity belts on the mares' vaginas.

Damu's perversion had its obverse in Sita's mental state. Dammed-up passion produced a case of severe hysteria in her. Not that anyone recognized it as hysteria at the time. But when her husband left her, Sita began to have bouts of madness. The sight of a young man seemed to make her lose control. She would make lewd overtures, tear off her clothes and run about naked. Her relatives would lock her up in the house. When she realized that her husband had taken another woman and had abandoned her in her parents' home, her condition got worse.

A woman who wandered around naked was in danger of losing her honour. She was to be branded as part of an exorcism and was brought in chains to the Maruti temple. When the fit was upon her, she had the strength of ten; she could easily fling off a couple of men. The manner of the exorcism was inhuman to say the least. When I think of it, my hair still stands on end. There was an old man in the village, quite famous for driving out evil spirits. His fame had spread and he was invited to other villages too. To me he seemed hardened; the kind of man who had spent his life hanging criminals. The person to be exorcised would have a fire of khair twigs lit right next to him. An iron rod would be heated until red hot. Then this would be brought forth and wielded with great energy. A crowd would gather to watch. Among them, me, my breath caught in my throat. When the brand was applied to Sita's head, to her temples, to the area near her ears—I still remember her shrieks and how they rent the sky. The brand left wounds as large as coins. Then they laid castor leaves smeared with ghee on the wounds to cool them down. Even so Sita's madness did not go away; in fact, it got worse. I found it odd that Shankar was not similarly treated.

But then the ethics of the village were of an entirely different order. Some Mahar youths had spent years working with rich villagers. Invariably, they would form relationships with the Maratha women. These women would allow the Mahar men to screw them; but they would serve them food or offer them water from the regulation distance to avoid pollution. This seemed rather odd.

The Thakars lived by a different code. Their affairs were conducted openly and without fuss. If a woman were known to be pregnant she would be brought before the panch. I remember one of those cases. The girl said without flinching, 'What do you want me to say? Was it a worm or a twig that went in? What do I know?' The panch fell silent. The girl was set free. Sometimes a girl would get married when she had a child on her knee. The groom knew better than to ask about the paternity of the child.

I remember another case that left a deep impression on me. The guiding principle of the white-collar world is secrecy and containment. Thus, if something untoward happened within the four walls of the home, that was where the matter had to be resolved and it could never be mentioned outside. But if something happened in a Mahar home, the matriarch would be the first to stand in the courtyard and announce her domestic problems to the world at large. One might hear her roaring at her daughter-in-law, 'You slut. Where did you go to eat shit?' Once, a strange event happened in the Maharwada. This time the daughter-in-law was not to blame; she was of upright character. Her husband was working in Mumbai. He had not found suitable accommodation there and so had not taken her with him. His father was a widower, an ordinary man. But one night he had made his way to where his daughter-in-law was sleeping. When she found her father-in-law at her side, his intent amorous, she raised a stink. In the morning, she sent a message to her mother's house. The groom was sent a telegram calling him home. The entire community had gathered to decide the matter. As head of the community, Javji Buwa was asked to judge the matter. The crowd was eager to know how the matter would be resolved. I still remember the story Javji Buwa told.

'Once upon a time,' he said, 'there was a king. He came to the court carrying a piece of flint wrapped in a kerchief. The court was filled with the learned and the armed. The king folded and twisted the cloth and said, "Look how pliable the flint is." All the court nodded in agreement. A wise man said, "It is not the flint that is pliable; it is the court."'

Javji Buwa looked around. He felt he had offered a parable and a resolution. But the bridegroom took this in a different spirit. He said: 'When I married this woman, she was meant to be common property between my father and me. Thus she belongs to my father as much as to me. I'm not going to hurt my father's feelings. If this is unacceptable, her family may take her back.'

This answer shocked everyone. No one knew what to say. The panch was stunned. They had come prepared to dispense justice. The father-in-law understood what he was supposed to understand. For a long while, I wondered how the young man could have taken such a maverick view of the case and how he could have had the courage to state it.

The elders often brought shame upon us with their behaviour. Take Sudam Buwa for example. Even though the Mahars had decided to refuse to go asking for food, Sudam Buwa could not be stopped from going to the village to beg for flour. 'Then you feed me and my wife,' he would say. Sudam Buwa was one of the elders with his own peculiar position. In one hand he carried the clappers and in the other hand the tambora and he would go into the village and sing bhajans. In return, he would get handfuls of flour. His clothes were also unique. On his head, a red turban; his forehead covered with red oxide of lead; Vithoba beads around his neck. When he was eating, he would hang the beads on a peg. In one of the pockets of his somewhat tattered coat was 'Mavshi', a rag doll who had ghunghroos tied to her feet and a knot of tangled hair on her head. She seemed to fill a need in Sudam Buwa who had no children. He would talk to Mavshi. He would make demands of her. When people said, 'His line will end with him,' his face did not change. He continued to look as he always did: cheerful and spirited. In our area, he was known to be able to give barren women the gift of a child, so what if he had none of his own? And so he always had a bevy of women around him.

He was a master of sleight of hand. None of us was very impressed when Satya Sai Baba began to pluck sacred ash, udi, out of the air. Sudam Buwa had been doing this for a while. In his hands, red oxide of lead would materialize. First he would show you that his hands were empty. Then he would ask you to present your palms. When you rubbed them together, vermilion! If he was in a good mood, he'd perform this miracle for us children too.

I saw Mavshi's power when I was a child. While Sudam Buwa's father was still around, he would play in his father's band. Once, he was asked to perform at a Thakar wedding and I went along. I was very hungry. After the wedding, sometime in the middle of the night, the musicians would be fed, rice or lhapshi, gruel of broken wheat. By this time I was almost in tears. Then a woman came up to ask Sudam Buwa for a talisman. Her husband was threatening to marry again as they had had no children. 'Make a chaanki of twelve eggs and put it under that mango tree. Also twelve ghee parathas. This is what Mavshi says. She will surely bless you.' With this he tapped her on the head with Mavshi. The lady went off and came back with the offerings. But before she returned, I had concealed myself behind the tree. As soon as she left I fell upon the food.

Once, it seemed that Mavshi's powers were failing. When the religious discourses of the month of Shravan were on in front of the Vithoba temple, Sudam Buwa walked into the mandap with his slippers on. That was it! Tempers flared and he was beaten mercilessly and tossed out. No one would give him flour now but that didn't change his behaviour at all. He just went to other villages to beg.

On the quiet, we would take flour from him. Call it a deed done in memory of my father or call it an offering to the orphan, but he would give us flour willingly. When he came home, it was time for tricks and jokes. At that time, a tamasha troupe had come to the village. One of the roles was that of the king of Pathardi. Why the village of Pathardi should have the reputation of being a village of eunuchs I do not know, but the role seemed to require the lead performer to prink and ponce about as if he were one. 'Shake it,' he would shout and the entire court would respond: 'Oh we're shaking it, your ladyship.' Sudam Buwa would imitate this actor and we'd fall about laughing. It was on his gleanings that we got through the lean days of Ashadh and Shravan. For we bore the brunt of the end of the practice of baluta and yeskar-pali, our share by right. We had no other means of earning a living. Aai was now slaving to keep us going but even when she went to forage in the jungle, the forest guards had to be paid off. After the harvest, she would glean the fields, and pick up the cobs that fell off the vehicles taking the crop to the threshing floor. On these slim pickings, we would survive.

It is true that I have never felt any deep appreciation of nature. Nature seemed to be like a rich man with a lot of property and I could only look down on the rich. The issues I had to confront left me no mindspace or time to stand and stare. Nature worship seemed to me to be for people whose stomachs are comfortably filled.

From time to time, I would go with Aai to Dhagya Hill. Climbing those rough-cut steps was difficult. From there we could see right up to the horizon. Mount Kalsubai was some distance away. The Mula ran far below us, a river of silver. But I was more interested in plucking karwandas than enjoying the view.

By night, we could see a forest fire raging. In the darkness, it was a thread of light. Here was another time when the whole notion of natural beauty proved to be false. In the morning a forest guard arrived to accost the Thakars and say, 'You lot started the fires.' Then he threatened them with a criminal record. For one may not cut down trees but it is allowed to take wood that has already been burned. The forest guards believed that the Thakar community started the fires so as to get hold of the burnt wood. But the Thakars were far from worldly wise. They knew nothing of money, for instance, recognizing only the four-anna coin. If someone were to offer them a rupee they'd refuse. 'Four annas it is,' they would say. I found it difficult to believe that such simple folk could think of such devious schemes.

I would sometimes visit the Thakarwadi, the settlement of the Thakars, because we had a small piece of land near it. Aai had guarded it with her life. To seize the land of a widow was an old patriarchal pastime. But Aai kept a sharp eye out for encroachers. She never gave the Marathas the right to sow on her land.

To begin with, the Maratha farmers were very greedy. 'To hell with your father, to hell with your mother,' they would say and grab the entire crop. If they gave us a couple of measures, that was out of the kindness of their hearts. They even took a share of the seeds. So Aai would give the Thakars the land to sow. Our Sarkati Thakar was an honest man. After the harvest he would come, bearing our share on his head. He would not forget to bring interest in the form of daal. Sometimes I would go over to his threshing-floor on work-related matters. It was in the Thakarwadi near his house. What has remained with me is the remarkable cleanliness of the Thakarwadi. The houses were small but neat. Bundles of hay were piled on the roof. The walls were red mud, ornamented with various vibrant designs in lime. The courtyards too were clean and well-kept. Everything, down to the water jugs, sparkled from scrubbing. You didn't see such cleanliness in the Maharwada.

But while they were clean, their ignorance was epic.

They would not send their children to school but put them to work as grazers and shepherds. When a doctor arrived in the village to inoculate the babies against smallpox, they would, if a child had been born, run and hide in the forest. In that sense, they were a long-suffering community, whose endurance was legendary, as was their inability to hurt anyone.

One thing annoyed me about the Thakars. They were Adivasis, or aboriginals, who saw themselves as descendants of Mahadeva or Shiva and so they thought we would pollute them. They would give us water to drink but pour it into our hands from above. If they gave us food, chatni and bhakri, they would scrupulously avoid physical contact. How did they come to practice casteism? Were they imitating the Marathas? That the Thakars should be aware of matters of purity and pollution was evidence of how the poison of casteism had spread through the village. The cities were supposed to be comparatively free of it.

Or were they? My school-mates may have changed but that didn't mean the residents of the taluka had. The first time I saw separate cups maintained for the untouchables was in a restaurant in the taluka. When did these cups vanish? I can't remember, but of one thing I am very sure, they remained for many years after India became independent. The law had changed but for years no one dared insist that it be followed. Then a Mang boy broke with tradition. The other untouchables followed his example.

As with the cups, so with the barbers. As boys we were

fascinated by the idea of going to the barber to get a haircut. One day, a Mahar took his courage in his hands and entered a barber's shop. Who knows how the owner recognized him. Surely it is not possible to read one's caste in one's face? The Mahar came back, tail between legs. When we were in school, Sudam Buwa cut our hair for us. But when we moved to the taluka school, his haircuts began to look a bit anarchic. After that we began to go to a man called Ramji in the Maharwada of the taluka. (When you don't get milk, you manage with whey.) Cutting hair didn't call for much skill. Later, barber's shops did open their doors to us but for a long time my heart would thunder as I stepped into one. In the cities we could always visit the saloons but in the village, for many years, the barbers would refuse to cut the hair of the Mahars and the Chambhars. I would think: they're happy to shave buffaloes; why not us? The barbers felt that the other castes would shun them if they touched us.

Around this time, an important change took place in my life. I passed the fifth-standard exam with good marks. I desperately wanted to study further. We had a teacher called Sonawane from the same caste. He kept an eye on my academic progress. He had made me write a request for admission into the taluka hostel. I wrote it and forgot all about it. Then I passed the exam and the application was passed at the local board office in Ahmednagar. I was very happy. Aai's burden would be lessened a little. It was as if someone had unclogged a stream.

The hostel was located at the spot where the weekly market was held. It was a long low white building with a tiled roof. Around it, a compound marked out by a wire fence. Next to it, the students' dining hall. A large well. We went to school in the village and lived in the hostel. Food was free. What more could I ask for? It seemed like a vision of heaven.

Not that it lasted. I could not even dream of what this hostel would serve up to me. It was known as the territory of Koli students; they were all Mahadev Kolis* from the Dang district. I was the first Mahar student to enter its portals. How strong caste pride can be, never mind how low your caste is supposed to be on the hierarchy. Arising out of that, there were slights whose power would last a lifetime.

On the first day itself, the hostelites gathered in groups to study me and mutter to each other. I was to share a room with an older boy, lame but otherwise robust. He already had facial hair. 'You can't sit with us for meals,' he warned me. 'You'll have to sit near the door.' The other students

---

*According to *The Castes and Tribes of H.E.H. The Nizam's Dominion* by Syed Siraj ul-Hassan, the Koli tribal people were divided into the Malhar Kolis (who take their name from the god Malhar, their tutelary deity, and who are balutedars) and the Mahadev Kolis (who take their name from Shiva and are found in greater numbers).

agreed with him. He seemed to be their leader. To me, he seemed like Taimur the Lame. I suffered much after that but the sting of that moment is with me still. Keeping company with books, my mind had become all the more sensitive. There was no question of complaining. The Superintendent was of the same caste as they. He stopped me as I made my way to the mess, my copper plate gleaming with the scrubbing I had given it. 'Look, you're a Mahar. If you go into the hall, you'll be beaten black and blue.' Quietly, I took a place close to the door, not neglecting to leave some space between me and everyone else. I looked at the students. They looked at me with the threatening eyes of bulls about to charge.

And then they would sing, 'Vadni kawal gheta naam ghyaa Shri Hariche' ('Think of Shri Hari when you take your first mouthful of food'), which seemed to add insult to injury.*

Really speaking, I didn't have to take this. If I had only stood up to them, their opposition might have crumbled. But it's easy enough to write revolutionary poems, poems that challenge the status quo. It's different when you must live the challenge. That I lived without self-respect is still a matter of regret for me. At the time I felt: Is it true? Am I really so spineless? Damn it, why am I such a cowardly custard? Who put this fear into me?

---

*'Vadni kawal...' is a prayer that Maharashtrian children are taught to say before meals. It means, roughly, 'Take thought for the Lord as you put the food into your mouth.'

I was an insect being teased by wanton boys for their sport, unable to respond, unable to retaliate. I chose not to strike back but to push on. Sometimes I would wonder how a mouthful of food could drain us of self-respect. Why could I not have the courage to oppose them, to refuse this aid and pay for my own education? I left the hall with my plate and glass, feeling like a convict sentenced to a lifetime of servitude. I could hear the fetters clanking hollowly: khoodam, khoodam... I would look into the lofty blue arch of the sky and wonder: Would there ever be room in it for free flight?

The hostel had a Saturday stotra to Hanuman. Bhajans would also be sung. It was here that I first heard Gandhiji's favourite bhajan. 'Vaishnav jan to tene kahiye je peed paraai jaane re' ('He alone can be called a Vaishnav who feels the pain of another'). I had a good voice so when I was alone I would sing it to my heart's content. I was one of the foremost bhajan singers at the hostel. The other Koli students would follow my lead. But when the prasad was being distributed the thali with its pieces of coconut would never be allowed into my hands. I swallowed these insults as one swallows one's spit. At such times, I always thought of how Hari's father, his body rotten with leprosy, was treated in the village. I would look at my own hands. Had the capillaries begun to burst? I would feel a scream welling up. But I swallowed that too. I shut my mouth and took the shit. Had I chosen to be another village cowherd, I should not have had to face these insults. Why, oh why had I started reading? I could have been a stone in a stream...

If these wounds were soothed even slightly, it was because of Pastor Kharat, one of our teachers. He was a Christian preacher, fair of face, a smile always playing about his lips, a pleasant person. I think he had once been a Mahar, for his speech sometimes revealed a Mahar turn of phrase. He was a Protestant and so he did not have to wear the robes that Roman Catholic priests must. He had a family and did his religious work. On the banks of the river, he had a small church next to his home. There, he sang bhajans to Christ in a fine voice and accompanied himself on the harmonium. He would go out of his way to meet me at the hostel. He was very affectionate, a new experience for me. I did go with him once or twice to church. When I moved to Sangamner to study, I would still meet him. I remember that I did not feel much love for the Hindu religion. Christianity did not seem, to my eyes, much concerned with caste. But Kharat never asked me to convert. Perhaps that is why I began to have a green and moist spot somewhere in my heart for Christianity. And now I think, truly, why didn't I become a Christian? In the district in which I was then living, a huge number of Mahars had converted. But no one in our district had.

But then there was the case of Uma-ajya's father. His name was Kadu; I could not have possibly seen him myself but the old folks had many colourful stories about him. This Kadu was about three feet tall; he would sport a turban and give his moustache a magnificent twist. He was part of the Mahar music players and was known for his excellence at the sambal. People would gather from far and wide to hear him. When he was travelling from one village to another, one of the other musicians would carry him on his shoulders. Kadu's wife was a strapping woman, built like a Pathan. This one I had seen. How did they manage? That was the question that everyone wanted to ask.

Kadu once went to Mumbai to see his relatives and then there was some explosive news: Kadu had been to a church and had been baptized. His version: 'I just ate some bread.' That was it! Forty villages around us decided to teach Kadu a traditional lesson by punishing our Maharwada. We were not allowed to share the hookah; we were not to be talked to. This was a powerful weapon that society could use at will. Seeing that the elders, the mehetars, of the forty villages had assembled at a general body meeting, the Mahars of our village humbled themselves and begged forgiveness for Kadu's offence. As penance, they were forced to hold the leaves of a neem tree in their mouths. In this way, they took his sin upon themselves. In addition, we had to host a feast. No ordinary one would do; it had to be gulwani and puris. When Javji Buwa was in the mood he would tell me stories about how this feast became famous in the district. These stories must have had their effect on me and that is why I began to avoid Kharat later.

The hostel food was abundant. I had never eaten so well in my life. So perhaps that is why I saw it as abundant. Every week or fortnight, we had a feast. That was bliss. Laddoos or jilebis were served. Mutton was never cooked in the hostel.

At the feasts, I would think of my mother and sister. Here I was eating sweetmeats while they must be dipping stale bhakri into tea. I would be tempted to hide a laddoo in my glass for my sister but I never dared. Had I been caught, I would have been called a thief. Each time I went home, I had to take my trunk and my school bag with me.

Sometimes Aai would come to the hostel to sell what she could. I never spoke to her in front of the other students. When the students had finished buying and she had left, I would run after her. I burn with shame as I tell you about how I would only speak to my mother in secret. For an education, I was willing to sever the umbilical cord.

Every student received a grant of twelve rupees a month. We shopped for ourselves and handed over the vouchers to the Superintendent. What was left at the end of the year was handed over to us. I think this system has ended in almost all the hostels. Only the superintendents know how much government money has been misused.

In those days, we were required to spin khadi, every morning and evening. If we did not meet the required quota, no food would be served. This cloth was used to make us pyjamas and vests. If we were made to weave at the hostel, at school, we were set to work in the fields. This was counted towards the final examination. We spent more time doing this than classwork. That didn't mean we did any actual physical labour; there were labourers for that. We were expected to go and keep an eye on things, check on the number of leaves and count the flowers. In our journals, we drew diagrams of the plants. Each of us filled a book of nearly four to five hundred pages with agricultural theory. I even took agriculture as a subject in my final examination and did well too, but it was all wasted. I never used any of it: not the spinning and weaving and not the nature study.

I learned to cycle but only because I was stubbornly determined to do so. I did not have enough money to hire a cycle, so I made out the week's receipts for the gram panchayat's weekly market and I got a commission on that. I enjoyed the work. My ancestors had spent their lives stripping carcasses; I was ripping receipts out of books.

I learned to swim in the same way. Behind the boarding school the Pravara River formed a dark deep lagoon. Every afternoon I would go for a swim. The pond was above the village. Whenever I went swimming I would think about the illogic of caste pollution. I was allowed to bathe here but the Mahars could only draw water from the lowest point possible. But when I bathed, did I not pollute all the upper castes simply by being in this water? The Koli boys cut through the pond, swimming strongly. I could never do this. All I could do was flounder in the shallows. For a long time, even looking into the cruel jaws of a well would send shivers down my spine. Finally, I just gave up.

Thinking about water bodies brings back a river story. In the running water, a cloth bundle is being carried along by the current. A boy jumps in and swims out and brings it back. He opens it and jumps back with a scream. It's a newborn, a modern Karna. News spreads in the village. The police arrive. A panchnama follows. The police go up-river to find 'Kunti'. Finally, a fair unmarried girl with a jaundiced look is caught. A doctor examines her and finds she has delivered a child recently. She is paraded on the road from the market to the government office area. The public follows, cursing and abusing. They say she was punished.

These daily dramas made me far more introverted than most other children my age. I did not understand all of what was happening but I did know that savage oppression was our lot. In Marathi class, I would lose myself in poetry. Our Marathi teacher's name was Khandge. He too would lose all sense of self as he read out poetry. He would sing the poems to us in his beautiful voice. Tilak's 'Kevde he kraurya?' ('How Much Cruelty?') and Kusumagraj's 'Ahi-Nakul' ('The Serpent and the Mongoose') or 'Zameen-Aag-gaadi' ('The Land and the Train') were my favourites. Alone, I would sing them aloud. My mind would fill with pain and rage. In the terrible reality of the hostel, these poems brought me some relief.

The first student to shake up the status quo was Tukaram Shirkande. I still remember his first appearance in school. His turban embroidered with gold thread, his brand-new coat smeared with haldi left over from his recent marriage; a dhotar completing the picture. Everyone looked at his clothes and burst into laughter. I told him of my plight in the hostel. On the first day itself, he marched straight into the Koli clique and sat down, thigh to thigh, with them. The boarding school couldn't get over this outrage. But then he was well-built, his eyes flashed a warning. After my experience with these boys, I watched all this with astonishment. He saw this and grinned mischievously. That day, Tukaram threw down a gauntlet. It got me thinking. Why had I lacked the courage? I felt ashamed of my cowardice. I can now understand how Tukaram could have such courage. His father worked at the mint in Mumbai. He had bought land in the village. Why would Tukaram be impressed by the abundant food of the hostel? He did not have to wriggle worm-like through the world as I did. He often gave his name as Shrikhande. He didn't like Shirkande as a surname; it revealed his caste.

Tukaram would take off to his village on the weekly holiday. On his return, he would give us chapter and verse of his encounters with his wife. Sometimes his father would come from Mumbai, bearing gifts: new clothes and sweets. Later, he failed the year. His father complained to me, 'He has failed every subject…at least he could have produced a child!' I could see he was far more grieved at that than at his son's lack of academic success.

On festive holidays, we could go to my uncle's place at Aurangapur, two miles from the taluka headquarters. We would amble along a road engulfed by the deep shadows of old banyan trees. If you left the road and began to follow one of the paths, on both sides were orchards and gardens, loaded with fruit. The creak of the water-wheel—but if you felt thirsty along the way, you didn't have the courage to stop and drink at a pond.

I preferred Aurangapur to my own village. The houses were all in a row. Even the Maharwada was remarkably clean. One of the common legends was that the Mughal emperor Aurangzeb had granted this village as upkeep to the widowed daughter-in-law of the patil. Many anecdotes were woven around this. My uncle's house was tiny. As you entered, a threshold at the door. Under the tiles lantana mulch had been stuffed and had stayed there for years. Black bits would fall off on to one's body. In front of his house, one could see the ruins of his son's house. The ground was seen as cursed so no new house was built there. Instead, they preferred to live in their hen coop in which they would often talk about the ruined house. It was the haunt of the Bhujang, they said. My grandfather had buried a treasure under it, they said. This was my maternal grandfather they were talking about. He had died when my mother was still a child. He had belonged to a gang of dacoits. Through his life, he had accumulated a fortune and buried his ill-gotten gains under the house; or so my uncle and grandmother said. At night, I would dream of the Bhujang. But more than the treasure, I was interested in the guns and swords he must also have hidden there. As I slept, these weapons would materialize in my hands and I would make savage and bloody war against the Koli boys in the hostel until victory was mine.

My grandfather—or to be more precise, my mother's uncle Tanaji—worked at the docks in Mumbai. Once when we were in Mumbai, he had come to meet Aai. My father was also working in the docks at the time. New workers were being taken on, new tokens were being issued. My father got his father-in-law a token, which meant, in effect, a job at the docks. This is a story of that time. Workers were not given permanent jobs; instead, they were often retrenched. Then it was Ajoba's turn. What could my father do? He got hold of a huge iron bar and dropped it on to Ajoba's finger. There was blood everywhere. Ajoba proceeded on medical leave. He was hurt on duty, he claimed. From then on, Ajoba would tell everyone proudly how his job had been saved by his son-in-law's quick wit. Ajoba had once got my father out of jail and so he had paid his debt!

From time to time, Ajoba would come to Mumbai. His entire focus was on the village, though. He had invested all that he had earned in land with rich black soil. He would send a regular money order. He would live frugally in the city through the year in order to afford this. His appearance was interesting. He had very dark skin. His dhotar stopped short of his knees. His body was covered by a waistcoat, often with its buttons missing. His chest was always bare. On his head, a black topi. When he came to the village, everyone walked in fear for those days. Even though he was now old, his wife dared not present herself before him, such was his aura. I was the only one who could tease him. He never lost his temper with me. I would say, 'Baba, you earn so much. Why not buy yourself a good wool coat?' He would only laugh. Other than tobacco, he had no addictions.

As he left for Mumbai, he would put an anna in each child's hand. He would also slip his married daughters an anna each. After he was gone, they would mock his miserliness.

About a dozen years ago, his end came in suspicious circumstances. At that time, I was living in the Sion Railway Quarters, as a sub-tenant. The old man would eat with us. The railway passed right beneath the building. There were many accidents involving commuters who climbed the fence and crossed the tracks. He would warn me: 'Walk a little more if you have to but don't cross the railway tracks.' When he had finished eating, Ajoba would feel the need for tea. He would go every night to the station for a cup. On one fateful night, he was knocked over by a train. When I arrived at the accident spot, there was not a drop of blood anywhere. It was the slamming that did it for him. The man who had warned me against crossing the tracks had crossed them himself that night.

As his only relative in the city, I had to go and get his corpse from the coroner. In the panchnama, the old man's clothes and chanchi—a cloth wallet in which betel leaf and tobacco is stored—had been all noted down. The police had no idea that he had any money with him. When I took some notes from the chor pocket, the police were quite taken aback.

We could not wait until my uncle and grandmother arrived from the village. I had to go into the cold room at the morgue later to claim the body. There was a pile of naked corpses there, emanating a life-threatening stench. I could not remain there for more than a moment. It wasn't difficult to identify the old man. That night, I lit his pyre.

When my grandmother and uncle arrived the next day, all the rituals were over. They went to the docks to see about his service fund. When they returned, they were laden with shopping. My uncle had a brand new shirt on. They had bought new saris for my grandmother and for my aunt. My uncle told us what happened: the workers had collected some money for him. I was shocked. My grandfather, who had slogged at the docks all his life, had not been dead a day and they could think of going shopping?

In a couple of years, my uncle managed to squander the money his old man had spent his life earning. He had never worked for a living. On the day that a money order arrived from Mumbai, he lived it up. In the next two or three years, he began to sell the land, piece by piece. His condition began to get increasingly wretched. Today, he does physical labour somewhere in Mumbai to earn his bread. He has brought his entire family to live in the city with him. He has a battalion of children. He once had the bearing of an elephant; now he looks like a dried-up stick of sugarcane.

In Aurangapur, Ranuji lived in the house in front of uncle's. My paternal grandmother, Aaji, lived there too. This was the house in which she had been born. (She shared a surname with her in-laws: Kasbe. I found that intriguing.) Ranuji was an old man, but stern. He was plagued by a string of boils but that didn't temper his tongue. However, he did have a soft spot for us. I longed to visit him but the two homes were at loggerheads. Ranu was poor. He worked as a bricklayer to look after his children. In reality, my uncle and Ranuji were first cousins, born into the same family. Now they were sworn enemies.

Ranu-ajya had a relative who lived in Vitthe. My uncle's family believed that he was a real live tantric, that he could kill a man with a single blow, that he was working his black magic on us. My uncle's mother-in-law came from Vashera. For a long time, she had not had any children. Later, my aunt had many children. But when she miscarried, she spread it abroad that it was the doing of this tantric from Vitthe. My aunt was prone to possession by the goddess. This would generally happen at night, after dinner. She became an awe-inspiring sight, this fair-skinned woman, her forehead adorned with a blood-red smear of koonkoo, her hair streaming behind her. When she started to spin, she terrified me. And then she would have to be appeased by encircling her with ash, whirling a cockerel in front of her to draw the spirit into it and then disposing of the body at a place where three roads met.

One rain-soaked night, it was really coming down. Lightning forked and flashed. It was so dark that you could see nothing, even if you stretched your eyes open with your fingers. That night, the goddess had told us, through my aunt, that Vitthya Bhagat was going to send us a curse. The whole house was on high alert. I was awake simply to see what form or shape this curse might take. Everyone was frozen with fear, waiting for someone to start vomiting blood. Eventually, we did fall asleep without even knowing when sleep descended. In the dawn, we woke to see that the wall in front of the house had collapsed. Everyone heaved a sigh of relief: the goddess had protected us, deflecting the curse and sacrificing the wall instead. Even though I was a child, I wondered if it was divine intervention or the force of the storm that had brought the wall tumbling down. Later, I began to find it all rather ridiculous, the idea that a fresh lime pricked with pins can come swirling through the ether to the life of a man.

Ranuji was a voluble member of the taluka. He would attend public meetings to heckle the speakers. He took an enthusiastic part in the Ambedkar movement in our taluka. This may have played some role in his determination to educate his children. He named his son Raosaheb. This Raosaheb Kasbe became a Dalit intellectual of much repute. Perhaps without knowing it, he absorbed this habit of inquiry from his father. Now he teaches political science at a college in Sangamner.

Ranuji's house had a goddess installed, by tradition. No one would worship the goddess except on festive occasions. The Maratha men and women would come and worship her, bringing offerings. I remember a funny story from Raosaheb's youth. He was going to the taluka school and was once covered with scabies. 'Your own devi has brought this on you,' the villagers would tease him. He was knee-high to a grasshopper but who knows what got into him? He took a hoe and uprooted the deity, a red-smeared stone that had been firmly anchored in the ground. He took the image and threw it on the garbage dump in front of the house. The whole village watched him, aghast. But Ranuji could barely contain his laughter. Now the goddess would wreak havoc upon the family, the villagers muttered to themselves. But after all these years, they seem to be doing fine. Perhaps they didn't get rich, but the tree of education took firm root there.

Aurangapur was the scene of a disaster that befell me. I had come down to my maternal uncle's house for the holidays. There was a crowd in front of the Maruti temple so I headed there. I saw a man with a slipper in his hand, running towards the deity. He was abusing in the most foul language. He seemed to be intent on making war on god. The villagers obviously thought he had a few screws loose. But I thought he had the right of it. It also occurred to me that if the villagers could tolerate this, how was it the end of the world if we went into the temple? I mixed with the crowd. Up to this point I had never been inside this temple. I climbed the stairs and sat on the outer platform. A Maratha man grew suspicious and asked: 'Whose son are you?' I replied: 'I've come to stay with the Kasbes. He's my uncle.' The Maratha was outraged. Curses sprang to his lips. 'Motherfucker, you've polluted god!' Everyone looked at me. God's assassin, the man with the slipper, was forgotten and they turned on me instead. Someone hit me, a sound one around the back of my head. I looked for god's abuser. Maybe he would help. Then my grandmother turned up, begged and pleaded and I was allowed to go.

Much later, I learned that the man abusing god was the propagandist of the Satyashodhak Samaaj.* In reality, the land on which the Maruti temple stood belonged to the Maharwada. The Mahars had also laboured to build the temple. But once Maruti was ensconced and the temple consecrated, the Mahars had to be kept away.

The Aurangapur Maharwada's struggle for water was interesting. In those days, there was no movement for 'One village, one water source'. But they must have got wind of the Mahad agitation** and been inspired by it.

The fight was however occasioned by a deeply felt need. The Mahars were only allowed to use a stream fed by rainwater. This was half a mile away. It dried up during the summer, making life hell. Right next to the Maruti temple was a well whose water was cold and sweet. It had a wheel

---

*The Satyashodhak Samaj was founded by Mahatma Jyotirao Phule in 1873 to liberate the oppressed.

**In 1927, Dr Babasaheb Ambedkar and others started the Mahad agitation to get access for the Dalits to a water tank that had been declared as a public water body but which was reserved, in reality, for upper-caste use. The struggle lasted ten long years until a court order opened the body for general use in 1937. Ambedkar called the Mahad agitation the beginning of the untouchable liberation movement.

that squeaked and squealed. Women from the Mahar and Mang communities would sit by the well, hour after hour, waiting for someone to feel a moment of pity. Then a pot might be drawn and poured into their thirsty pots. In one sense, tradition was on the side of the Mahars, the land being theirs. They had asked the administration to intervene but the government was unmoved. One day, they cracked. They got together, all of them, and lowered their buckets into the well. The women, their loins girded for action, were at the forefront of the agitation. The village was in an uproar. The possibility of a separate tank was mooted but the Mahars were having none of it. 'We don't want separate taps. We want to fill our pots at the well too,' they said. Finally, a panchayat was called. The Mahars were allowed to fit another pulley on the well. It was all right for a Mahar pot and a Maratha pot to hobnob in the water but they could not be hoisted from the same pulley for, this would offend the Marathas' caste sensibilities. They still have separate pulleys.

I saw my first Bohada in Aurangapur. It was danced around a Holi bonfire. The dancers painted themselves as characters from the *Ramayana* and *Mahabharata*. Their faces were covered by ferocious masks, and on their backs they had circular frames of bamboo and straw. Their hands were sometimes tied to these frames, sometimes they bore weapons. Their feet had ghunghroos. The chorus went, 'Dance, Ganpati, dance, for Sarja [Saraswati] is following you.' They would be accompanied by musicians or the Mang daf and pipe. The songs would have a single rhythm. To play the role of Raavan was a big honour, for one had to manage his ten heads. One had to make a big donation to secure that role. Mahar boys were not allowed to participate. Etched in my memory are those ferocious faces, those tongues dripping blood, and the glinting weapons. When I went to Calicut in the South, I saw a somewhat refined version of Bohada. It told the story of the Aryan conquest, the subjugation of our land; these were the last traces left in the twentieth century.

I was to be married into a family in Aurangapur. The village was my uncle's territory. When I went there, the women would tease me: our son-in-law has arrived, they would say. The mukadam's daughter had come of age. She was dark and well-built. Hers was one of the richer families in the Maharwada. Their house was awash with milk and butter; it was covered in English tiles. The girl's father had many acres of land. He was a supervisor in the docks. His wife, strapping as a Pathan, was always swathed in gold ornaments. They would have me over for a cup of tea when I went home. When I was young, I had been bitten by a dog in their courtyard.

At that age, my voice was still thin. The mukadam's wife would imitate my voice to tease me. At these moments, his daughter, trying her best to manage a bulky nine-yard sari, would be hanging around, giggling. She would whisper to other girls her age, making it obvious that she was talking about me. I never raised my eyes to her. I knew that everyone wanted me to marry into that house. But even at that age, I felt a deep hatred for the rich. I would not let myself be sold off to them. And then, I didn't want a dark-skinned wife. I was dreaming white-skin dreams. I would dream of children who looked like Brahmin-Baniya children.

The girl's brother was well to do. He would mock the idea of education. 'What's an educated man going to do in our house? Count the bags of grain?' he would ask. This made me uncomfortable. One day, the girl kicked a puppy and sent it flying. It ran away, whining. It wrung my heart but I was silent. I thought: It will be my turn next. Only my grandmother was not in favour of this match. She did not want me at someone else's mercy.

—

It was impossible to forget Mumbai, city of freedom. Even with my father gone, Tatya was there. Sometimes, I would go to meet him or he would come to the village for a change of air. When he came, he brought my aunt and Aaji with him. He was on his second marriage. His wife was very beautiful. When she visited, she would be wearing a peacock-coloured Paithani sari and would have gold ornaments such as a nose ring and a vajratika, three golden beads as an ornament, and silver anklets. The whole village watched her progress with bated breath. When she came home, she sat around as if she were a guest and we, the rather inferior hosts. Aai had to do all the work. Aai's old sari, her lined face, her bare forehead, would come into focus. She also suffered from scrofula. As soon as one pustule burst and healed, another would burgeon. This would get infected and bring wracking pain and high fevers. But who could tell this city-bred aunt to help? I would burn with unspoken rage. Aai would bear her pain silently and keep on working.

Tatya came to the village in high style. With his woollen coat, shining shoes and hair slicked back, he looked like a film star. On our way to the Agasti village fair, we took a breather at the Mahar kund. And then a dark-skinned woman began to hover around us. Aai seemed to recognize the woman. She was Tatya's first wife, whom he had abandoned. Who knows what happened to Tatya, but suddenly he was on his feet. A cart full of sugarcane was standing there. He took a sturdy stick from it and began to beat the woman, as if she were an animal. The other pilgrims got in the way and freed the woman. Perhaps she had hurt his pride. That she should appear before him so boldly must have angered him. People said she deserved it. For a long time, I could not help thinking about this abandoned aunt.

Apart from that, Tatya was a good man. He took great care of us. He helped us hold our tattered dignity together. His arrival in the village meant new clothes for me and my sister. Once he bought me new slippers and I lost them on the same day. He didn't get angry; he just bought me another pair. He would bring us dates and pao from Bombay. And such bread—the crisp brun pao of Mumbai! To dunk it in tea, that was bliss. He would arrive laden with goodies: dried Bombay duck, shrimp and the small but tasty mandeli fish. When those arrived, we'd have a shaguti. Mutton would be bought at the village or a chicken barbaat would appear. Every year, we waited for the day when he came down from the city.

During the Diwali vacation, I went to Mumbai. It was always a double-bind. Tatya's wife Kaku didn't like having us visit and made her dislike clear. But Aai would force us to go. For one, we would all get a couple of sets of new clothes that would last us through the year. Additionally, there would be money for books. When I went alone, Kaku would be savage. 'Why are you helping them? When he grows up is he going to piss in your mouth?' she would ask Tatya. These vitriolic words would sear my soul. I would feel like going somewhere, anywhere, so that I could be alone to weep my rage and hurt.

But then, am I looking after Kaku and her son today? I find it difficult to make two ends meet for my own family. How did these elders stretch what they had to include everyone? Today, our relationships have all but snapped. My cousins and I do not share the kind of bond that my father and Tatya shared right up to the end. Who built these walls between us?

I once went to Mumbai with the Marathas of the village. Vithoba had a tinning business. As a Warkari,* he had a

---

*The Warkaris of Maharashtra and North Karnataka worship Vithoba, held to be a form of Krishna. They go on an annual pilgrimage (a wari) to Pandharpur where they gather on Ekadashi of the month of Ashadh.

Vithoba garland around his neck, his forehead was marked with sandalwood paste. He lived in Sangappa Chawl in Parel. All the Marathas of the village lived in that area. He was supposed to take me to Kawakhana, to Tatya's place. At dawn, we were at Sangappa Chawl. Because I am a Mahar, he would not let me enter his house. I washed my face at the outside tap and sat in the shadow of the building. Slowly, the day began to warm up. My food was brought to me there. It occurred to me as I ate: now Vithoba's wife will take my plate back into the house and she will scald it in the fire, for it has been polluted. I ate with my eyes downcast. I was dying to get away, to go to Kawakhana; it seemed odd that even the water from Mumbai's crooked taps could not change Vithoba.

Kawakhana has changed dramatically. I remember what it was in my youth. It had a huge wooden door, a door that could belong in a fort, a door with bolts and bars that were drawn in the night. It had a smaller door set in it that found maximum use. When I was young, I was witness to a number of Hindu-Muslim riots here. Sometimes curfew would be imposed on the city. If you stepped out at such times, a bullet might come whistling through the dark, a bullet with your name on it. When a riot began, the big door was kept closed. But as children, we were in and out of the door—that was somehow allowed from the little door. We saw some terrible violence. The Irani restaurant would be raided for chairs and bottles. Soda-water bottles would come down like rain. And blood. There was always a drizzle of blood.

A thrilling moment from those times: Five or six thugs have encircled a slightly built man. In their hands, the glitter of knives. The young man seems done for. But then, like lightning, he breaks through the ring and leaps on to a Victoria, grabs the long whip and slashes it through the air, slashes it at the goons. He cuts faces open. Blood begins to flow. The knives wilt impotently in their hands.

Another incident—a man with a knife sticking out of his middle, as he tries to ram his way through the smaller door of Kawakhana. Someone has stuck him in the stomach and pulled out his intestines. I am very young then and look on with curious, innocent eyes as his guts unravel like a ball of thread. Then someone clips me on the head from behind and I run off inside.

Today, that door is only a frame. The carrot-red Jews drinking kahwa have been replaced by brown sahibs who demonstrate their skill at cards or billiards. It brings back the time when we would watch the Jews playing snooker and wonder at how they could use those long sticks to get the colourful balls into the pockets. Now anyone can play. And there's an abundance of dives and gambling dens.

Speaking of betting, Chander comes to mind. He was two years older than I. He came from my mother's birth village. He had only studied up to the fourth or fifth standard but his streetsmarts made him a Plato among men. His mother did domestic work in some bungalows, but how could she bring up three children on that? And so Chander began to take bets for a bookie. Money was always dancing across his palm. When I came to Mumbai we would spend hours together. He would buy us movie tickets, using his own money. We would dine in restaurants on exciting dishes, all new to me. That I was still in school was a matter of pride to him.

I didn't know much about betting. But it all had something to do with the prices of cotton in America. Those were the numbers on which people laid bets in Kawakhana. 'Open', 'closed', 'mendi' were all words I heard. You could make nine rupees on a single rupee. And if an 'open' number turned out to be 'closed', you could make a bundle. The old folks were totally addicted.

One day, Chander got caught. While the panchnama was being made, he swiftly exchanged pencils. He changed his copying pencil for an ordinary one. In court he defended himself. He proved that he had not written what was shown on the betting sheet. That was Chander. We were in awe of his sharp wits. After that, he began to write his numbers on the walls. They could not be presented in court as evidence.

Chander's fame did not rest on gambling alone. He had magic in his hands. When everyone was asleep, he would use coal and coloured chalks to draw beautiful pictures on the streets and pavements. He had no English but a great love of Hollywood. The drawings would often star Hollywood's finest. Sometimes he would paint cinema hoardings. It seemed that he might one day become a renowned painter. Later, I came to Mumbai to find a job. At that time, the Bhimjyot* was travelling all over Maharashtra. Along with it went a huge oil painting of Dr Ambedkar. This had been painted by Chander. Now when I meet him in Fort or Colaba, he's carrying a sack containing a hammer, a chisel, a saw, that kind of thing. He repairs the rolling shutters of shops. And I wonder, who killed the Husain in Chander's hands?

Chander's marriage. That's another story. Next to us lived Manjula, Chander's mother-in-law. She was a doughty woman who had been widowed young. Like all the other women, she too went rag-picking. She was known to be a fighter, something like Champa in Vijay Tendular's play *Sakharam Binder*. She had a peculiar way of walking, and spitting with a 'pachkan' sound. Even the men were wary of her. You couldn't tell when she might attack, grabbing a fistful of your shirt. Her abuse was also colourful. Her stance, in a fight, was masculine in its aggression. She would tuck in her sari and scream something like, 'You pimp, I'll grab your balls and swing from them,' or 'I'll stretch your

---

*Ten years after the demise of Dr Babasaheb Ambedkar a Bhim-Jyoti rally to commemorate his life and thought was organized from Mhow in Madhya Pradesh (Dr Ambedkar's birth place) to Chaityabhoomi, Dadar, Mumbai (where he was cremated), under the leadership of Dadasaheb Gaekwad, Dr Ambedkar's political heir. Bhaiyyasaheb Ambedkar, Dr Ambedkar's only son, also participated in the rally.

shame like a rubber band,' with appropriate accompanying gestures. The ferocity and inventiveness of her abuse stunned me.

She had three daughters and a son. One of the daughters had just attained puberty, the other two were still young. The son was the youngest. The eldest daughter was the nicest of them. She had not been affected by her mother's nature. That she was different was the result of another story. Vithabai the albino had no children and longed for one. And so she had looked after Manjula's eldest, treating her as her own, bringing her up in comfort. Since she had been brought up in Vithabai's care, in her clean and well-cared-for home, this girl did not seem to be Manjula's child at all. She was also fairer than her mother. This was the girl Chander wanted to marry. It had been a dream he had nursed from childhood. Vithabai also thought it might be a good match. But then she was not the girl's real mother.

When the child came of age, Manjula asserted her rights. She claimed her daughter from Vithabai. She had no intention of letting her daughter marry Chander. She would say: 'He has no home of his own, he's a vagrant.'

It was then that I saw the destructive power of love at first hand. Chander could never sit idle. Next to the toilets there was a large open space where everyone threw their garbage and the little ones squatted to shit. Chander put all the children to work. In a couple of days, he had the entire ground cleaned. In a month, he had turned it into a beautiful garden. Rose shrubs began to bloom. Then Chander prepared for Diwali, working for a week or more. He set lamps in front of his door, strung up fairy lights and paper buntings. He erected a terracotta fort as well. We were all admiration for his handiwork. But then he heard that Manjula's eldest daughter was engaged to another. The news destroyed him. He trashed his decorations. Like a madman, he ravaged the garden that had been such a delight to our eyes. He uprooted the bushes. In minutes, he had turned it into a wasteland again. This was a new side to Chander. Otherwise, he had seemed a peaceable fellow, with a smile on his face, always willing to help anyone who came his way.

For a long while afterwards, he didn't say much to anyone. He was nursing his psychic wounds. Then he turned his attention to Manjula's second daughter. She was very young, barely ten or twelve years old. But Chander waited for the next two or three years. Perhaps he had made up his mind that he would only marry one of Manjula's daughters, any one of them—who knows? But he did manage it. He married the second daughter. Manjula had mellowed too. She offered no real opposition to the match.

Meanwhile, Vithabai's life took a tragic turn. The loss of a child that she had taken as her own daughter broke her. When her husband died, she fell on bad times. He left no savings. Slowly, the furniture and the household goods began to find their way into the Marwari's shop. In a short time, the well-appointed house emptied. Chander used to live in Vithabai's house earlier. He began to look after her now. He brought her food from time to time. On the day she died, a number of young Muslim men gathered in the mohalla to claim her body. One of them announced that his father had married Vithabai and that he considered her his mother. This was explosive news in the basti. No one in Kawakhana knew that she had remarried and become a Muslim. Until the end, she had dressed as a Hindu woman. She had never used a veil nor had she worn a salwar-kameez. Had she made this compromise as a matter of survival?

I was touched by the sight of her young Muslim adoptive son raising her bier to his shoulder behind his father. As I raised her body, I found I had tears in my eyes. I could not forget her kindness to me when I had been a lad.

On one side of our alley in Kawakhana was the police station; on the other, Kamathipura, the red-light area. The Mahars went to school in Sunder Gully, a filthy area, beautiful only in name. It was covered with piles of rubbish, puddles of dirty water. In the middle of all this was an akhara, a sand pit where the students of Sakharam Ustad practised stick fighting. Sakharam Ustad was one of Kaku's relatives. He was an influential figure in the area. The school teacher and Sakharam Ustad were leaders of the Ambedkar movement there. Naigaon had Daji, Colaba had Badshah, Nagpada had Sakharam. He brought the youth together and would organize the Samta Sainik Dal, an equality brigade.

I remember that every once in a while, on small pretexts, fights would begin. Sometimes it would be Untouchables versus Caste Hindus; sometimes it would be Muslims versus

Untouchables. But when it was only a Hindu versus Muslim riot, the Muslims did not touch us. 'Jai-Bhimwaale'* was a term of approval with them.

I remember a Mahar versus Muslim riot in Kamathipura. I can't tell you now what caused it, but I do remember Sakharam Ustad during the riot, his head shaved, his chest bare, his powerful body on display. With an iron rod in his hand, he's chasing down the Muslims, and the Muslims are running helter-skelter, even though they are armed with the shining choppers they use to slice open animals.

One thing did happen as a result of Sakaharam's akhara. The Muslims who had been accustomed to seeing Dalit women as easy pickings were now more respectful. They kept their distance.

There were other fights. Once, the young men of our area took on the police in an all-out battle. If the police had batons, the boys had stones. The police were put to flight, the boys pursued them; it was a comic scene. But then the maddened police returned in vans. Now they had rifles. They fired in the air, but all the young men had vanished. That unarmed boys could challenge the police was an eye-opener. That day my biceps too seemed to swell up.

Any reason was good enough to start a riot between the upper castes and untouchables. During the immersion of

---

*Jai Bhimwaale was used to describe those Mahars who followed Dr Ambedkar into Buddhism. Now it is the preferred nomenclature among the community too, as seen in the epic documentary *Jai Bhim Comrade* (Anand Patwardhan, 2011).

Ganpati, there was a fight to make sure that the Mahar Ganpati did not take precedence over the upper-caste Ganpati. Or the Mahars would take out a procession for the book *Pandavpratap* and the upper castes would object.

The complete *Pandavpratap* was read non-stop in a cycle of ritual readings. That we were of the same race as the Pandavas of the *Mahabharata* was a legend I had heard. That there was a Pandava throne in Delhi, a throne so hot that grain would pop if tossed on it, a throne of glowing embers, a throne on which only Babasaheb could sit. Such were the oral stories I had heard right from childhood.

Kaku would sometimes use Sakharam Ustad as a threat because Tatya was scared of him. He was from her mother's side of the family. When my father had been alive, Tatya never touched a drop. He would go to the akhara, he would exercise with clubs, he would practice dandpatta and, with his eyes closed, slice a sour lime in two with the naked blade. But once my father died, it was as if some kind of handover happened. Tatya took his place as the family alcoholic. He would come home drunk and beat his wife. Once, he felt the cups and saucers on the drying board had not been properly washed, so he broke all the cups and saucers in the house. Every time Kaku got beaten, she would go and sulk in her mother's house for a few days. She was not very fond of Tatya and she was deeply attached to her mother's home. One day, Sakharam Ustad's boys gave Tatya a salutary beating after he had beaten Kaku. That made him drink even more. He always had some money in his pocket. When he came home drunk, Kaku would take whatever money was left. When he found his money missing, he would suspect it was her doing, but Kaku was clever enough to conceal her crimes.

One unforgettable day, Tatya gets up in the morning, finds his money missing. He gets angry, seizes his new wool coat and shreds it, turning it into rags. We watch all this from a safe distance. No one dares to stop him. He gets up in a hurry and whisks me off to Chor Bazaar, where he gets hold of a clothes vendor. He chooses one of the best woollen coats, shoves it into my hands and signals with his eyes that I am to slip away. I cut out of there. From a distant corner I watch the fun. The stall owner and Tatya argue heatedly. I can see him showing his empty hands, claiming he had taken no coat at all. A crowd gathers. Tatya is released from the stall owner's clutches. He is delighted to have stolen from a thief. He comes up to me, bubbling with mischief. 'We got our money's worth, didn't we?' he says. I am bemused. First he tore his own coat. Then he stole one. What had he profited from this?

In some ways, he was a simpleton. He was very proud that I was getting an education. He had always regretted his own lack of opportunity. Once, on pay day, he came home a little more far gone than usual. He shoved me out of the door. 'Let's get you some new clothes,' he said. I was delighted. In those days we would shop for clothes at Pila House, in those shops with their glittering windows. We climbs the stairs of just such a shop. Tatya told the shopkeeper he wanted heavy clothes. By that, he meant fashionable ones. In those days, bush shirts sported horses or elephants on them. The chest was one colour, the sleeves another. I really didn't like these clothes. In such a shirt, I would look like I were decked out for a Shimga performance.* I told Tatya so. He said, 'Look, next year you're going to a school where you will learn English. What kind of clothes do you want? You have to look like you belong.' I wanted to laugh but I suppressed it. In truth, I wanted blue trousers and a white shirt. But who could argue with Tatya? Unhappily, I took the clothes. How could I wear them in the taluka, I wondered miserably. Carrying my parcel, we walked down Golpitha. There were brothels on both sides of the road. On the first floors of some buildings, there were numbers and red lights. It was now getting on for evening. Business had not yet begun. Some of the women had just woken up. Some were going to brush their teeth. Some sat in their doorways, doing their hair, braiding flowers into their plaits.

One of them calls to Tatya by name. That there should be a woman who lives in this area and knows Tatya seems odd. I look at this woman. She's drying her long hair. She's dark but voluptuous. She seems to be from Karnataka. Her nose ring is glittering like the noonday sun. She stands there,

---

*A folk dance performance performed at the Holi festival. The gods are placed in a palkhi (a palanquin) and, carried on the shoulders of the men, brought to the homes of the village.

talking to Tatya. 'This is my nephew. He studies in the village school,' he says. The woman looks at me affectionately. I am embarrassed. I don't want to stay here a second longer. Without stopping to think, I leave the two of them standing there and go back to Kawakhana. Tatya comes home much later. He's more drunk than usual. As soon as he sees me, he calls my name. He abuses me roundly. He says, 'You cunt, if your uncle goes to eat shit, will he take you as well? You're sly, just like your mother.'

That he could abuse my mother as well hurt me deeply. Circumstances had made us vulnerable; we were not allowed to defend ourselves. We had to bow our heads and listen. That hurt, that deep and grievous hurt, stayed with me for a long while. I decided that I would never come back to Mumbai for the holidays. I kept this promise to myself. I came next to the city for his last journey.

In Kawakhana, it was no big deal for a man to bring a sex worker from Golpitha to live with him. One young man threw his ripe young bride out on the streets while he cootchie-cooed in his home with a prostitute. When she came to stay, the prostitute would bring the children new clothes and fine things to eat. Tatya went beyond this tradition too: he brought home a real live hijra. The hijra was very good looking. He had all the airs and graces of a woman. Unless you looked very carefully, you couldn't tell he was a hijra. Everyone felt sorry for Tatya as it was generally known that his wife, Kaku, treated him badly; she did not let him touch her in the night. But Kaku maintained an outward air of calm through all of this. On such occasions, she went and sat on the footpath.

I too had an encounter with a hijra, but not in the same way. His name was Sahadba. Like Tatya, he was related to me, but distantly. He was from my village. He worked in a mill in Mumbai. He wore men's clothes but behaved in an effeminate manner. When he was in the mood, he would clap in the characteristic manner of the hijras. One day, he came to meet us in Kawakhana. He was surprised at how big I had grown. 'Come, let's go for a movie,' he said. I was ashamed to be seen with him but Aaji also insisted that I go. When we left, passers-by looked at us suspiciously; I was terribly embarrassed.

That day we watched a film at some filthy fleabag at Pila House. We were sitting in the balcony. I couldn't get involved with the film. All I could think of was how to get away from my 'uncle'. After the film, Sahadba took me to a restaurant and ordered some assorted cakes.

As we made our way home through Golpitha, Sahadba remembered something. 'Arré, do you remember your Jamuna Maushi? She lives here. Let's go see her.' That one of my aunts could be living in this warren of brothels was not something that had ever occurred to me. I could not remember my mother ever mentioning a sister called Jamuna. On both sides of Golpitha, there were cages, iron-barred, such as those built for lions. Behind these bars, half-naked women. Some were wearing short frocks, their juicy thighs on display to excite the lust of clients. They seemed like hungry tigers, waiting for meat. Sahadba took me into one of their cages.

This was the first time I had ever visited a brothel. A twelve-by-ten-foot room. A cloth curtain cutting off one side of it. A small shrine to Yellamma on the wall. A wooden contribution box under it. I was astonished to see a photograph of Babasaheb Ambedkar on the wall.

Sahadba introduced me to a slim woman, Jamuna. Her basically fair skin seemed jaundiced but she had a good sari on and her fingernails were painted. Under the loads of make-up, she was an attractive woman. When she heard that I was Sakhu's son, her eyes filled with tears. She hugged me affectionately and then she asked someone to get me a cold drink. She told me I must come again the next day. 'I'll get you some good clothes,' she said. As we were leaving, she pushed some money into my hand. I didn't want to refuse. Outside, I asked Sahadba about Jamuna. 'She's your mother's step-sister. One mother but different fathers,' he said.

'How did she land up here?'

Jamuna had been living close by with her husband in the loft of a shack. Her beauty made her husband suspicious. He would beat her often. It was he who had brought her here and sold her. I found it difficult to believe that a man could sell his own wife.

I spent the night in a restless debate about whether I should go back to visit Jamuna or not. I still cannot tell whether it was any feeling for Jamuna Maushi or the lure of new clothes, but the truth of it is that I did go there alone the next day. She had bought me some rather good clothes and took me for a long ride in a horse carriage. 'The next time you come on a holiday, be sure to visit,' she said.

But I never sought her out again. I did not tell anyone who gave me the new clothes, not even my mother. I was frightened of what she might say. After that, I heard tales of Jamuna often: that she had left the business, that she was now begging on the streets, that she had lost her mind, and so on.

Then, two or three years ago, I am walking under the Dadar bridge with some rather illustrious writer friends. The bridge shelters a large gathering of beggars. Some of them have knocked together temporary shelters. In the middle of this crowd, I see Jamuna. Although she is in rags, her hair loose and unkempt, her face ravaged, it is her. Even after so many years, she must have recognized me. She keeps staring at me. I keep turning around to look at her as I walk away. I still feel her eyes on my back.

I couldn't even manage a few lines of ordinary, everyday conversation. I felt: In these Terylene clothes, how bourgeois I've become. What could I have told my friends about her? And even if I had talked to her and then taken her home with me, would my wife, my very educated [second] wife, have let her in? My second wife, who washes the house four or five times a day, keeps its surfaces relentlessly mirror-like. And Jamuna in that state, the filth caked on her.

I did not sleep well that night. Her gaze lanced through the darkness.

Later I met my one of my cousins on my mother's side. He gave me some startling news:

'When her time was up, Jamuna came back to the village to die.'

How did she find her way back? What of her madness? My cousin reported that her husband performed the last rites himself and he also fed the village when the time came.

—

I would often meet people from my village when I began to live in Mumbai. Aambu and Sadashiv were among my favourites. They were both four or five years older than I. They were working in Mumbai but behaved with me as if I were an equal. They would amuse themselves by taking me to Golpitha. I would object: 'When a man is seen sitting under a toddy palm, it is assumed that he is drinking.' Aambu was jocular, always making people laugh, while Sadashiv never spoke in jest. And yet there was an unbreakable bond between them. Aambu was good-looking, well-groomed. He was illiterate but when he started speaking, he could mesmerize even the educated. His hobby was mimicry; he would perform at public shows. His patent joke was his imitation of the Konkan accent, a big hit at Jayanti celebrations.

Aambu was a boarder with Kaku. In the morning, when he was leaving for work, he would praise her tea to the skies,

'The tea you make, Parvatibai! I can taste it right up to the company gate.' Everyone got the sarcasm. Everything he did and said was infected with the same good spirits. And then one day those good spirits evaporated. He had contracted tuberculosis. At first, he hid the signs. But his cough and his weight loss brought it to our attention. Now he began to worry that he had not married; and that when he died, he would go to the cremation ground alone.

He did get married, not once, but twice. His second wife looked after him to the very end. But fear of his imminent end swallowed his laughter, his jokes, his conversation. The mark of death was upon him and it made him difficult to look at. The news that he had died came when I was in the village. Death held no novelty; I had witnessed it as a child. But that day, Aambu's death came as a shock.

Sadashiv's tragedy was different, it was a political one. I remember him from the time before he came to Mumbai. He was a ploughman. He would work in the fields, his dhotar tied so it ended at his knees, a banian covering his upper body. His relatives came and took him to the city. They stuck him into a job in the tram company. The largely unlettered Sadashiv—he had studied only up to the sixth or seventh standard—changed under Mumbai's malign influence. When he came to the village, we were all astonished by his style, his heron-white clothes, his backswept hair. He always had a book in his hand and he would tell tall tales in what seemed to us to be chaste Marathi. Even if he was still dark of skin, he seemed very dashing. He could play Shivaji— or so we thought.

In the beginning, his hobby was to get together with some enthusiasts and stage plays. Rehearsals were held in an institution in Kamathipura. I remember him staging *Ajoba* (Grandfather). I went for the rehearsals too, when I was visiting the city. One of the actors was a beautiful Brahmin girl from Girgaon. All the other actors vied for a chance to talk to her. To go to her home and fetch her in a taxi was a big thrill.

There was also an actor with a gold tooth. He was married but he threw away a great deal of money on the Brahmin actress. He would buy her saris and blouses—or so they said. But these actresses are smart cookies. No one is allowed to touch them. Their admirers are like the guard dog at the sweet shop who may smell but not taste. Sadashiv was different. He was mad about theatre. During rehearsal, the actress once suddenly experienced a resurgence of caste pride.

'What pronunciation!' she said. 'But then you're a Mahar. You'll never learn.'

That was it. Sadashiv turned on the actress. With the same contempt he said, 'Madam, if you're so proud of your caste, why put bells on your feet and come here to dance with the Mahars?' That cut her to the quick. She began to sniffle, her plump cheeks turned red, as did the tip of her nose.

I can't tell you how Sadashiv got involved in union work. But sitting still was not in his nature. He began to give speeches at the gate meetings of the bus company in Colaba. He lost his job in the BEST strike. He was now on the street.

He got his things together and returned to the village. He began to take a role in the political life of the taluka. Everyone called him 'MLA' (Member of the Legislative Assembly) but this was an honorific conferred on him by the people. In truth, he'd never been elected. But whether it was a government loan or a case of marital discord, Sadashiv was your man. His work began when he took out a morcha to the local government offices. While people would treat him with respect, take him home, sit him down, offer him tea, he found it offensive that they would treat others from the Maharwada with contempt.

Once, he caused a commotion in the village. There would be a big fair at Ram Navami. Everyone was invited to a meal. 'We don't want your free food. Take a contribution from the Maharwada too,' he said. A collection was duly made in the Maharwada. That evening the first guests sat down at the Maruti temple. The Mahars were not invited to this seating. Sadashiv was furious. So what did he do? He tucked in his dhotar and went to serve the food. The Maratha youth restrained him. They said to him: 'These old so-and-sos won't listen. All the food will go to waste.' Sadashiv was in no mood to listen. Finally, they had to lock him up. When the first guests had finished, the rest of the young men got ready to eat. Sadashiv refused to eat; he had been profoundly insulted. No one from the Maharwada went to the feast that night.

Sadashiv was a member of the Republican Party of India (RPI). After several years, the Congress and the RPI came together. Then came the Zilla Parishad elections. The Congress wanted Sadashiv to stand but the RPI leaders opposed the idea. Sadashiv was denied the ticket. His political career crashed and burned. His ability was unlimited but he was outspoken. He was not one to latch on to someone's coat-tails. When the Samyukta Maharashtra Movement* was on, he had called a public meeting with its leaders. When he was refused a ticket for the elections, he was deeply hurt.

'Arré, there was once an alpha male in a troupe of monkeys. To eliminate any competition, he killed and ate all the male babies that were born and let only the females live. That's politics for you.' He knew whom he was calling an alpha male.

Sadashiv's life became impossible. His family was growing and they were all starving. And so Sadashiv joined Dadu Indurikar's tamasha troupe. He was appointed manager but 'manager' means doing whatever needs to be done. One day he came home to invite us for a show of *Gaadvaacha Lagna*

---

*In 1956, the Samyukta Maharashtra Movement sought the formation of a separate Maharashtra state, to be carved out of the erstwhile State of Bombay. This state was to have Bombay as its capital. Morarji Desai was of the opinion that the city of Bombay should be a union territory. The Samyukta Maharashtra Movement sought the inclusion of Dharwar, Belgaum and Goa into the state of Maharashtra. In January 1960, several protestors were shot and killed at Flora Fountain, in South Mumbai. The dead included an eleven-year-old girl. These are the martyrs after whom the Hutatma Chowk (as Flora Fountain is now called) is named.

(The Marriage of the Ass). I went to the theatre in Lalbaug. The laavnis seemed to have ended. Sadashiv appeared from somewhere, in a hurry. He sat me in the front of row. The vagh began. Dadu Indurikar's performance as Sawlya Kumbhaar was greeted with much laugher. After that, some donkeys come on to the stage. They were men in costume, bent over double. I was quite shocked by the scene, for one of the donkeys was Sadashiv. Through the entire play, he was in this position. No dialogue. The man whose tongue was like a sword was forced here into silence. What was he feeling? I couldn't bear it for too long. I came out and stood for a while.

After his work was done, Sadashiv came out too. He took me to a restaurant nearby. He told me heart-rending stories of the exploitation tamasgirs suffered. The contractors extracted every last bit of work, wringing workers out like sugarcane, while they built mansions for themselves. He would tell me he dreamt of starting a tamasgir union.

Sadashiv is still a tamasgir. He has not achieved his goal, he hasn't set up a union. But when I meet him, he is still optimistic. His son, Sharad, has also been destroyed by the same social conditions. In the beginning, he was a gofer for the young Dalit Panther leaders. He worked as a bodyguard. But his life too has ended in the dumps.

All these people played important roles in my life. Remove them and there's not much of me left. They make patterns in my life, like those of oil on water…Chander, Aambu,

Sadashiv. They were my professors in this peculiar university of life.

It was the opposite with Dadasaheb. He had also left his mark on me, but in another way entirely. I wanted to shine in public life as he did, make speeches... If I had begun to see social problems in the light of Dr Ambedkar's teachings, it was through Dadasaheb. I believed that all the young men of my age in the hostel should follow the ideals he espoused.

Dadasaheb would come to the hostel—I'm not talking about the Koli boarding school now. This is the Siddharth Hostel I'm talking about. Dadasaheb would come and spend time with the students. He would be one of them, he would sing, play the dholki. When he got into the mood, he would tell naughty jokes, in Mahar style. We would laugh until our tummies hurt. I still remember a song we would sing: 'Kaarya kara re tarunaanon', whose lines went something like this: 'Do not shirk work, O Youth/Walk in the ways of truth/Gather the brave and form a band/Remember Tanaji and Bajirao, Young Man.' My hair would stand on end when he sang this song.

We were all also deeply interested in Dadasaheb's personal life. His wife was beautiful, fair-skinned, light-eyed, like a Brahmin girl from Sadashiv Peth, Pune. In his heart of hearts, each of us wanted a wife like his.

—

For the seventh-standard examination, we had to go to the Zilla School. I had to go to Ahmednagar. Aai had to beg my fare from many people. The Maratha boys were placed in the agricultural school boarding, I was in the Party office. My clothes were all a bit ragged. At that time, I had a remarkable shirt of some glittery cloth, with buttons on the shoulders. Aaji had sent it with some villager. Perhaps one of the rich women whose bungalows she cleaned in the city had given it to her. I was deeply embarrassed about it. In the Party office, there was a man called Savle Mama. Every morning he sat down with *The Times* and a dictionary. He had never studied English in school but he learned it using *The Times* and a dictionary. Later he acquired a Master's degree. He and his son would go to college together. For a long time he was the headmaster of a Marathi high school. Even at that age, I was impressed by his determination.

The Party office was in a Muslim-dominated area. On the first day itself, there was a disaster. I was brushing my teeth in the morning, standing on the terrace. Beneath, was a group of hijras. I don't know what came over me but I began telling a neighbour's child something about hijras when one of them caught sight of me and realized I was commenting on them. Furious, the hijra shouted: 'Bastard! Die, you low-caste boy...' The Party worker also took umbrage. I couldn't understand what I had done wrong. And in that shaken state, I wrote the examination. Then we went off to see the city. It seemed like a large village. We saw the fort in which Pandit Nehru had been detained. But I was much more excited by Chand Bibi's palace. They say that there was an underground route between her palace and the city.

I was generally a forbearing soul. I would swallow insults and offences and hold my peace. But as time passed, a mischievous side began to emerge as well. Perhaps this was the result of education. I would wonder later: how could I have spoken like that? Once, we went to a village called Rajur to see an exhibition of animals. In the evening, we went to see the Marathi-medium school there. Since there was no teacher, chaos reigned. Everyone was fighting with each other. I was with a friend. I said, perhaps a little too loudly: 'Wah, what discipline this school has.' That was it. The students stopped fighting amongst themselves and turned on me. My friend vanished. That night I got it from those boys.

The other example can still make my hair stand. I was studying in the high school then. There were two famous gangsters at the time: Babban and Savji. They had some kind of hold over everyone. It was said that they ran a wholesale opium and ganja business. They also controlled the local Congress Party. One of them was handsome, fair, strapping. He would walk down the road as if ready for a wrestling match. It was said that he had dressed up as a prince and defrauded some rich people in Kashmir. The other was gaunt but swift as a water snake. When they walked down the road together, even the crows shat themselves. One day, I was standing at a street corner chatting with some upper-caste boys. I was telling stories, spinning yarns from my storehouse of experience. Then the two gangsters passed by in their vehicle. Because of the crowd, the car swerved close enough to give us a fright. I shouted abuse at them loud enough for them to hear. That was it. The boys, upper-class, cowardly, were now terrified. Where did I get the courage that day? The thugs got out of the car. The whole city feared them and this little boy thought he could get away with abusing them? There was no hope left for me. The earth seemed to be slipping away under my feet. I didn't want to run, so I braced for a beating. It didn't happen. I was saved that day. The boys I was with, they were sons of important people. The goons knew their parents.

I remember another example of my tongue's valour. This happened in Mumbai. I was quite grown up. I had passed the SSC. In Mumbai, one of Sadashiv's relatives was getting married. The goddess had marked her face but she had found herself a fair, handsome boy. When the wedding party arrived, I discovered that the groom's younger brother was in high school with me. Since we were from the girl's side, we did whatever little jobs had to be done. But right from the beginning I could see that the brother of the bridegroom was a little snooty. He was always hanging around the girls.

The wedding took place. The food was served. The boy's side was chatting away. The stage was empty, with a microphone on it. I got on the stage. I took the mike and talked to the wedding party: 'Brothers and sisters, now let me tell you about the groom's brother.' And I told them a tale out of school.

'It's assembly time. All of us boys and girls are standing in line. And then, panting, gasping, he runs up, wearing a shirt with some odd designs all over it. In Sangamner, this shirt looks like something a clown might wear. The kids begin to laugh. The principal is annoyed at this interruption and plucks him out of the line. Orders him to class. He's scared, runs in the direction of the class, slips, falls, scatters his books. The kids begin to laugh again.'

The wedding party also began to laugh. They thought it was entertainment put on for them. The funny thing was that the bridegroom's side also joined in the laughter.

The boy had the wedding party's money. In a temper, he took it and vanished. Chaos ensued. Those who were laughing at my jokes were now looking for me. Sadashiv slipped me into a house and hid me under a bed. The search went on all night. The panic ended only when the boy was found, cajoled and persuaded to come back. Morning finally broke and the women of the wedding party sought me out in a group. 'What a fellow-and-a-half you are!' their eyes said. They looked at me as one might at an animal in a zoo!

In later years, in my public life, such spontaneous overflows of emotion would often happen, the result, perhaps, of suppressed rebellious urges. Dadasaheb had become a minister. I read of it in the paper and on an ordinary post card, I wrote him a message: 'Up to now all the Dalits who have become ministers have been corrupt. As minister, you will have to erase that and act as a candidate who has genuine compassion for the poor.' This was a rather pompous thing for a small man like me to write. Dadasaheb met many of our common friends but he did not mention the letter. I got only a cycslostyled form letter as an acknowledgement. Once, I went to his Malabar Hill bungalow on the occasion of his birthday. Many people had gathered there. The lawns were lit up. Some luminaries from the film world were also present. I went only because of our long-standing relationship. He noticed me and decided to ask me to speak. When it was my turn, my mind was a blank. Finally I decided to say what was in my heart. 'I have seen Dadasaheb in the thick of movements, morchas and meetings. That I should see him as a minister now seems almost improbable. Today, my mind seems unwilling to accept him in this new avatar. The love I feel for him is the love born of revolution—love for the man who taught us to fight, the man who showed us the power of the Ambedkar movement.' I sat down, exhausted. I felt I had no reason to be there. But Dadasaheb proved his greatness then. In front of everyone, he sang my praises. He said he was proud of how bravely I had spoken in front of a minister. The next time I went to his bungalow for his birthday, he had lost his ministry. There were no celebrations, only an air of gloom. The harvest had ended; the birds had flown.

Once or twice he had said about me in public, 'He keeps

away from me. I would like him to come close, I want to draw him to me with affection.'

Dadasaheb got many Party workers housing-board flats in Mumbai, but I never felt tempted to ask for one. I can never forget the help he had offered during my dark days: I was not of much use to him in his political life, but he had given me some principles which I still hold dear. It is not in my nature to deceive myself and so I stayed away, heeding my inner voice. Madness? Naivete? Who knows? The war continues in my head today.

—

The final examination results were out. I got good marks but I didn't know what to do next. I wanted to study further. After the finals, I could have, with a little extra effort, become a school teacher, but I didn't want to rot in a village. I did not want to live with constant references, all slighting, to my caste origins. To get out of all this, I had to study.

And then I heard that in a neighbouring taluka there was a hostel for Dalits. Dadasaheb was the director. I wrote out an application. Dadasaheb had a meeting in the taluka. At the end of it, I handed him my application. When the holidays ended, I got a call to a test. I went for it with the Gandhi cap I customarily wore. The assistant director of the institute asked me my caste. When I said 'Harijan,' everyone looked at me suspiciously. Someone said, 'Don't say Harijan. Say Mahar. Harijan is a term of abuse invented for us by

Gandhi.' My head began to spin. Up to now, whenever I had said I was a Mahar, whether in school or at the Koli hostel, the upper-caste teacher had said, 'Say Harijan!' And now this lot was insisting on Mahar.

I explained this quandary to the assistant director. Perhaps this bit of intelligence turned the tide. I was told to bring a trunk, a plate, a tumbler and my own bedding. I was delighted.

The hostel was on the Sangamner-Pune road. To get there, you had to cross a river. It was in an area called Dhakta Sangamner, or Little Sangamner. Which high-caste person would rent a building to house Dalit students? The building belonged to a Muslim. He lived behind it with his family. Along the wall were our tin trunks. Next door was a tin shed, the mess. Behind it, a well. At meal times, there was always a crowd of students milling around, washing their plates. We used the same tumblers to drink water and when we went to the toilet.

The hostel got a government grant, so our stay and our food was free. We studied at the big school. The Gokhale Education Society also had a grand Petit School. Outside the village there was a Christian school but save for a couple of students, no one took admission there.

The majority of the hostel was Mahar. There was a sprinkling of Mangs, Chambars and Mahadev Kolis. There were about fifty or sixty students on the rolls. It was the organization's first hostel and so the workers had slaved to make it a reality. In the beginning, there were no grants, so many of the founders had pawned their wives' ornaments to raise the necessary funds. Their sacrifices were now well known. They tried to uphold the principles of Bhaurao Patil who founded the Rayat Education Society in 1919. The network spread through the zilla. They set up fifteen to twenty hostels. Their names too were revolution-inspired. There was the Shambuk Hostel in Shrirampur and in Agasti, the Rama-Yashodhara. Ours was Siddharth, a name chosen by Dadasaheb. This was his true political constitution. They say the organization's budget crossed a lakh of rupees.

But this was also where I first encountered the fault lines of the Dalit movement. In this Mahar hostel, students of other castes went in fear of us. This became apparent when some of the Koli boys from the hostel came here. In the Koli-dominated hostel they had been tigers; here they turned into kitty cats. In the mess, the students ate in caste-based cliques and everyone mocked the behaviour of other castes.

I remember my first day at high school, my first in such a grand building. Every hour, the teacher changed and this was a novelty too. The teachers were committed idealists who made a deep impression on me. In the eighth, we began to study English. Our teacher was a Brahmin; fair, sturdy of body. He would wear a dhotar and shirt and a Gandhi topi; his forehead would be anointed with sandalwood paste. He was strict but loving. We had come from the villages and found pronunciation difficult. He would put a pencil in our mouths and make us speak. The phobia about English I developed in the eighth standard would stay with me right up to the SSC. The other subjects were easy.

There was one important difference between me and the other students in the hostel. I did not mix with the village children. They sat together in their own clique. I would invariably find myself talking to the upper-caste students. I was not in their division; I did not try to join the division in which the boarding-school students were.

Ours was the house in the lead. The kids who were in the top ten ranks were in our division. My friends Bhagat and Bharitkar were leagues ahead of the rest. I also remember Khambekar, a Shimpi. He was very fond of me. All these boys were from rich families. They wore neatly ironed clothes. I must have looked quite slovenly by comparison. But because of my sweet nature and my habit of chattering away, they did not keep their distance.

I was also theatre-mad. As a child, I thought I should like to be a tamasgir when I grew up. In high school, I wanted to act again. But who would let me? No one from the boarding school had ever been so honoured. There was a variety programme at the school, performed by the students where some plays were also presented. In front of the stage, in the press of students, I too was a viewer. Suddenly my basic nature came to the fore. There was an interval between acts. I knew Katkar Sir so I went and asked him whether I could present something. He looked at me for a moment. He realized I was a boarding-school student but he gave permission. At the Marathi school, our set texts included some scenes from famous plays. I marched on to the stage and recited Sudhakar's monologue, 'Hya rikaamya pyaalat kaay distay tula?' ('What do you see in this empty glass?') from R.G. Gadkari's *Ekach Pyaala*. I did this with great confidence. When it was over, I heard a huge round of applause. For the next few days, I walked on air. I had found a hitherto unsuspected ability. My stock rose in the school, and after that I took on every role with huge intensity. In those days Diwakar's monologues were included in the text books. Once, even before I was in the tenth standard, I studied a one of his monologues from our SSC textbook, 'Tevdach dnyanaprakashat' ('In the light of that much knowledge') and performed it in front of the tenth standard, speaking from memory.

Around that time, I read Shirwadkar's play *Bajirao aani Mastaani* (Bajirao and Mastani) for the first time. I was impressed by the language as much as by the fantastic exposition of the theme of love, and I wanted this play performed at the school's annual event. I got hold of a copy and went to meet the principal, a certain Upasni, fair skinned and slim of build. He would stalk the streets with a military gait, each turn executed at a right angle. All the students were terrified of him. Now, he looked at me bemused. He didn't get angry. He tried to explain: 'Arré, who's going to play Mastani?' I understood what he meant. Sangamner was a puritanical village. The idea that girls might act in a play with boys had not occurred to anyone. But I had already convinced a pretty Brahmin boy to play Mastani. I suggested his name. The principal, however, had a school to run. He refused permission. Crestfallen, I left his office.

My passion for theatre ended over a risible matter. It was, as I remember it, in my last year at school. That year, *Raja Ashok* had been chosen as the school play. I expected to get a good role as I had done in previous years. But when I tried out for the title role, I was refused. 'For Ashoka the King, we need someone fair. You're too black,' said the teacher. I was offered the role of his minister. I was enraged. And in that mood, I met the principal. He diverted my attention with another question. 'This is your final year. Poor students shouldn't be taking part in plays. That's for the rich.' Why did I feel so acutely the nature of my predicament that day? My zest evaporated. I did not even go to see the play.

I had always tried to participate in extracurricular activities. Specially speeches, essays, races, sports, et cetera. When there was a public-speaking competition in the village and I gave my name, the boarders began to taunt me. 'Fancies himself another Ambedkar,' they sneered. 'Thinks he can speak in public.'

You've probably heard a lot recently about ragging in colleges. I too had my share. It was the second day of Holi and at the boarding school, colour was being splashed about. If the boys couldn't lay their hands on coloured powder, they used muck. It was also the day of my Sanskrit examination, an extracurricular subject I had chosen over drawing and Hindi. I got ready, putting on my clothes. Outside, the students were waiting to pounce, their colour and filth at the ready. I began to sweat. Finally, I threw open the door and made a dash for it. That I saved myself from their colours was my only satisfaction.

The ragging increased in intensity. But I brought this on myself. When I went home for the holidays, I found it heartbreaking the way my mother and sister lived, hand to mouth. At around that time, the old woman who cooked for us in the hostel retired, claiming fatigue. I met the director and asked if my mother could have the job. He agreed and I returned from the very next holiday with my mother and sister in tow. Aai was paid thirty rupees a month and her food as well as my sister's board. She had to cook for fifty or sixty boys. But Aai always said, 'This is better than doing free work for the village. I just have to sit in one place and slap on the bhakris.' Aai's old scrofula problem resurfaced. One by one, the boils would appear and the wounds would suppurate and refuse to dry up.

Now the boarders began to harass me even more. Some of them were nice but the bullies were aggressive. They were from the upper classes. No one spoke politely to me. And to this were added accusations of food theft. Rumour had it that my mother was feeding me additional quantities. When I sat down to eat, everyone would look daggers at me. So it became impossible for me to go to the kitchen and say a couple of words to my own mother. An invisible wall rose between us.

It was hard work for Aai. The same job was handled by two women in the local Koli boarding school. There were fewer students in that hostel, and the pay was higher. I could see my mother was being exploited. But if I complained, I knew they would say, 'She wants the work, she does it. Or she can shove off.' And so Aai worked like a bull at the wheel of an oil press. All she had was the satisfaction of having her children close by. She had to rise before dawn to get the breakfast usal going. Barely had the boarders finished with that and Aai would have to make twelve to fifteen seers of bhakris.

There wasn't much variety in the food served. It was generally bhakri and something wet to get it down. The boarders would say: 'What kind of gravy is this? You can see the ceiling in it.' Poor Aai, what could she do? She worked there for three or four years. No casual leave, no paid leave. All day long, she sat in front of a roaring stove. The kitchen would fill with smoke, a veritable gas chamber. It was only when the school vacation began that she got a break. And then she was only a prisoner out on parole.

The residue of sorrow on my face began to settle then. I did not spend much time in the boarding school. I came in only for meals. Otherwise, I'd be with my upper-caste friends. I would visit their homes, Khambekar's in particular. His family was also very affectionate. I did not mention the fact that my mother was the cook at the hostel but I think now that most of my friends probably knew this. No one mentioned it, though, perhaps so as not to hurt my feelings. Once Khambekar's mother asked me about Aai. My face flushed. I must have looked like a thief caught red-handed.

I began to avoid Dadasaheb too, for no good reason. I suppose I was simply working out my anger against other things happening in my life. When he was supposed to come to the hostel, I would head to the village. Once when it was announced that he was coming, I stayed at a friend's house on purpose. I returned when I thought he would have left, only to encounter him at the door. He was very angry. 'You've been given free admission and food and you're not observing the discipline of the place,' he said. But it pleased me to feel that I was bold enough to ignore his standing and behave badly with him. In truth I was angry only at the social structures that had brought me to this pass. Dadasaheb could not understand this and it brought us into conflict.

Although I was the kind to turn the other cheek, one day I snapped. I was quite shocked at my own behaviour that day. It was as if a volcano erupted, spewing lava. I am coming back from school one day, hungry and tired. When I get to the hostel, I hear boys singing in a closed room. Someone is beating accompaniment on a tin. This is no new thing at the hostel. I peer in, casually, through a crack in the door. What I see makes me explode. My nine- or ten-year-old sister is dancing and the boys are watching her, delighting in it. They are singing an erotic laavni number: 'Kaathewaadi ghodyavarti pudyat ghya ho mala; Raajsa, zhaau ya Jejurila'. ('Set me on your Kathiawari horse, Raja, and let's be off to Jejuri'.) I cannot take this. The blood vessels in my head begin to pulse. I kick the door furiously. The boys open it, wondering what's come over me. I curse them: 'You cunts, why don't you make your mothers and sisters dance for you?' No one says a word. They begin to leave, one by one. That I should get angry at something so ordinary probably surprises them. I hug my sister and sob. All day, I am disturbed.

The story I'm going to tell you now still has the power to disturb me. How much the boys were to blame is debatable. Indian culture has us all in its vise-like grip; how can the Dalit escape? And yet I feel no hatred for all those who played a role in this miniature *Ramayana*. Some of them are now officials of high rank. One heads the Zilla Parishad. When I meet them, they ask after Aai. They speak respectfully of her. There were some for whom my mother has shown more affection than she does for me.

This is how it happened. Aai had not even been working a month in the hostel when she began her period. She was a traditional woman so she wondered how she was supposed to cook when she was in a state of ritual uncleanness. She took her dilemma to the Superintendent. He had no answers. There was no way he was going to pay someone else to work for four days each month. What of it? he said and forced her to go back to the kitchen. How did word of her condition spread to the students? That must remain a mystery.

When I enter the mess, plate and tumbler in hand, I am greeted by a chorus: 'Shame, shame.' No one is willing to eat. I have no idea what this is about. I think the curry might have gone bad, for the students are always griping about it; sometimes it is too salty, sometimes too thin. Some take an unholy delight in summoning my mother for a scolding while I am there. And then there are some truly perverse types. Once or twice, they have thrown fistfuls of salt into the curry behind her back. When it all gets too much for me, I sometimes steal to my mother's side in the middle of the night and we weep together. At that age, tears are never far away. A few words can bring on sobs. Sane Guruji has done a good job of describing tears. But so many tears flow that my eyes begin to dry up.

Ignoring everyone now I force down a couple of mouthfuls. Then I get up from my seat and go to find out what has happened. Aai tells me. I want the earth to swallow us. I am too young to realize that it was the same society that had made us untouchable that deemed the woman's body as unclean in the menses.

At another time, Aai was accused of robbery. And what was she accused of robbing? Flour. Not that she had anything to do with it. The real thief was the Superintendent. His marriage had just been fixed in Little Sangamner. He was a man of some years, a widower, and the girl was much younger.

His new relatives-to-be lived in the outhouse of a dak banglow with many children and much paraphernalia. Morning and evening, he'd be off for there, grinding his gums. Perhaps the age difference made him generous, for the provisions meant for the hostel began to be sent there on the Superintendent's orders. One day, one of the students caught one of the Superintendent's future relatives leaving via the back door, with a towel full of flour. This crime was laid at Aai's doorstep. Since the Superintendent had the upper hand over us, neither of us could say anything. We could not afford to anger him. And so when the students had their kangaroo court and accused Aai, I could not say a word in her defence. Nor could she. The world, it seemed, was against us.

Among our relatives was a boy called Dethe, tall and well-built. Whenever we were taunted or persecuted, he would take it personally. This repressed rage found expression in an odd manner. Before joining school, he had been a cowherd, taking the animals to forage. This meant he was admitted to school a few years late, which made him larger than most of the children in his class. While herding cattle, he had seen the other cowherds playing a strange game. Put a leaf of the gui plant into your ear, and you go mad for a little while. Now whether he actually did experience such a bout of madness or he was only pretending, there was no knowing. I never dared try it. One night, he put some gui leaf into his ear. When you do this, it seems, you begin to spin like a bhagat, an exorcist. He kept chanting: 'The thorn of the gui! The thorn of the gui!' In his hand he clutched a thorny branch of the taarwadi with which he would whip people who got in his way. This started a commotion at the hostel. In all this, I did not fail to notice one thing. When under the influence of the gui, Dethe attacked students at random but he never turned on either Aai or me. His main targets were the bullies. For a long time, I wondered whether these fits were the real thing.

—

Each boy in the hostel was rich in experience. Most of them had come from the lowest of the low strata of the villages. They had arrived here as the sum total of the multiple influences that had worked on them, some good, some bad. How could they free themselves from their backgrounds? Fights, arguments were always breaking out.

In the middle of all this, there was a Mumbai boy, the son of a rich father, a delicate, beautiful lad. It seemed that he might bleed if you so much as pinched him. He was the smallest boy in the hostel. His father was foreman of the works in a factory in the city and sent him a money order every month. He was always in fancy clothes. He would eat a couple of bites in the hostel and then go to a restaurant. His two elder brothers were uneducated; they were on the fringe of a gang. That was why their father had tried to isolate his youngest son. All the students fawned over him. They yearned to borrow his fashionable clothes and took advantage of him to go to the cinema and eat at restaurants.

There were always quarrels with the hostel officials over food. They were particularly fierce on feast days. Without the authorities knowing, the boarders would check the account books. They knew the grant amounts by heart. When the hostel officials stopped the morning serving of usal, there was widespread resentment and things often boiled over. I felt rather sorry for the officials. They had to walk a tight-rope—balancing the trustees and the students. The grant money would often arrive late, which meant buying provisions on credit for two or three months at a stretch. Some days we even went hungry. The boarders would abuse the trustees and the masters. If a trustee came to a meeting, the complaints were only about food.

The society was mismanaged, its accounts puffed. The government subsidy often did not suffice. And in any case, by the time the money got to the hostel, much of it had leaked away. The government felt that the organization should also raise funds from the public; the hostel officials were routinely accused of stealing the money. When prices rose and things got expensive, the local hoods would threaten the shopkeepers. That was what happened on certain important days, including Dr Ambedkar's birthday. There would be a feast. If it were not declared, the students would force the issue by gheraoing the officials. A feast meant laddoos and jilebi added to the menu. No one would touch the rice or chapattis that day. The students would take bets.

I remember one of these. A student from a higher class ate twenty or twenty-five fist-sized laddoos at a single sitting to the shock and awe of all of us.

We would be served a mutton barbaat once a week. You were lucky to get a piece of meat in your serving. Once, the students in charge of the shopping bought sheep meat by mistake. It didn't take long for word to spread. The students refused to touch the fatty and fibrous meat. Only a few of us ate. The rest had to be fed with bhel and laddoos bought at a restaurant. A teacher said, 'When you're corrupt to the core, why worry about your skin?'

I remember one of the superintendents of the boarding school, Bhagwat Master, who was a man of ideals. His food was no different from ours; he ate with the students. The boys had had bad experiences with his predecessors, whom they nearly drove away, but for Bhagwat Master they had only respect. He kept the needs of the students in mind and fought to protect their interests. He lived a simple life, never showing off or putting himself forward. He was wiry of form, his hair elegantly parted so that a lock fell across his forehead. He held the tail end of his dhotar in one hand as he walked. One of his front teeth was missing. At some time in the past, he had served in the military. That explained his love of exercise. He wanted the students to be fit, to play sports. If you didn't show up for games, he got your food stopped.

One of the boys, Sonawane, was in the habit of chewing

tobacco which he would always be scrubbing in the palm of his hand. One day, Bhagwat Master had him bodily lifted and carried to the playground. Sonawane simply squatted on the ground, like a buffalo in a pond. He refused to play; he was adamant in his apathy to physical activity. Finally Bhagwat gave up on him. In the beginning, he had wanted to impose military discipline on us. He would rise at dawn to take us on parade. We went running on the Sangamner-Pune Road with Bhagwat leading the pack. Once, he showed us how to fall to the ground in case of an air raid. In doing so, he hurt his chest so badly that he was ill for a couple of months. His chest was all bound up with bandages, to our great amusement. Thereafter, dawn parades were no longer mentioned.

The boys of the boarding discussed the girls of the high school endlessly. These were all upper-caste girls. Their saris and make-up were subjects of fascination. Some boys even counted the saris each girl had. Perhaps that was because many of the boys had just a couple of pairs of clothes. So this almost endless parade of saris was nothing short of mind-blowing. There were many cases of unrequited love. If textbooks were exchanged, the boys would be elevated to seventh heaven. Pathare, one of the students, had the style of a film hero. On Saturdays, he would bring a steam iron from a rich friend in his village so that he could go to school in high style. Some of his friends knew that he was madly in love with a Brahmin girl. He would explode if he were teased about it. One day the boys wrote a letter in the girl's handwriting and tucked it into his book. She had 'invited' him to meet her at the State Transport Bus Stand that evening. It is difficult to describe Pathare's delight. Of course he dressed up to the nines. Of course she did not show up. Of course he was terribly disappointed and came back dejected. The rest of us toyed with him, as a cat torments a mouse. Poor fellow, he was close to tears.

Then there was Rokade. He was one of the better students at the boarding school. He was terribly poor. His parents were labourers. His books and clothes were in tatters. No one would lend him their books during the day, so he would get up to study in the night when all the others were sleeping, so that he might use their books. He was good at all the subjects but he scored full marks in Sanskrit and mathematics. He always stood first or second in class. In his class there was a sweet, fat girl called Kulkarni. They got to know each other by pretending to talk about studies. In the evening she would take her aged grandfather for a walk and steer him over to the hostel. Rokade would, quite coincidentally of course, happen to be around. They would exchange a few words about school work. Kulkarni was pretty: plump cheeks, short but of a neat and shapely build, sparkling eyes, skin the colour of ketaki. Rokade would talk about her for hours when we were alone. He and I looked a bit similar, in face and physique. We could even use each other's clothes, so people thought he was my younger brother. It is difficult to say how far he and that girl Kulkarni went but when there was a send-off after the SSC examinations, both wept copiously.

Then Rokade comes to Bombay. Kulkarni goes to Pune. Rokade joins college but he does not forget. After four long years, he meets her suddenly in Thane. She has graduated as well. He reminds her of their love. 'Let's get married,' he urges. Kulkarni gives this a cool reception. 'Where were you all these years?' she asks. 'I had forgotten all about you. Did you really set such store by what happened in school?' Poor Rokade was devastated. But he was not willing to give up so easily. He even went and met her family. They refused the match on the basis of his caste. Rokade was broken as if he had been thrown from a great height.

—

At that time, an inter-caste marriage in Sangamner was the focus of all attention. The boy was a Brahmin. The girl was a Mahar from the Sangamner Maharwada. I think her name was Hansa, and she was as beautiful as the swan her name suggested. This was no love match; it was an old-fashioned formal arranged marriage.

Deshpande was a Brahmin high-school teacher known for his progressive beliefs. He had asked for Hansa's hand in marriage for his only son. This caused an explosion of comment in the village. Some thought he was eccentric. Others said, 'The boy has tuberculosis. No one in his caste is willing to give him their daughter so he's trying to find a Mahar wife.' The marriage was celebrated in great style.

Many dignitaries and leaders attended, including the Collector. But it ended sadly. After a child was born, Deshpande died. Hansa returned to the Maharwada, her hair wild.

This was also the time when my passions began to get unruly. But the incident with Banoo in the junior school had left me scared—a man scalded by hot milk will even blow on buttermilk to cool it. I did not have the courage to strike up a friendship with the upper-caste girls in my class. But how could I hide the attraction I felt for them? Khambekar and I sat on a bench right behind the girls. I could smell their perfume, their make-up. I felt like reaching out and stroking their hair. I would tell sexy jokes to Khambekar. The girls would be embarrassed and move to sit somewhere else. None of them spoke to the boys. In the lunch-break, not one would linger. They would take flight in a large girlish flock. When they left, I ruled the class. The boys would gather to listen to my off-colour jokes. This was the time when I began writing songs. 'Vargaatlya, Bai, chaar muli/Buddhi maazhi karti khuli' ('Lady, there are four girls in my class; they drive me mad') is one that I remember. It was a spoof of a famous bhavgeet. Each verse ended in a raunchy description of a bodily feature. I remember mentioning 'Sapaat lotion', a play on the popular anti-bacterial 'Sapat lotion', sapaat being the Marathi word for flat or level. It was used to describe a girl's flat chest. This became a catchphrase among the boys. Oh yes—and that reminds me of some phrases that belong to that time, that place, those boys. One such phrase was 'laakda zhaali'; it meant 'he lost his wicket', something that fizzled out.

Ever since I can remember I have been mad about reading. I would lose all sense of hunger and thirst if I were immersed in a book. I never felt such hunger for food as I did for books. 'He'll read a paper covered in shit,' they would say about me. When I was young Uma-ajya would not let me read the yellow-cellophane-covered pamphlets he brought home. That made me determined, I suspect, to read whatever came to hand. I didn't have the money to join a library. That had one result. There were certain obscene monthly magazines that my rich friends bought—*Masti* (Excitement) and *Unmaad (*Arousal*)*. They featured pictures of nude women. *These Eighty-four Asanas* was another book of the kind I began to have a taste for. Saturday afternoons were free. I would read these books in those free afternoons. Sometimes I would bring them back to the boarding school. I would not show them to anyone. Then Bhagwat Master caught me reading one, hidden in a school book. I was embarrassed but I could not shake the habit for a long while. As I read them, lust would flame across my body.

At around this time, I began to be friends with a shepherd girl, a Vadarin called Gaoo. Why her? I have no idea. Perhaps it was just something to do with my age or with proximity. Close to the boarding house, there were some Vadari tents, built around stick frames on waste land. To enter, you had to bend right over. In one of these lived Gaoo. She had only an aged mother for family. Her elder sister was married and lived in the next tent. She had no children even after years of marriage. Her husband was black, the colour of a demon. He had his bloodshot eye on Gaoo. He wanted to marry her to have children by her. Gaoo hated the idea.

In a way, Gaoo was pretty. She was well-built, straight as a cornstalk. Fair, a coppery brightness to her skin. She wore the traditional clothes of a Vadarin: a nine-yard sari pulled tight between her legs as a dancer might drape it. The upper end of her sari was similarly drawn tight against her bare breasts. In the afternoons, Gaoo would come to chat with Aai. She would share her worries about her future. At these times, I would hang around, pretending to read, but for once the words would not hold my attention. For I was aware that Gaoo was staring at me. This made me break out in gooseflesh. Sometimes Gaoo would lend Aai a hand with cooking or with smearing the mess floor with cow dung. I enjoyed watching her, both hands wet with dung, a lock of hair falling over her face. She would smile gently at me and on the floor she would draw lotus petals. The petals would begin to merge with each other and her bangles would tinkle as she drew. I can see her clearly, even today.

I did not have the courage to make advances. I could see the invitation in her eyes but I could also feel Aai's eyes on me. 'Eventually, you'll turn out like your father,' she would say and it would sting. I would shrink into my shell like a tortoise.

I enjoyed talking to Gaoo. She was uneducated but she

knew a good deal about the world and its workings. She had been doing physical labour ever since she could remember. Once or twice, I took her hands in mine to see what they felt like. They were rough and dry. It was like taking an iron rod in your hands. My palms were soft in comparison. But her naked arms looked as soft as the heart of a lotus and aroused my lust.

I remember asking her once, 'Why don't you wear a choli?' In truth, she would have liked to. But the rules of her caste panchayat were strict. She would be ostracized if she were to put one on. Why they didn't wear cholis is another story.

'In the *Ramayana*, Sita didn't get the deerskin she wanted to make her blouse and since then we haven't worn any.' This made me laugh, for I had cast her brother-in-law in the role of Raavan to her Sita. I was suspicious of his motives. As he passed, he would look at me out of those reddened eyes. On his shoulder he carried a sharp, gleaming axe.

Later, Gaoo did marry her brother-in-law. He called a caste panchayat and served alcohol. Gaoo had no father. Her poor mother, how long could she oppose the match? Now she had to leave her mother's tent. At the time of the marriage, a pig was slaughtered. Its shrieks and squeals filled the entire boarding school. The next few nights, I was restless. Every night I could hear the pig's squeals. And behind that Gaoo's innocent face. A few days later, the settlement was dismantled. Their work had ended and they moved on. I never saw Gaoo again. When I see Vadari women at work on the road or a dam, I look for Gaoo. I know it's stupid but still I look for her.

Aai and I had a good relationship. We could speak freely to each other. I was not in the habit of hiding things from her. She taught me that at least one person should know the whole truth about you, good or bad. Where had she got this idea from? But it had a profound impact on me. All that I tell you today is an offering to her memory. Even as a big lug, I would sleep with my head in her lap. She would run her fingers through my hair. In a beautiful voice, she would hum to me. I enjoyed listening to her ovis—her grinding-stone songs—when I was in the village. When she had some free time from her work at the hostel, I would read to her out of a book. A short story called 'Manini' brought back memories of her mother's home, about Dubalwadi and how she was treated there. She had never forgotten how they had wanted to marry her off when her husband had died. She had felt like a splinter in someone's foot; to be plucked out swiftly and thrown away.

Whether for this reason or some other, she would never mention Aurangapur when it was holiday time. Mumbai was out of the question. So we would go to her sister and brother-in-law who were poor but loving. I enjoyed going to this farming village that always seemed green. The water in the canal would burble along merrily. At dawn, women would grind the grain for the day and sing beautifully, as if records were playing. It was almost as if they were competing with each other. The men went from village to village, playing their instruments as a group. In the evening, they would sing laavnis. Not one of the men did any physical labour. The women worked in the houses of the rich and powerful.

The Mahars married young. In their eyes, I was old enough and so the villagers were always teasing Aai about getting me married. Every time a girl was chosen for me, I would delay it. They would feign disgust and tell Aai that the young girls had their eyes on me. But I was too bookish to take advantage of any of it. That one incident had scared me off. I would tell Aai all this.

'Aayé, let's get out of here. This village frightens me.'

Aai would laugh at my state: 'A widow's son must have the smarts,' she would say. I had heard this said even as a child. There was a thread of mockery in it but I began to take it as a compliment. I began to feel, 'Sure I have the smarts, or how would I have come through?' Perhaps that's why my face, even in childhood, began to carry a look of adult gravitas. My expression indicated that I could not possibly be playing with other children my age; instead I should be sitting with the adults. We went rarely to our own village. There I was treated with respect because I was now studying in high school. Our condition had improved a little. With her earnings, Aai could afford new clothes. My behaviour had also begun to differ from that of the Maharwada children. Other jobs occurred to me. I could write letters on behalf of the Maharwada or teach the children or even sweep up the place. I did not think it important now to learn the dholak or the tuntuna. I gave my father's clappers, the kanda, to a cousin who lived nearby. Today I regret that I did not bother to acquire such home-grown knowledge. I had abandoned quite casually our own traditions of knowledge. Today I cannot play any instrument. My father played the dholki beautifully; he could play the shehnai too. But he earned no money nor did he make a success of it. When I see my six-year-old son playing on a chair, keeping time and beat perfectly, I am astonished. Will he be able to rejoin the chain of tradition?

Since we did not live in the village anymore, our house would be a shambles. The thorny bushes in front would turn into an overgrown jungle. Some of the tiles would be missing when we came back. The beams in front of the house would have been ripped out by unknown hands. Without so much as a by-your-leave, the village shepherds had started using the house as a goat pen. We could not even decide to whom we could entrust the house. In front of us was Javji Buwa's towering house with its wooden ceilings. He said that it was only because of him that our house was still standing but we also knew that he had uprooted the threshold of an inside room and taken it home. He said he had done this to prevent anyone else from stealing it. But when he installed doors inside his house, our doorframes and threshold gleamed brazenly in their new setting. We said nothing for we knew the old expression: What leaks away in a trickle does not return in a flood.

Javji Buwa's house was a prosperous one, the kind with its own cowshed. Ours was the kind that lacked even a henhouse. When I came to the village, Javji Buwa would rub my nose in this. 'Give the boy some milk,' he would tell his wife and with great condescension, he would invite me to a meal. I have never liked milk and could only eat their food with great difficulty.

Javji Buwa's home was a conservative one. He had a reputation for discipline. When he entered the house, everyone fell silent. Every morning he would get dressed in immaculate white clothes. Even his turban was a beacon of white, as befitted a leader of the taluka. He'd tuck his umbrella under his arm and march off to the taluka meetings. He was always meeting someone or the other. All the other leaders from the places around would gather there. It was Javji Buwa's pleasure to sit and chat with any 'Mamai'walla who had come and get a cup of tea off him. Later, when I got a job in Mumbai and came home, he would circle, vulture-like. 'What a father he had!' he would say, in my hearing. 'Such a philanthropist, he was. In comparison, his son is nothing.' He would leave only after I had bought a round of tea.

Javji Buwa's mother was still alive. She was completely blind in both eyes. Her name was Chandrav. Her hair hung down in grey ropes. Her eyebrows were grey too. The flesh of her arms hung in loose flaps. I liked Chandrav and could not bear the way the old lady was tormented by everyone in the house. She would not be given her meals on time. No one, not even the children, would take her to the outhouse. I would help her to go, supported by a stick.

She had a great stock of stories. A story, once started, could last a week. As she would tell her tales, I would look into the sockets of her eyes, crevasses of darkness. She and I played a little game. She could not get her tongue around the word 'cinema': she would say 'cidema'. However much she tried, she could not get it. I deeply regretted that I was not in the village when she died. They say she was asking for me.

Javji Buwa and his only son Baban were locked in a dramatic struggle. The father would admonish the Mahars not to do traditional demeaning jobs; meanwhile his son would be surreptitiously stripping carcasses. The father thought playing music for the upper castes as part of the Mahars' duties was tantamount to bondage; the son played the shehnai beautifully. His troupe was famous in the taluka. Opposing his father seemed to be a habit with Baban. But where Javji Buwa was a tough old bird with a constitution of iron, Baban looked like a stick. He was stunted, as a sapling growing in the shade of a vast, spreading tree might be. While the father was seen to be of good character, the son saw nothing as forbidden. He was a gambler, a drinker, a womanizer. His father had married him off when he was a boy. When his wife came of age, the old man did not want his son to go and fetch her. The old man stood guard over his son for he believed that having children could ruin a man's body. Despite this, Baban managed to produce three or four pretty daughters. Later Javji Buwa would get his granddaughters married off, but Baban's lifelong complaint was that his father had done nothing for his girls.

As long as Baban's mother was alive, Javji Buwa could keep his son in the village, but once the old lady was shoved into the earth, Baban upped and went to Mumbai. He built a hut on the footpath and lived there. He started an old paper business. Alone in the village, Javji Buwa began to suffer. Baban refused to help his father. He would not send him a paisa. His father asked him to send one of his daughters to look after him but Baban refused even this simple demand. The old man was also stubborn. Right up to his death, he refused to sacrifice his self-respect. He sold everything in the house to buy food and when that was gone, he sold the land, bit by bit.

When a neighbour came to sell him water, he found Javji Buwa dead. He had died alone. Hearing about his funeral procession made my heart ache. When Javji Buwa died, the Maharwada had emptied. Everyone had gone to Mumbai to fill their stomachs. And so there were only a couple of aged widows in the village to accompany him. All the other houses were locked up. The old women dragged the old man's body to the burial grounds. The Marathas watched the fun. Who among them would touch a Mahar corpse? Who would pay for a nice new shroud? He was buried, wrapped in old gunny sacks.

I would meet Baban in Mumbai on occasion. He would come to the office, always very drunk. He would be swaying, his clothes filthy. Sometimes he would have footwear, sometimes none. When he arrived like this, the clerical staff would look askance at me. I could not bring myself to say, 'Don't come to the office in this state next time.' When he came, he would abuse his old man. He would accuse him of squandering the estate or some such nonsense...

'Now all that's left is that one-storey house. Once it's sold I'm free!' he would say. To get his last daughter married, he did sell the house. Everyone in the village had been waiting for that to happen. The huge beams were made of teak. The villagers must have taken all the good stuff at throwaway prices.

Baban loved all his daughters. He had only one regret: not one of them was happy in her marriage. I was witness to his elder daughter Venu's tragedy. Her wedding had been celebrated in grand style in the village. Venu was as pretty as a picture. She had inherited her fair skin from her parents. A rich home had been found for her. The groom's father was foreman in a company in Mumbai. The boy was a strapping fellow who looked after the fields. But right from the beginning, he began to harass Venu. He would not let her sleep at night. When he went to the fields, he would lock her up in the house. When I was in school, I tried to save her once or twice from this persecution. For no reason at all, he would get angry at her. He behaved as if she were an animal, his chattel. Finally Baban brought her home on the pretext of celebrating a festival and did not send her back. Her husband went mad. He came armed with a naked knife and stood in front of Baban's door. Baban was no muscle man but this time he stood firm. Later he sought assistance from the Ramoshis, a tribe that was famous as 'muscle for hire'. His daughter announced in court to the faujdar: 'Saahib, take me and throw me in the well. I will kill myself but I won't go back to him.' She got a divorce; later, she married a much older man. Why did she give up such riches? Why marry an old man? Why choose such a life of toil and labour? These were questions to which I found no answers. Today Venu's old husband has lost his job. Venu works as an ayah and supports him and their infant children. Baban-tatya could never forget how Venu's life had been destroyed.

I remember him coming with an invitation to another daughter's wedding. He did not forget to say: 'Now don't come alone. Bring the wife and children along.' The wedding was to be held in Gautamnagar, Mulund. Although the name sounded impressive, it was a huge slum. Those who had been uprooted from Kamathipura and Nagpada had settled here. A Mahar community was like an island. Individuals did not move even in the industrial age, the island moved. When I came home and told my wife, she snapped: 'You go if you want. Catch me taking my children to a slum.' She wanted to forget her past too. But however hard I tried, I found these bonds were unbreakable. So I went alone. Baban's wife was disappointed. 'You came alone?' she asked. Baban-tatya just hugged me.

I can never forget Baban-tatya as he was that day. There was some time for the wedding but he was already tight. He was blabbering, bubbling over with words. I tried to remonstrate with him: 'Tatya, at least today you shouldn't be drinking. The wedding isn't over yet.' Looking at me, he began to abuse the boy and his family. 'I'll dance when his mother finally gets married...' I began to laugh. They were familiar curses, Satva's curses now on Baban-tatya's lips. That he was drunk didn't seem to worry the boy's family. Many of those assembled were in the same state. One of Baban-tatya's relatives brought his station wagon along. Your car is my car, Tatya thought as he looked at it. He began to boast about it to the wedding party. The Patil's horses are the Mahar's ornaments, as they say. The groom was taken for a spin. I thought: Some of this generation of Dalits have made economic progress. But the rest live in caves. A deep chasm of consciousness separates these two lots.

Baban-tatya led the procession. He had a troupe of musicians as a village wedding would. When he began to play the shehnai, he clean forgot he was the father of the bride. Now he was a musician, his shehnai in his hands. He began to play the old songs with zest. The other players picked up his tune.

I was reminded of my father: the same energy, the same music.

It was monsoon time. The slum was thick with mud and muck. The wedding took place according to Bouddha rituals. We sat down to eat, not very far from the mud and muck. I had to eat because Baban-tatya had invited me. We got usal and lhapsi porridge on banana-leaf plates. I no longer had a taste for this kind of food but I shovelled it down anyway. When I left, in the night, Baban-tatya and his wife sent me off with a nice new sari for my very educated wife. It was a five-yard sari, a modern one. 'We bought it for your wife. If she had come, we'd have got her to put it on.' And suddenly I was struck by how large their hearts were. I was deeply saddened by the way our lives were diverging.

Baban-tatya was the last of his generation and it was clear that he too was on his last legs. Like his forefathers, he too destroyed himself with drink. I had seen many young men die in the Maharwada. Now when I go back to the village, the Maharwada seems silent and still, a husk of its former self, a threshing floor for ghosts. Dogs and pigs wander at will through the broken walls of the houses. Only one or two homes are still in use. At each open door, a decrepit old woman sits, looking like she might belong in a ghost story. Her hair grey and wild, she mumbles to herself, punctuating this with angry gestures. My heart aches. Such giants lived in the Maharwada once. Where did they go? Did they just fly away into the air? The Marathas say: 'Black magic. Someone cursed the Maharwada.' Is that it? During the last twenty-five or thirty years, the village has burgeoned like Gokul, the birthplace of Krishna; it is vital, full of energy, spilling out of the land allotted to it. The homes now have British-style tiles, the Panchayat is an impressive building, there is a new school. The village has spread into the area where, in our youth, we would go to shit. Then it was full of rocks, some of the boulders as large as elephants. A thick cactus forest grew all around. Now the forest has vanished, the rocks have been levelled. Wealthy Maratha families have built their pretty bungalows here and set up threshing floors so clean and shiny that you could eat off them.

In the old days, every Mahar home had its own patch of bone-yard. Now there's a race on to see who can grab as much of that land as possible. If an acre of village land goes for a thousand, an acre in the Maharwada goes for five hundred. In the last twenty to twenty-five years, the Mahars have been driven off their land, as if by conspiracy. They would no longer do the work that was assigned to them by tradition but they were given no other work either. They no longer had any share in the village turnover, in its produce. They absconded to Mumbai to keep body and soul together. In bad times, they began to pawn their patches of land. Some sold their land outright. I too had a little land in the village. When I went to collect the crop, I'd spend more than it was worth just travelling there. It was like spending a rupee on the masala with which to cook twenty-five paise of chicken.

Two years ago when I needed money for my daughter's wedding, I raised a thousand rupees on my patch of land, pawning it to a Maratha farmer. I haven't been back since. But I did have a soft spot for the house in which I was born. Then last year, a close relation advertised an auction of the house. The next rains would have completely annihilated it, he said, and I agreed with him. My wife was annoyed at how emotional I became. 'What's this? The fall of some great house?' she asked.

—

But we digress. We'll have to backtrack a bit.

Poetry saved me from madness. I remember my first moment of recognition. There was a public meeting in the school. I was asked to sing a song. I recited Lok-kavi Waman Kardak's poem on Dr Ambedkar. The touching composition and the use of dialect led the teacher to believe that I had written the song. He praised me publicly. I got no chance to tell the truth. All night I tossed and turned; I felt guilty of literary theft. The next morning, I went straight to the teacher and confessed. He shrugged, said, 'Arré, what's so special about that? You can be a poet too.' This was encouraging. Me? A poet?

I began to write some songs. Lok-kavi Waman Kardak came regularly to our hostel. On special occasions, he did public readings. Once he came alone, without his usual accompanists. Some of the students stood in for them. His songs were composed as qawwalis. I began to write songs in his style. In the beginning, I would base them on film songs. *Albela* was the biggest hit of those times. I remember I composed a song based on one of its tunes. I remember the first lines: 'Slap your arms, don't sit quiet, it's time to rise.' The song was full of meaningless rhymes. 'My lovely rose, come a little close, strike a pose.' That kind of thing. Every Saturday night we would have a programme in the hostel.

The beat of empty tins and pots would accompany me as I sang. That someone, *anyone*, was singing my songs was thrill enough. I never thought any special use would be made of my song. But when the holidays started, the students would return home.

Going home meant starvation for us. In that time, we would accompany Bhagwat Master to various villages asking for donations in kind for the hostel. When we arrived in a village, our first stop would be the village square. I would sing to bring people together. It never occurred to me that I was doing social service of a kind. In the ninth or tenth standard, I remember some poems of mine being published in Babasaheb's weekly *Janata*. They were a child's work. But there was no false consciousness in them either. Then, ten or fifteen years ago, a Dalit writers' conference had been organized with Kusumagraj as chairman. The inaugural speaker was Dadasaheb Gaekwad. I was one of the organizers. In a spare moment, I hesitantly slid my book of poems under Kusumagraj's nose. There were love poems and poems on social issues. Kusumagraj liked one of them; it was a poem of social comment. It's still in an old notebook. It's called *Zhool*, or the brocade with which an animal is covered for a procession. It goes like this:

> For a chance at the brass ring,
> How humanity cuts capers,
> Acts out roles
> Splashes out colour.

Bodies roll in the dirt.
No one here seems wise.
All are corrupt
I am not exempt.

When you yank that rich
Brocade of social service
Down to cover your feet,
It slips off your back
And the hollow shell beneath
Is exposed.

When there's as much wrong as right
How do you choose?
If I too belong here
Who am I?

This scorpion of doubt seems to have always had a home in my head. It was not as if I too had not sought the help of 'the great and the good'. And yet, I cannot figure out when I gave up their support. You might think that this sounds like ingratitude but I was attracted, lodestone-like, towards mentors, towards well-known people. Like blotting paper, I wanted to absorb everything I could from their personalities. But then I would see that I could no longer draw any benefit from them, and then I felt I had to go it alone. This caused me no end of confusion about myself. Some would suspect me of Rightist leanings and some would think me Left-leaning. They would say affectionately, 'Arré, take a position. Choose a side. The middle of the road is a good place to become roadkill.'

But to tell you the truth, I found it difficult to choose between the leaders and the parties of the Right and the Left. That I had often seen Leftist parties behaving in a Rightist way added to my confusion. In this turmoil of principle and practice, one thing seemed clear: I should try, as those who were on the lowest rungs of society did, to stay faithful to the side I chose.

A story to illustrate how I was often misunderstood: Hamid Dalwai, the Socialist leader and writer, had a serious kidney problem. Dadasaheb was a minister then and I went with him to see Dalwai. Hamid sees me in a minister's car and erupts with laughter. 'I thought an elder was arriving,' he says. 'You are everywhere. You are never anywhere. I ought to learn this trick from you.'

Hamid's back-handed compliment leaves me nonplussed. I begin to wonder: What do I want of my life? What have I lost? Why this constant motion? My wife, my sternest critic, says of me: 'You're the dog's tail, tick-tock, tick-tock. Tick is good and tock is also good.' I must ask her what she means.

—

That I had a different world view from that of the upper-caste children became clear to me in school. An essay competition was announced. The subject: Sane Guruji's*

---

*Pandurang Sadashiv Sane wrote more than seventy books, among which was *Shyamchi Aai* (Shyam's Mother) which was made into a film directed by P.K. Atre that won the National Award for the Best Film.

Indian Culture. When I read it, it drove me crazy. In the essay, I mocked his concept of Indian culture. Our teacher, Kulkarni, was deeply disturbed by my essay. 'Your views show a deep hatred for your country.' I remember that I argued with him vehemently.

The last day of the SSC year was called Students' Day. The students became teachers and ran the school while the teachers sat in the classrooms. Everyone from principal to peon became a student. I remember the lessons I taught in the garb of a teacher. I chose Marathi and history as subjects to teach. In the Marathi class, I taught poetry by singing it. In the history hour, I explained the origins of the caste system. At that time, explaining the roots of caste, I attacked *Manusmriti*, the Hindu holy book. In my head, this scene plays out clearly: the Brahmin teachers who were playing students keep obstructing me by asking questions and I reply in an aggressive style.

In truth, these were not my beliefs. I had read Dr Babasaheb Ambedkar's *Who Were the Shudras?* Additionally, the boarding school subscribed to *Janata*. The editorials in it would give me strength; they seemed to be echoing my thoughts. They helped me become aware of how we were being exploited.

Around this time, I began to love literature. I've mentioned Kulkarni Sir—but I feel I didn't do him justice. Kulkarni taught Marathi beautifully. He was a short man. He wore a dhotar, well-washed, and a coat. On his head, a white topi. His Kolhapuri slippers would announce his arrival in class—scritch-scratch. He was rather handsome. You felt that if you pinched him, he might bleed, so soft was his skin. He had done badly at the MA and so ended up teaching in a high school. This had left him somewhat discontented. I had the feeling that the poet Shanta Shelke had been in college with him. When we chatted, he would often talk about her. When he taught a poem by her, he really got into it. As soon as he came into class, we would ask him to do a poem by Shanta Shelke.

When he was angry with a student, he would hit him on the hand with a pencil. As if that made a jot of difference! But one of his pedagogic methods was rather terrifying. If he got angry with a student, he would ask him questions but without looking at him. The boy would end up on the verge of tears. (I experienced something similar at the hands of a well-known leader. He would say, 'In a political fight even a nonentity can be useful.' At such times, he would draw this 'nonentity' close. When he was done, he would drop him.) Kulkarni Sir sometimes wrote monologues and short stories. Once or twice, I saw these printed in the monthly magazines. When I asked if I could borrow a copy, he said, 'They're not meant for school children.' I wanted to laugh. What could he have written that he thought was unfit for my eyes? What had I not experienced already?

Even if Kulkarni Sir dismissed me as a callow schoolboy, I had lived through many ups and downs. Around that time, a certain event changed the course of my life. But before recounting it, perhaps I need to give you some background. Tatya was seriously ill in Mumbai. I was sent for by telegram. The question was: who would perform his last rites if he were to die? His son was too young. As his nephew, I was the next best choice.

When I arrived, Tatya was struggling for breath. Like my father, he had destroyed his liver with spirit. It was likely that his intestine was ulcerated too. Tatya had poured water into my father's dying mouth; it was my turn to perform this last ritual for him.

I was not shocked by Tatya's death. I could almost have predicted it. Aaji was sobbing her heart out. She loved him far more than she had ever loved my father. I was dry-eyed. I had not forgotten his vicious words. But my behaviour was ordinary in comparison with his wife's. Everyone knew that Kaku would not look at a corpse, never mind whose it was. Dead bodies filled her with horror. She wore a talisman around her neck against them. But to ignore her own husband? The whole of Kawakhana was talking. The last bath was the wife's last duty, so tradition said. But Kaku refused to perform this rite. Perhaps she just felt, 'Good riddance.'

This was a first for me, raising a bier to my shoulder. In those days, we Mahars buried our dead; we did not cremate them as we do now. When we watched Babasaheb being cremated at Chaityabhoomi, we were watching the end of a tradition. The graveyard had special gravediggers, also Mahars. They were rumoured to strip the clothes off the corpses. Tatya's corpse was gently lowered into the earth of Sonapur at Worli. Mud was heaved in with spades. Water was poured into his mouth. I have no idea why one circumambulated the grave or why it was necessary to shout and scream while breaking pots. We washed our hands and feet at a tap where someone was sitting with neem leaves which we placed in our mouth. Then all the mourners had to be given tea at the restaurant across the road, and also chewing tobacco and betel leaf. That day, the bereaved did not cook. Their relatives brought them vegetables and bhakri. When my father died, I was too young to remember much. I do remember that on the thirteenth day, I was eager to avoid having my head shaved.

Even then I remember thinking of these rituals as nonsense. The idea of offerings to the dead seemed ridiculous. A measure of flour would be placed where the person had died. On the thirteenth day, the elders would study the marks that would be naturally produced in the flour and tell us into which womb the deceased would take birth. This too seemed risible. Very often, they would say that the dead one had gone on to become a crow or a snake. Someone might like to make a study of whether anyone in the last seventeen generations of their families had ever read the *Bhagvad Gita*. But the belief in reincarnation was bone deep.

—

I could see that Tatya had forged a way in the world for himself. But when I consider the path he had rough-hewn for me, I don't know what to make of it. When I started down this road, I had no idea that one's own flesh and blood could let one down in such a manner. Not that Tatya did this deliberately either. The road to my hell was paved with his good intentions.

Without consulting me or my mother, Tatya arranged my marriage. He offered betel nut to the panch members, an announcement of the marital alliance. Aai said, 'Son, don't break his word. You can't lick up what you've spat. And look at the girl chosen for you: she could be a Brahmin or a baniya. Her face commands the moon to give up rising; it tells the sun to forget about shining.' The women of Kawakhana offered their support. The leaders seemed to be the wives of my cousins. The girl's guardians and relatives were completely sold on the idea. The credit of getting this marriage fixed must redound to them. The two houses had strong ties—so was I supposed to be the sacrificial goat whose blood would seal these bonds for all time? I was also vastly disgusted that they should have conspired to get me married before I had even seen the girl. She was illiterate, the kind who used a thumb impression for a signature.

Yes, she was very fair, but what did that matter? I did not want to be weighed down by marriage so soon. A young man married is a young man marred, or so I feared.

And at the same time, in one corner of my mind, a picture of this woman, my wife, began to form. This image, could it represent the truth? I began to think about her. That would have pleased my mother. She was eager to see her grandsons.

The girl's village was five or six kilometres from Sangamner. We had a half-holiday on Saturday and we would all go to the bazaar at her village. Once, in the hurly-burly of the bazaar, a relative pointed her out to me. It was hot enough to pop corn that day. I won't say that the heat turned into cool moonlight at the sight of her, but I can say that I liked what I saw. Local farmers would bring their wares and sit in long lines as wedding guests do at the feast. She too had a basket in front of her, produce from her parents' kitchen garden. Her mother was with her. She was weighing the goods for the customers. From a safe distance, I kept staring at her. She was wearing a chintz skirt and blouse. Her hair, in delightful disarray, would fall on to her forehead. Her cheeks were flushed in the dry heat. She was slender and very pretty, her eyes had a bluish tinge, her nose was straight and sharp as a knife, her colouring a light pink. I was dazzled. She must have been about ten to twelve years old. Could this be an angel from heaven, selling veggies in the market at Sangamner? I wondered. Then the thought: Were she dressed in the clothes of one of the girls in my class, no one would be able to hold a candle to her. Going up to her and talking was out of the question. When I came back to the hostel, my heart had taken wing. That she had never been to school, that she could not read and write, all this no longer mattered.

So now I was determined: if I was to marry, I would marry only her. I waited for Saturdays so that I could watch her from afar. Right to the end, she remained unaware of my surveillance.

In my mind, I named her Saee. It was a name with the flavour of the village, but it suited her. Later, I managed a darshan in the Devgarh festival. The pilgrims' route went past the hostel. The festival generally took place in the month of Chaitra. Our relatives from Mumbai would come down, bringing their families. This Devgarh, two or three miles from Sangamner, had a famous wish-granting Khandoba temple. For generations, the Mahars had been going there. It was a family tradition to make the pilgrimage to our protector. Each family offered a cock or a goat. The cousins always sacrificed a goat. I wasn't terribly interested in the religious aspects of all this; I enjoyed the excitement of the fair and the sting of the spicy barbaat that followed the sacrifice. But Khandoba's love story, a traditional tale handed down from generations, was something I also cherished. Khandoba was, by caste, a baniya. He fell in love with a Dhangar* girl, Mhalsa. Apparently, he would often go to the Dhangar settlement to meet her. But Mhalsa was never placed by his side in the temple as other consorts were. Her shrine would be set apart, always at a lower level. The place next to Khandoba was reserved for his lawfully wedded wife. But Mhalsa took the offerings, or so it was believed.

At Devgarh, we'd stop for the ritual of the iron chains. When the Waghyas—men dressed as tigers—were possessed by spirits, they would snap iron chains as if they were straw.

---

*Dhangars are herders. They were classified as a Nomadic Tribe in 2014.

The dance of the Muralis—women who had been 'offered' to Khandoba by their families—was also worth watching. They would sing songs like 'Bhandaar bhogya ruh, bhogya Maludeva' ('Enjoy the feast, Lord of Mhalsa'). At that age, it was all a thrill.

I met Saee at this festival. Okay, 'met' may be overstating it. I saw her there. She was decked up in a gaudy nine-yard sari that bunched and billowed around her. She saw me and blushed. Her friends said, 'Hey, it's your husband.' She ran off but I could see that I had met with her approval. Talking to your future spouse was not allowed so we did not dare to speak to each other. But wherever I went I was sure to find her hanging about. I saw a newly wedded husband carrying his wife up the steps of the temple. I felt: Would I have to carry Saee like that? Would I be able to bear her weight?

Then an opportunity to go to her village arose. I was to accompany Aaji to Saee's village. Evening had fallen; I kept an eye out but there was no sign of her. I spent a disturbed night. When I woke up in the morning, it was to see her playing with a lamb. She saw me and rushed back into the house. This brought back memories of *Shakuntala*, a film I had seen in Mumbai. It had a scene in which the heroine plays with a fawn and a calf in just such a manner. For a long time after that, these two scenes would merge in my head.

Saee's home was a prosperous one. Four or five brothers lived there together. They had a sheepfold that was full to bursting. The sheep would be allowed into the local fields which they would manure. In return for this fertilizer they would be given the leaves from the babul trees that grew around the fields as fodder. At the end of the year, they would be shorn. Since it was a joint family, each brother tried to get as much as he could out of their holdings. They were always squabbling over this. Saee's father was different. He was dark as tar. When he smiled, his teeth flashed in his dark face. He was sturdy of frame and always dressed in white. He did not work on the fields. He was a foreman with the roadworks of the Public Works Department. His job was to fill the potholes that appeared after the rains. Looking at his colour, I would wonder how he could have produced such a fair daughter. But if you looked at his wife, you had your answer. She was as fair as Saee. But those bluish eyes? They made her look like a Konkanastha Brahmin.

Aaji could not believe her grandson's luck.

—

Whether it was this distraction or something else, I don't know, but I failed the SSC examinations. This was the first time I had ever failed. When the results were declared, I was at my uncle's village. I began to bawl. My uncle and mother tried to console me. 'The gods don't age if you fail in one pilgrimage,' they said. I could not understand how I had failed. I wasn't a duffer. But when I looked at my marksheet, I understood. I had got through five or six subjects but scored only 28 marks in English.

English had been a problem from the eighth standard. Each year, I would scrape through by the skin of my teeth. I never got my head around the sahibs' language; it would torment me for the rest of my life. They say that one year all the BA answer scripts were lost in a fire. Everyone was passed. These students came to be known as the Burnt BAs. A whole generation had been ruined. That was about my case. I had been studying English for four years and I could not speak or write a single line without errors. The rich could take extra coaching to make up. That was impossible for me. I began to detest Morarjibhai Desai. He was a minister in Maharashtra at the time when the government decided to change the system. Until then, students would learn English from the third standard and come out, after eight years, with a good command of the language. They say it was Desai who had initiated the system of education by which we started studying English only in the eighth standard.

I felt as much hate for him then as when he plucked the rifles out of our hands. For a year, I was in the National Cadet Corps in school. I had learned how to fire a gun there. We had had a camp at Lohgaon once. 'Next year, we'll get you up in an aeroplane,' the organizers had assured us. There had been no 'next year'. Morarjibhai shut down the NCC and our dreams of flying crash-landed.

Failure crushed my zest for life. The desire to study further was extinguished. My fear of English thwarted everything. Despair grew inside me. Failures were not allowed to stay in the hostel but I had nowhere else to go. My life now would have the direction and use of tumbleweed. Again I fell at the feet of the directors. Perhaps they felt that if I were thrown out my mother would also leave so a special case was made and I was allowed to stay. As a failure, I had no rights. The boys ragged me even more. I could see how we had bartered our right to self-respect for a handful of grain.

I grew angry with myself. I began to avoid meeting the eyes of the other students. I would only go to the hostel to eat. Not very far from the boarding school was a hen coop, about the height of a man. It was empty so I began to spend most of my time there. It was a peaceful place to study. I even stopped going to the Saturday market. I was good at rote learning, having acquired the skill while learning lines for plays. I started learning the English texts by heart.

I had to go into town again to clear the paper I had failed. That October, I sat for the examinations again and passed. Oddly, I got more than sixty marks in English. That shows you the power of rote learning. I never dreamed I could get such marks.

Now our time at the boarding was truly over. I felt like a convict released from rigorous imprisonment. But who does a convict turn to? What route could I take? What did the future hold? My love of Mumbai resurfaced. The city beckoned. I felt I would find my way in this siren city. Some of my friends had already found work in offices there as clerks. Being a clerk in charge of advances meant a glorious salary. And such respect! You were called 'Bhausahib', or respected brother. Everyone turned lickspittle in front of you. You were served special tea, betel leaf was ordered. I was not drawn by all this. Nor did I want to be a teacher. I felt that my life would end in a rut in a school or a zilla parishad office. A life spent like this would be the kiss of death.

—

And so Aai and my sister and I set out for Mumbai.

Kawakhana was waiting.

Mumbai was in my blood. After all these years, I wonder: what has the city given me? As Krishna sundered Jarasandha and tossed his two halves in different directions to defeat him, this city has split me down the middle too, and each half has been tossed into a different world. Where I came home to sleep, each night was a veritable hell. The world I saw from afar, that was an illusion of heaven. The city seemed like a precious stone set in a ring on a rich man's hand. It would gleam an invitation at you, but it would never end up on your finger.

I felt no regret at all at leaving Sangamner. Aai had slaved at the hostel. She had in all that time baked a mountain of bhakris.

The years spent in the blazing heat and smoke of the fireplace had left her with asthma. Now even a short walk left her breathless. She had ulcers and, I suspect, a problem with her blood pressure too.

It was only in Kawakhana that we had any place to call our own. Aaji was still alive then; she could not turn us away. But Kaku was unhappy at our return. We had no idea how much suffering we would have to endure.

On the rare occasions that we went back to the village, we would get off the bus at Sangamner. I would feel no desire to visit the village. My schoolmates had all moved on, settled down in their various stations in life.

Once, later, I hopped on to a cycle and went to Little Sangamner. I could see the hostel building at a distance. In my mind, a host of emotions. Four or five years of my life had been spent there. Memories of my mother also came back to haunt me. I should go there, I thought, see the kitchen where my mother worked, the place where I studied, where I slept, chat to the students. No one recognized me at the hostel. I caught two or three students gambling at cards and startled them. They thought I was a government official on inspection. The floor of the mess had holes in it, as if it were a cattle pen. The kitchen was in a similar state. In the dormitory, the students' bedding dangled forlornly from the sills of the windows. In our time, it had not been so ramshackle. I didn't feel like speaking to any of the students. Depressed, I walked down the stairs. The boarding house had been started with certain ideals. It was now a business.

An interesting story about the Petit High School. Raosaheb Kasbe had been a lecturer in the Sangamner College. If I ever got to the village, I would try and meet him. Once the Maharashtra Sahitya Parishad asked me to read my poetry and discuss Dalit literature at Sangamner at that very school. No one seemed to know that I was an alumnus but then no one now knew me by the name Dagdu. When I got to the venue, I found that Marhalkar was presiding over the function. The man who taught me Marathi poetry, Gandhe Master, was sitting in the front row. I was embarrassed to speak of literature in front of these men.

No Mumbai or Pune audience, however sophisticated or literary, would have made me feel this way. But here I was supposed to speak to the teacher who had taught me Marathi with a gentle, almost maternal love. But it is also true that for a while, I drew them all into a new world. I have participated in many programmes since then but this one is fresh in my memory.

Getting a job as soon as one arrived in Mumbai was impossible. Aai went back to the grind of daily work: scavenging and sorting scrap. One did not need capital for this. Carrying bundles of discarded paper, Aai would come home in the night, tired and worn. This paper was sold to make paper bags for shops to use. The godowns that bought the paper were behind Kawakhana. They also bought rags. The women of the area always knew where things could be sold: any old iron here, glass there, copper and brass at a third place. When she returned, Aai would always bring something strange to eat. She knew where to get cake crumbs or broken biscuits cheap. The restaurants would dry their used tea leaves and sell them cheap. We used these to make tea at home.

I was terribly ashamed that my mother was still scavenging. Damn it, I had studied so much but I was still living on my mother's earnings. What was her work? The hardscrabble of collecting and selling paper? What dignity did society offer her for her labour? This question of dignity had been put into my head by my education. No one around me seemed much concerned by it. When you don't know that you're supposed to be unhappy, you can chug along quite well; only I was being hollowed out from within, as a tree is by termites.

I climbed up the steps of the Employment Exchange; I climbed down again. Each time, I came home disappointed. There was a separate list for Scheduled Castes. It wasn't as bad as it is today. I would get letters calling me to interviews; and that was where I would stumble: at the interview. Those well-appointed offices. Those velvety carpets underfoot. Those sibilant 'Hellos' issuing from the glossy red lips of the receptionists. This seemed like a dream world, far removed from Kawakhana.

Mine was a world rich with cuss words and torn quilts, wreathed in the smoke of coal fires, a suffocating place where I was only a sub-tenant. I was not fluent in English. When the questions began, I could only manage 'Yes' or 'No'. I would be drenched in sweat.

I am called to the Police Commissioner's office for an interview. The atmosphere is starchy with discipline. When it is my turn to be interviewed, I find a military-style gent sitting there, his moustaches bristling. When he sees good marks in English, he begins to ask complicated questions in that language. I cannot answer. This makes him sure that I have brought someone else's mark sheet with me. I swear it is mine. I tell him that my mother does physical labour. With my heart in my eyes, I tell him how much I need this job. But the officer continues to make sport of me. My eyes begin to fill. When he tells me that in his opinion, I would never be fit for a clerk's job, my self-confidence is crushed. It feels as if I have left my breath behind in that office. I want to go somewhere to be alone so as to weep my shame and frustration.

I apply to Akashwani for a job. There my wicket is taken on the grounds that I do not know how to type.

My idleness was eating into my soul. I had always loved reading right from childhood. Only, I could not lay my hands on the kind of books I wanted. Yes, I was as hungry for books as I was for food. Some of my hunger for reading was assuaged by a neighbourhood library. Near Kawakhana, across the road, was a large church. There was a library run by missionaries right next to it. The librarian's name was Rao. I built up an acquaintance with him. He would let me borrow whatever book I wanted. He did not charge a fee. Anyway, I could not have afforded it. In five or six months, I had worked my way through the entire collection. The author who hit me hardest was Sharatchandra. His *Shrikant* totally possessed me. The protagonist's personality seemed to be, I don't know why, very familiar. Another book that affected me similarly was Rahul Sankrutayan's travelogue *From the Volga to the Ganga*. I read Russell's political works here. No one else read the Marathi poetry books. I enjoyed humming verses from the Marathi translation of Omar Khayyam's *Rubaiyyat*. Some of the Marathi novels I read out of the huge hoard still remain with me. None of the reviewers had ever mentioned these. Dr Ranganath Deshpande's *Aagya Mohol* and Manohar Talhar's *Maanus*, for instance, showed no resemblance to my life. But perhaps that was why I enjoyed them.

Culturally, Kawakhana seemed to have remained unchanged, although my relatives seemed to have bettered their lot. One of my cousins had a job in Burmah Shell. I called him Baba. He gave loans to people on interest. So he always had some money in his pockets. He was showy in speech, he sported a gold ring, a watch gleamed on his wrist. His wife was draped in gold ornaments—nose ring, vajratika—but only on festive days. On other days, she looked just as shabby as all the other women with whom she went out to scavenge. I found this odd. I wondered why he would send his wife out when there was no pressing economic need. His son was two or three years younger than I, in the ninth or tenth standard. He did not care for his father's usury.

All of us paid rent and so we were entitled to having our names on the rent receipts, but our two or three rooms were all in Baba's name. This meant that technically we were his tenants. Neither Tatya nor my father had thought it necessary to have their rooms on their own names. As a result, the family went in awe of Baba. Kaku did not like us coming back to live with them. But her fear of Baba kept her in check.

In the night Aaji would suddenly long for a cup of tea, an old habit. It was said that her need for tea was so strong that she would think of nothing of breaking a hundred-rupee note to assuage it. Now in her declining years she could quench her thirst in Baba's home. Tea was not made in the night; it had to be ordered from outside. (That became another fad: ordering food in. If the curry wasn't any good, she'd ask for kheema-pao.) For Aaji a slug of tea before bed was as good as a meal. As she sipped, she would begin to gossip. At around this time, my uncles got together to plan the construction of a two-storey building in the village, complete with British tiles. In a voice that no one could fail to hear, Aaji would announce: 'My Dagdu will also build such a house.' Baba would sneer at her: 'Tell him to wake up and wash his ugly mug first. You have to be asleep and dreaming if you think either getting marrying or building a house is easy.'

I concealed my rage and smiled and said, 'Baba, when you came to Mumbai, you were doing physical labour. I have an education. When I get a job, the basic pay will be three-four hundred rupees. Why shouldn't I build a house then?' Now I know that I spoke from the shaky foundation of hope. Today I see how foolhardy my words were. Far from building a home of my own, I have not even been able to repair my ancestral home. I have not been able to buy myself a flat in Mumbai. I still live in a home with walls of tin. The value of the rupee has fallen; it has been stripped of all dignity. I am tired now of all this firefighting. It is a familiar fatigue. I remember it from the time I was looking for a job. Only I know how many times I have told my sob story to try and secure even a rented flat.

When Dadasaheb was an MLA, my wife said: 'You know him personally. Can't he do this small thing for you?' I swallowed my pride and went to meet him. He called me to the MLA quarters the next day. When I arrived in the morning, he said he had been invited by a high-ranking official to breakfast at Sarang, the State Guest House. 'Come with me,' he said. 'But you'll have to wait outside. I'll be back in ten-fifteen minutes.' I stood in front of Sarang, watching the tumult of the waves. When Dadasaheb came downstairs, the high-ranking official was with him. He had forgotten me; perhaps I had simply dropped off his radar. I found myself bereft of words as he got into the official's car and zipped off, right in front of me. I was left standing there like a fool, watching the car recede. Even today the memory stings.

In the vacations, gambling dens would open in the houses around us. If you let someone gamble in your home, you could pay the rent from the money they gave you. Sometimes the police would raid a house or two and scoop the gamblers up. The residents would have to scramble to make the case go away.

I am thinking now of Mahadoo from my village. He was

a dyed-in-the-wool gambler. He made a passion out of throwing his money away. No one had ever seen him do a day's work. Later, he was extradited from Mumbai, by police order. He was a character even if his main occupation was petty theft: umbrellas, clothes from off the line, that kind of thing. When the bits and bobs grew too large, the police would pack him off to the village. There too he would get the youngsters together and set up a game. When he got a chance, he was a fine talker. He had a fund of odd experiences. I would wonder how such a fine fellow had ended up a thief. But it is true that his face did not show his real circumstances. All he wanted to do was gamble and hang out with the tantric exorcists who came by Kawakhana, spinning and keening.

The sound the exorcists made as they spun was scary. There were different groups that came and went. Some walked on burning coals; others swallowed flaming camphor. They would begin by drawing a circle around the person possessed who was called 'the tree'. The bhagat would begin beating 'the tree' in rapid strokes and 'the tree' would shriek in heart-rending tones. No one could intervene; it was just not allowed.

An aghori would also turn up. He would vomit spontaneously, and then he would turn and whirl and turn and whirl and lick up his vomit.

If there was a fascination with the doings of the exorcists, there was also the desire to create gold. Baba was at the cutting edge of these alchemical pursuits. He would light a fire and throw all kinds of interesting things into it. But I remember only misshapen lumps of iron ever coming out. When we were children we would make fun of all this.

Once a Vaidabai, a witch, turned up. She promised to double any gold she was given. All the women of Kawakhana stripped their necks bare and turned over their gold to her. When she returned their gold in double measure, they were delighted. But not so delighted to find, a little later, that the gold was now all brass.

Sex was discussed openly in Kawakhana. No one thought of such matters as obscene or dirty. There was a man called Sayaji who lived there. He was so thin you could count his bones. He seemed to suffer from asthmatic fits. They say that at some unspecified time in the past he had even been married. But which Fool gets a Cordelia? His young and shapely wife abandoned him. But Sayaji didn't turn out such a fool. He found himself a voluptuous fair woman and set her up as his mistress. This woman sold bananas on the footpath. During the rains, she would switch to roasting corn on the cob. The two of them even had a photograph taken together. Sayaji was an orphan; he had no family. What he did have was a job in the railways but his salary all went to the upkeep of the banana-seller.

One day, the women of the tenement began to tease him about his mistress. And so Sayaji told them his tale of woe. His banana-seller would not let him lay a hand on her. Yes, she would take his money. Yes, she would drape herself in shiny new saris that he bought. It was obvious that she was exploiting him. The women decided to help Sayaji get his money's worth. That night, after dinner, a storage room was emptied. Then Sayaji was sent in for his honeymoon night. But the lady was no fool. She screamed and screamed and screamed until Kawakhana could not bear the noise. The ladies were having none of this. With Manjula in the lead, they marched into the honeymoon suite. One of them got her by the legs; one secured her head, and so on until she was pinned down. Then Sayaji was called to his just desserts. We were watching all this through the window. The woman began to struggle when suddenly Baba erupted from out of the darkness. The women ran away. Grabbing her sari to her bosom, the lady vanished into the night. After this Sayaji scrupulously avoided feminine company.

Just as there was always some gambling going on, there was also an illegal still somewhere in Kawakhana, run by the Muslim thugs of the area. The raw material for the brew would cook in tins, set on top of a flaming stove. A stone slab would be placed on top of the container. They always set up their illicit breweries right near the toilets. After nine or ten p.m., no one dared 'go'. The women, especially, were terrified. One night, a woman was bathing at a tap, under cover of darkness. Suddenly a stream of hot water began to rain down on her. The woman was puzzled; she had been bathing in cold water. Where had this hot stream come from? She looked up and found that one of the goons was pissing on her.

One day, I was seized of a powerful urge to clean up

Kawakhana. I had imbibed some new ideals at school and so I went alone to Bombay Central station and dialled the police. When I got home, the police were smashing the still. They confiscated everything but did not nab a single distiller. I slept well that night, for I felt I had done something positive. Next evening, I was walking home to Kawakhana with my new college friends when a goon, his eyes aflame, stopped in front of me.

'What do you want?' I asked in Hindi.

Without a word, he delivered himself of a ringing slap under my ear. For a moment I saw stars. None of my friends said a word. All of us walked on as if nothing had happened. Did he know I had complained to the vigilance squad? This thought keep me awake all night. After this, the urge to reform Kawakhana dissolved like a clod of mud in a stream.

—

All my relatives kept asking when I was getting married. My question was: How could I marry when I was unemployed? Their relatives would incite Aaji and Aai, saying, 'The girl has grown up. She's come of age. What's all this about a job? One day, he'll get something. If god gives us mouths, he also gives us something to put into them.'

We did not have a spare paisa for such a wedding. But my relatives were willing to pay. Or to be more precise, they were willing to loan us the money. The job that I'd get one day? I could repay them from my salary. As a favour, no interest would be charged. On the one hand then, Saee's face, her eloquent eyes, her fair skin tantalized me. On the other, my economic circumstances foretold disaster.

Finally, Saee won. I still don't understand how I could have announced I was ready to marry when I had no job. Her family was called to Mumbai. The wedding would take place in the village but the basta, the wedding chest, had to be filled in Mumbai.

At that time, the basta was filled in an interesting way. The groom and the bride, their relatives and friends, all got together. The central event was the buying of clothes for the young couple. Everyone gathered in a group outside a shop in Matharpakadi, Dadar or Dongri. Then ten or twenty of the most respected members of both sides would go in and choose. One or two of these would be women. The shopkeepers knew what was going on and stood apart as the two sides got ready to ambush each other. Whatever one side so much as touched would have to be bought by the other. This meant loud, heated discussions. Sometimes the marriage was even called off at this point. The shopkeepers held fast to their prices. When it was done, they would magnanimously order tea for everybody. No one knew that the cost of the tea had already been factored into the bill. After the bundles were scooped up, the two sides would go to cool off in a park. Laddoos would be bought at a sweetshop and everyone got a laddoo. If you missed the occasion, the laddoos would be delivered home. Basta!

When I think about the filling of my wedding chest, my hair still stands on end. Even before it began, a fight broke out. I had some well-educated friends, among whom was Sadashiv. He felt that the groom was an educated man so the girl's side should buy him a suit. The fun of it was that opposition arose from my own family, speaking on behalf of Saee's family. 'We should buy the clothes of our tradition: a coat, a dhotar, turban and slippers,' they argued. We had bought Saee a shalu, a heavy silk sari. 'Whatever you spend on the girl's clothes, we'll spend half that on the boy's,' they said. This was also part of the tradition. And so the battle began. I was not prepared to back down. There was chaos in front of the shop. We did some quick calculations and said, 'What you're willing to spend will cover the cost of a suit.' And though the girl's side saw the logic of this, my side was still adamant.

Deadlock.

And then Baba's rage overflowed. He began to abuse me, using whatever foul words came to his tongue. Before I could do anything to forestall him, he slapped me across the face.

For a second, I could not respond. Then I lost my temper too. 'The wedding is off,' I announced. Everyone went home with only the girl's clothes bought.

That night, what struck me as strange was my future father-in-law's behaviour. He had not participated in the discussion. He had not taken my side either. Did he feel that what had happened, had happened for the best? I tossed and turned all night. I have a contrary streak in my nature, the results of which became apparent in the next few days.

Kawakhana was quiet. No one would speak to me. Everyone assumed that the wedding was off. My anger began to abate. I began to wonder what Saee's future would be like. It was common knowledge that our wedding had been fixed. Now who would marry her? This question began to plague me. I had lost her now. This worried me too. I was obsessed with her beauty. Which of these motives was the most important I do not know but I went, head bowed, to meet my father-in-law. 'I'm willing to accept whatever offer you make. Give me the clothes of your choice or don't give me any, I don't mind. I can wear my own clothes to the wedding.'

Perhaps my father-in-law had been sure of the power of his daughter's beauty. Perhaps he was savvy enough to know I would not allow the wedding to be called off like that. But this time they got together and bought me a suit. I do not know how this change of heart happened. I could only think how grand I would look in the suit at the wedding. This was the first time that I'd ever worn one as an adult. If I hadn't been delighted, it would have been odd.

Which year was this? I don't remember. Let's see; I passed my SSC in October 1954. Five or six months later, I got married. The Mahars had not converted to Buddhism yet and so the marriage was conducted according to the old tradition. I was one of the last to get married in this way. Today the Mahars as Boudhs finish off a marriage ceremony in one or two hours. There's a triple supplication, the reiteration of the five principles and the vows and you're done. My wedding celebration took two or three days. But education had given me new ideas.

I refused to let them smear my body with haldi; I would not let them deck me up with the bashin, a headgear from which beads and pieces of coconut dangled in front of my face like a curtain. I thought I would look like a bull on parade. The wedding party was quite shocked at my appearance. Perhaps this was the first progressive groom they had seen. They began to complain. Aai began to weep and hit herself around the face in grief at my appearance. Finally I compromised just to keep her happy and agreed to have haldi smeared on my hands and feet and allowed a headgear with a couple of strings to be tied to my head.

On the day of this haldi ceremony, it was the custom to serve a meal. You paid your debts with this meal, cancelling off any meals you and your family had eaten at others' expense. Now your relatives had you where they wanted you. If they refused to come to the wedding, you were reduced in status to a loafer. They knew that they were your respectability receipt and held it over your head. We had no debts of this kind to pay. We had fed the required number on the required days after the death of my father and uncle. As a meal, if you served kadaaknya and jaggery syrup, it was considered a sumptuous feast. Kadaaknya? Puris deep-fried in oil and served steaming hot.

I remember that meal given on the day of the haldi ceremony. All the shopping had been done on the advice of the relatives in the taluka. In the village square, a cooking pit had been dug. Puris were being fried. Grandfather Tanaji was keeping a crow's beady eye on the provisions. Who knows how Tannya Baba began to suspect the relatives of theft but he did. So he went and checked the loft of the public meeting hall. There, kilos of jaggery and bags of flour had been hidden away. Tannya Baba lost his temper. He began to abuse everyone, accusing them of sleeping with their mothers and sisters. He said they wanted to sabotage the wedding feast. He said they wanted him to be the laughing stock of the village. This was not something new to me. I had witnessed these kerfuffles since childhood. This wedding-time bad behaviour would continue when they sat down to eat. Some would tuck puris under their thighs. 'My son's in Mumbai. Throw in his share too,' one woman would say as she was being served. 'How you ate at my son's wedding!' another would say. 'Such a stream of food that the plate could not contain it!' My head ached thinking about all this but if you took offence at this ugliness, you would be mocked, so everyone zipped their lips. As soon as they had been fed and watered, the whole lot would troop off to the girl's village to be fed.

I remember another problem: only one bullock cart had been hired that day. How would the whole party fit? Everyone in the Maharwada wanted transport—ten or twelve miles separated our village and Saee's—and they were going to stand on their rights. No one knew what to do. Tannya Baba tried to cajole people: 'Why insist on these things at the wedding of a fatherless waif?' Finally he paid everyone's bus fare. With the money in their hands, their faces lit up.

When the groom's bullock cart departed, Tannya Baba did not forget to break a coconut. I must have looked a sight. I had a katiyar, a ceremonial knife, in my hand, with a sour-lime impaled on its tip. This was to ward off the ghosts said to be attracted by the haldi. The bridesmaids kept nagging me to be careful with it. The bullock-cart driver was singing: 'My horses, my horses, how smooth are your strides/ Run, my fine horses, or I'll whip your fat sides.'

In one sense, the wedding was fun. I tried to keep things light, cracking jokes. I know that my face is now rather sombre but I kept the entire wedding party laughing. After the wedding we went in the bullock cart for a ramble about the village, my haldi-smeared bride at my side. I began to feel the desire to pinch my wife on the sly. Saee pulled the mundavli aside and glared her disapproval of my bad behaviour. Suddenly, Javji Buwa came up and said, 'Sit with dignity.' His opinion was: 'This girl is a little too big for my boy. Why burden this poor fellow with this yoke?' I didn't quite understand what he was saying but it was true that when I had seen Saee a year ago, her body had been as slender as a reed. Now she had filled out quite a bit. I might not have recognized her.

When dinner was done, a bucket of fried stuff was prepared by both mothers-in-law and set aside. These would be crunched and broken by the mothers-in-law on each other's heads and they would recite naughty ukhanas, rhymes containing the names of each other's spouses. Another of the acts was the buffalo act; there would be four men who would be under the hide of an animal, dancing and prancing. The musicians would be banging away and under cover of the noise, the men would be pinching the mothers-in-law and their protests would go unheeded.

That kind of thing.

In the morning, the bride and groom were taken to the river, accompanied by musicians. There we were bathed, and each of us was supposed to hold a betel nut in one hand; I was supposed to get it from her. Then we would eat coconut and spit on each other's faces. I suspected I would not be able to extricate the supari from Saee's grasp and everyone would laugh at me. So in a stage whisper, I pleaded with her to release the supari and everyone laughed with me rather than at me.

After the bath, another tradition required the groom to carry the bride. I walked up to her, then I pretended to lose heart, to turn away as if discouraged by the impossibility of picking her up. More laughter. I really doubted whether I would be able to sweep her up into my arms in the required fashion. The wedding party had probably never encountered such a comical groom before. Javji Buwa looked a little sad: 'I wonder how this is going to turn out. I hope the marriage won't end up a joke.' Why did he say this when everyone else was so happy?

On the night of the marriage procession, it was the tradition to dance the dhega. This is an odd custom. Men lift up the bride and groom and carry them around. Rotis made without oil are put into the bride's hands and everyone dances around her in a circle, as the musicians play. At this time, I remember, the wife is allowed to belabour her husband with her slippers. Perhaps this custom was developed to allow the woman an opportunity to even the score, for in most cases, it will be the husband who will beat his wife.

In Marathi films, you see elaborate preparations for the honeymoon night. There's the heroine climbing the stairs with a glass of milk in one hand, her heart pounding. There's the hero, standing at the open window, gazing at the full moon. The bed is covered with flowers. Nothing like this was arranged for us. When the girl comes to her husband's house, her stern grandmother comes with her. The boy gets no sleep. His bride sleeps with the old lady. The house is full of people. He finds it difficult to even exchange a few words with his wife. After a couple of days, the girl goes back to her mother's home. She looks at him with mischievous eyes and he looks at her with the eyes of a starving man who is offered food and then has it snatched away. She is expected to return in a week or so. At that time, the boy hopes to satisfy all the longing he has built up; but then a telegram arrives from Mumbai. He has been summoned to an interview. Going by previous experiences, he feels deeply depressed at the thought of another disaster.

'The girl's a lucky omen. She came into the family and you got a call,' his mother says.

The 'next time' is postponed indefinitely.

—

Finally, I did manage to get a job. But it was a bizarre job at the Parel Veterinary College with the alarming title of clerk-cum-laboratory assistant.

On the first day I understood how I got the job. No upper-caste person would have taken it. From the various districts of Maharashtra, samples of the shit of sick animals would arrive at the laboratory. Every morning, I was supposed to open these parcels, make a note of them in the register, transfer the contents into glass jars using a glass rod, change the water in them every hour, remove the sediment and when the water ran clear, transfer the remains into a glass phial. After lunch, the doctors would examine the specimens under the microscope. They would write down their diagnoses and I would have to send off the reports.

The other department, Anatomy, was where animals were dissected. The carcasses were hung on hooks, the skin stripped off. My job was to prevent them from decomposing by injecting their blood vessels with alcohol. My subordinate, a Class IV employee, was also a Mahar, from the Konkan. He was better than the qualified vets at stripping an animal. After all, it was his traditional occupation.

In the afternoon, swathed in swan-white gowns, the student veterinarians would arrive. I felt a terrible distaste for them. I wished their white gowns could be drenched in animal blood. In truth, my rage was misplaced; my position was not their fault. But what else could I vent my unhappiness upon? My head seemed fit to explode with the pressure of my resentment. I would think: 'Damn it, after all this education, here I am doing the work that my forefathers did.' I would begin to wonder if this were not my destiny. This was when I began to feel a true horror for the way society was organized. These experiences sowed the seeds of revolution in me. I felt like a gravedigger, turning up corpses, and I longed to see the roles reversed.

At this time, I had joined Ruparel College. Morning classes. At ten o'clock I would come racing into the office. There was nothing romantic about my time in college. I sat at the back of the class as a matter of convenience; I only wanted to answer the roll class, get through a couple of hours and then slip out to work. I remember a Sanskrit professor by the name of Desai, very fair, tall and sturdy, with a personality to match. He taught us Kalidas's *Meghdoot*. Listening to him declaim erotic poetry, there would be muffled explosions of giggles all over the class.

I was never enthused by these erotic verses. I just didn't want to miss the muster. I couldn't afford an umbrella in the monsoon so I would go to the office in wet clothes, hang them to dry, put them on again when they had dried and then plunge into that world of shit. Even today, I'm surprised that I bore all of it. Truly, I was being split into two.

—

My wife comes to Mumbai. Her father brings her. When there's a break in the rains, I toss my bedding on the footpath. There are just too many people in the house. If it begins to rain suddenly, I swoop down on my pillows and sheets and run for it. Then I must fit myself in somewhere.

Seven or eight days pass. My wife's body, polished with haldi, shines with a new brilliance. I try to catch her eye in the middle of our crowded home. No one seems to have noticed that we've just got married, we have no privacy, no place to sleep marked off for us. All day, the women are busy with housework and in the night, Saee goes to Tatya's home, next door, to sleep. Tatya and Kaku sleep on the bed; Saee underneath.

One day, the rain comes down when I'm sleeping on the footpath. I have never felt such happiness at a shower in the middle of the night as I do then. This time I wasn't swearing as I scooped up my pillows and sheets and made my way back into the house. Only this time, I go to Tatya's house. I drop on to the floor and send out my foot to explore. I make contact with a woman's foot. Cat-eyed, I peer through the darkness. She's moving about restlessly. She's awake. Our feet brush each other's. It sets off electric sparks across my body. I pick up the rag used to wipe the floors and chuck it at her. She chucks it back. I dare not go any closer. What a life. My lawfully wedded wife and I are reduced to this.

Finally the ladies of the chawl took pity on me. They shouted at my aunt. This question had always caused friction between my aunt and my mother. It was decided that we would have the house to ourselves for a few days. Kawakhana's first nights were once legendary. The newly wedded bride was never 'ready and willing'; often she would not allow her husband to lay a finger on her. There would be a huge commotion, much outraged shrieking, even a sound beating.

So the groom would often feed his wife some opium, mixing it surreptitiously with her food. Generally, she would have no idea that this was happening but some smart young woman who had heard the rumours would take the trouble to eat separately; or she would ask permission to share her mother-in-law's or sister-in-law's plate. In which case, the portion that was spiked was presented to her. The old ladies became expert at spinning the plate.

As a child, I had heard the stories of how Shiva-tatya had fed his newly wed wife, who had just reached puberty, opium in this way. At least in Mumbai, a marriage bed could be arranged for the newly-weds. No such luck in the village. If the couple lived in a joint family, it was even worse. When the husband arrived for dinner, he would pretend he had forgotten his chanchi or his turban. He announced this and his wife decoded the message. She slipped out and they got together on the sly, in a ditch or trench. Was this the unexpected result of the saints' philosophical teachings?

Giving a woman opium struck me as bestial behaviour. Nor could the women of the chawl do this for me. From the evening, excitement fluttered inside me. In truth, this would be the first time I had touched a woman. The reading I had done on the subject left me with the idea of keeping the light on in the room. Saee took one look at me and began to weep. In the rough and tumble of it, her bangles broke. That terrified her. Her body had a rustic smell, as the earth exudes after rain. It was deeply seductive. I tried to explain things to her.

'If you object, I will not touch you,' I said. This was what I had learned from reading. After a long speech, Saee fell silent and turned introspective.

When I got up in the morning, I heard the ladies talking. 'Dagdu's a smart one! How he got around his new wife!' and then it became clear. The women had been in the next room all night. The light being on, my long lectures, they had witnessed it all. I regretted now that silly decision to leave the light on and then to talk on and on. All day, I walked around with the face of a thief caught red-handed.

I would pine for Saee's company. I would wait for the night to fall but that was not enough. We slept under Kaku's cot. We may not even sit on her bed.

Each night Kaku sat on the footpath, chatting to the other women. We had to wait for her to come in to put out the light. She was a very young woman for all she was my aunt. But after Tatya, she preserved her chastity as a widow with great effort. The body has its needs, its hungers. She realized this and every morning she would drink neem-leaf juice. This was her honest attempt to rid herself of passion. She ate her food without salt too, and yet she would sit outside for hours. I did not understand this. Surely she could not be deriving pleasure out of tormenting us? Was it her intention to drive us out of the house? Sometimes it would be midnight before she came in. We couldn't even put off the light before that.

Once, we switched off the light and waited. But how long can you wait? Kaku walked in suddenly and put on the light. Chaos ensued. We had a difficult time trying to cover up our naked bodies with the sheets. Perhaps Aai too knew how Kaku tormented us. She would say it first thing in the morning. She gave vent to her anger by abusing the dogs and cats.

Then one day there's a terrible fight. Unrepeatable insults and abuse are hurled. 'We have a share in this house,' Aai claims.

'When you ran off to the village to fill your bellies, we looked after the house,' Kaku shouts back.

I was fed up of this fighting. Once Aai must have said something unforgivable to Kaku for she came running up to me and grabbed me and said, 'Come on, boy, here, do what you must. Get your satisfaction! At least your mother will calm down.'

My arms and legs began to quiver.

These displays of our culture seem like demon dances. I do not want to show my face to anyone in the chawl. My wife and mother get in between us and set me free.

Rahul Sankrutayan talks about the aggressive power of primitive women in *From the Volga to the Ganga*. This performance causes all his descriptions to fade. I wonder how I've managed to land in hell.

—

So why didn't we leave? In one sense, there was some truth in what Kaku said: we were parasites.

Could we not have found some other place to lay our heads in such a big city? We almost certainly could. At one point, we found a room in a slum in Koliwada. We had even paid the earnest money of fifty rupees. But Aaji and Aai were opposed to the move. 'You're going to take such a beautiful wife and go and live in a slum? It's full of goons and thugs. Dens of vice. Speakeasies. Matka-number runners. Fights that end in bloodshed.' In reality, slums are not filled with thugs and criminals. But at that time, it is true, I was worried that some Alauddin Khilji might abduct my beautiful Saee. So I decided that Saee would be safe in this illusion of home. That my mother and grandmother did not wish me to leave was another reason.

Saee had a very sweet nature. She followed me around like a shadow. She did not like my friends coming over. She would get very angry at me when I went out to roam with my friends on Saturdays or Sundays or when they came over. Once, when a friend was about to bear me off, she abused him roundly in her rustic language. This was a new vision of Saee. During this period, I was always tired: wakeful nights followed by morning classes and then my job at the veterinary college. In the evenings when I tried to study, she would snatch the book from my hands.

My friends were all praise for her beauty. One day she complained about a friend of mine. This was a garrulous fellow, a union leader, an effective speaker. 'When he comes over he always asks for water and when I give it to him, he pinches my palms,' she said. I would try to explain. 'Arré, you are so beautiful, anyone might lose control. Is there any sin in you? No, right? Then forget about it.' Saee thought my behaviour moronic. If a man in my village had heard of such behaviour towards his wife, blood would have been shed. In her sights, I was behaving like a laggard in love. I suppose I lived in the world of books. I thought of myself as modern, so I assumed that if one of my friends conceived of a passion for my wife, what of it?

The Jewish and Muslim gamblers at the club would often wave banknotes at Saee. She would complain to me at night about that too but I paid her no mind. She was forced to speak to the elders of the community about this, since her husband didn't seem to care. I still don't know why I behaved in such an imbecilic fashion.

That Saee had eased my loneliness and so taken charge of my life did not sit well with Aai at all. As long as I was at home, Saee behaved very well. But as soon as I set foot out of the house, Aai and Saee would begin to fight. I could not figure out how someone who behaved so sweetly with me could be so venomous with my mother and sister. When I returned every evening, Aai would tell me her saga of Saee's deeds. There were no huge crimes, most of the arguments arose over household chores. Aai's loving nature also began to change. In a voice that everyone could hear, she would call me a bull, meaning I was as love-blind as a bull in heat.

I was not used to this. I had always been the apple of Aai's eye. She resented Saee who had drawn me away from her so quickly. I did not understand Aai in this. Because I was educated and because I had read a few books, I thought to treat women with respect and not as men of earlier generations had done. This caused huge dissent. The general belief in our community was that a woman should know that she had the same place as a pair of slippers. 'Set her on your head,' Aai would say, 'and she'll shit on it.'

Aai wanted to rescue me but I was treating Saee with kid gloves. I wanted her to feel no pain, no discomfort of any kind. She was so madly in love with me, she would hang around just to be in my company. I too became happier in her company.

Now that I had a job, I didn't think it right that Aai should scavenge. I told her again and again that it did my prestige no good. I would insist and she would reassure me saying, 'Who, me? Scavenging?' But as soon as I left for the office, she would hoist her basket to her head and set off. Of course, Saee would tell all when I returned home.

I would ask Aai about it. She would tell me that she had a girl in the house to marry off. 'You don't have to worry about her,' I would say but she turned a deaf ear.

The constant warfare between wife and mother wrecked my peace of mind. Damn it, why had I got married? They said I would live happily ever after. Instead I found myself in charge of a field of poisonous thorn bushes. If I mowed them down in the morning, they were in luxuriant bloom by evening. One day, I could take it no more. There was a large mirror on the wall of the house. I picked it up that evening and began to jerk and spasm as I held it. Then I smashed it on the floor.

'My boy's run mad,' Aai lamented.

I extracted a promise from both of them that they would not fight and only then did I cool down. But they didn't really need a cause. Anything would do.

'You buy your wife these fancy saris and you buy me these ordinary ones,' my mother would complain. But even when I bought her an expensive sari, one that had cost me five or ten rupees more than a sari for Saee, she would not believe that she had the better one. Finally, I started taking her to the shops with me so that she could choose.

I longed to see Saee wearing a five-yard sari, instead of the nine-yard sari in the traditional Mahar style. But Aai would have none of it. I wanted my wife to look like she belonged to the Brahmin or Baniya castes. But that never became a reality. I felt aggrieved, for many of my friends had wives who dressed in the latest fashions and I couldn't even get my wife the kind of sari I wanted her to wear.

One day, the dabbawala did not arrive on time to fetch my lunch. Worried that her husband would have nothing to eat that day, Saeee came to the office with my sister and my lunch. I was ambivalent about this. On the one hand, I was touched by this gesture; on the other hand, I worried about what my friends in the office would think of her. But since they did not recognize her as my wife, they took her to be a servant.

'You sly dog! You've got a hot one as a maid,' one of them said. I was embarrassed. I didn't have the courage to tell them the truth. I had never taken my colleagues home, nor had I ever taken her out, not even for a cup of tea.

I had a friend by the name of Jadhav who also lived in Kawakhana. I got to know him when he was my aunt's—Kaku's—tenant. He was a great raconteur. He could have you laughing for hours. He had finished his SSC and had taken a job selling stamp paper at the Law Courts. Five or six years later, he joined college as a mature student. He had had a number of strange experiences. His nature had an odd aggressive streak, which I could not understand. If the rest of us live with the burden of what others think of us, Jadhav was unconcerned about the opinions of the world.

One day, he caused a storm in the office. Every day, he had to sell court stamps to the tune of fifteen thousand rupees. There was a famous lawyer who practised in that court. Even judges were respectful of him. This lawyer arrives one day at Jadhav's stall with a fat bundle of currency notes. Jadhav looks out of his small window. The lawyer does not bother to join the queue. He simply demands to be served first. He is shouting, demanding his stamps. He places the stack of notes on the sill. Jadhav loses his temper. He flings the money on the floor outside his stall, as if the notes are playing cards. The lawyer leaps to the floor to gather his money up. Jadhav grabs a stick and attacks him. The entire queue watches, completely stunned. Jadhav tells us the story later:

'So the judge calls me. This could mean I might lose my job. I throw myself at the judge's feet and I weep. So the judge forgives me.'

He adds a codicil.

'Yes, I wept at the judge's feet, but who was there to see me humbling myself? And didn't everyone talk about it? Didn't I show some valour?'

This silences me.

Around this time, Jadhav got married. His wife looked like a porcelain doll. I went to the wedding in Pune. He lived in a slum, just like those of Kamathipura, where I lived in those days. Ten-twelve brothers and sisters lived with their mother and father in a loft. His father was an accomplished keertankaar; he sang devotional songs. The name of Rama was never far from his lips. His son was quite different. He talked to his father as if he were a friend. He got his father to put on the wool coat he had had stitched for himself for the wedding and said, 'Baap, you look every inch the hero.' Jadhav Sr directed some perfunctory abuse at his son but he was also smiling. The other brothers, whether elder or younger, had much the same relationship but I noticed that once they started drinking, they fell to fighting as if they were mortal enemies. In the morning, no shadows of the night before or its fights lingered. It was an intriguing mix of happiness and hatred.

Jadhav turned his wedding into high comedy. All those practices that I saw as uncivilized—the smearing of haldi, the spitting of coconut, the tying of the marital headgear—he seemed to be able to enjoy wholeheartedly. Like a latter-day Krishna, he preened among the bridesmaids. I can never forget the sight of his young friends, all dancing in the style of Bhagwan Dada,* down to the bandanas tied around their heads, a band accompanying them. The song 'The blooms of zai and zui fill the courtyard but my husband is not by my side' was parodied by one of his friends as 'The bulls have filled the courtyard with dung but my husband is not by my side.' He sang it in a tragic voice and got a huge round of applause.

After the wedding, Jadhav found accommodation a problem. Finding a suitable room in the big city was asking for a miracle. He lived in Colaba; his elder sister worked in a home there. It was a fancy building, full of office quarters. All the flats had servants quarters attached. Every night there were inspections. The servants were not allowed to bring their relatives to live with them. But the chowkidars could be silenced with bribes. 'Damn it, can't even use the lift. We have to sneak in by the back door,' Jadhav would say, lacing his words with ripe abuse.

---

*Bhagwan Dada (1913-2002) patented a certain dance style in *Albela* (Bhagwan Dada, 1951), his most successful film. This can be described as a slow bounce and it was so successful that almost every dancing star from Amitabh Bachchan to Rishi Kapoor used it.

While he was living there, he did something startling. When his sister was not at home, he got a domestic help to bring him a Christian lady's outfit. He made his wife dress in the skirt and high heels, told her to do her face and then took her for a stroll by the sea. We saw him, walking like a sahib, his arm around her, whistling away. His wife was embarrassed when she saw us. When his sister heard about this, she cursed him roundly.

But Jadhav was a law unto himself. I, on the other hand, could not get my wife to wear a sari in the manner I wanted, and I still regret this.

Once when I met Jadhav, he seemed to be the worse for drink. And then he was not to be seen for a while. I found myself missing him and so I went to his office. Now he was the head clerk, and completely normal, a sea at rest. He was talking now of spiritual matters! He spoke with obvious pride of how even the Brahmin clerks addressed him as 'Pundit'. He told me of how he had once chosen the winning number in a lottery simply by pointing at it with a pen. This change shocked me. He said he had begun to acquire supernatural powers. I asked him about what I should do if I knew I was fated to face a problem the next day, should I take steps to avoid it or stay and face it? His answer was evasive. That this hedonist should turn to spirituality startled me. It was as if an RSS youngster were suddenly to turn Marxist. When he claimed that he no longer touched alcohol, I could not believe my ears.

—

In the movement in which I grew up,* the lines between political and social work were always hazy. You were given your party card at birth. The social forces behind this were so strong that even if one wanted to join another party, one could not. One would be ostracized if one tried. Nobody would even join one's funeral procession. Rankhambe of Vinchur,** Abbasaheb Khairmode*** (Babasaheb's biographer), and Comrade More† were prime examples. When I was studying in the village, I remember doing election duty. The Praja Socialist Party and the Scheduled Caste Federation formed by Babasaheb Ambedkar in 1942 had an electoral agreement. The PSP's symbol was a tree. On the day of the election, I went with the other Socialists to spread the word. Each student at the boarding school had

---

*Pawar is referring to the Ambedkarite movement.

**This probably refers to Amrutrao Rankhambe, one of the organisers of the Yeola Conference. Denied a ticket by Dr Ambedkar in the elections, he moved away from the Republican Party of India (RPI).

***Changdeo Bhavanrao Khairmode (1901-1971) was Babasaheb Ambedkar's biographer. He began work on his fifteen-work biography in 1923 and completed it just before his death.

†Comrade R.B. More was a committed Communist but he was also close to Babasaheb Ambedkar, which makes him something of an anomaly, for Ambedkar had little time for the Communists in general. More was one of the organisers of the Mahad agitation in 1927, in which thousands of Mahars drank water from a lake that had been declared public but which in reality was reserved for upper-caste use.

been assigned a village. When it was time for lunch, I was sent to the Maharwada. I wondered where the other Socialists were eating.

Our zilla was a bastion of the Communist movement. Our village and some others were known to be Communist. During the Telangana Movement,* a blanket ban was imposed on the Communist Party and the police reserves were called in to enforce it. Camps were set up everywhere. Whatever was to be spent on these camps was to be recovered through fines imposed on villages known to have Communist sympathies. Sakeerwadi, Navalewadi and Vashere were to bear the brunt of this.

At this time I remember seeing the social reformer and writer Annabhau Sathe's *Akalechi Gosht* (The Dimwit's Tale) performed in front of the temple. This had also been banned. We did not know when the police would arrive and arrest the performers. This satire was like no other we had seen; it had no kings and queens. It spoke of the exploitation we saw around us, offering an aesthetic analysis of our situation. It played all night and we learned some new songs. 'Daulatichya raja, utoon Sarjya, haak de shejaaryaala re, shivari chalaa' ('Oh kings of wealth, Sarjya, wake up, listen to what your neighbours say, let's go back to the fields') and 'Aamhi dhartichya lekra bhaagyavaan' ('We are the fortunate sons of

---

*The Communists led a movement in the Telangana area of the State of Hyderabad for land reform between 1946 and 1951. This led to them being banned during the Second World War.

the earth'). These songs were never far from our lips. Our taluka had public programmes by Annabhau Sathe, the poet Atmaram Gavankar and the famous revolutionary singer Amarsheikh. People would come as for a festival, a storm of them, riding in on bullock carts. In spite of all this, none of us actually joined the Communist Party, although our village was sympathetic to the cause if not to the comrades. We were told the comrades were a violent bunch and so we stayed away from them. Until recently, most of us hadn't even heard of Marx's name, never mind reading his philosophy.

Dadasaheb was the leader in the zilla. However, he was very close to the Communist leader Annasaheb Shinde. We found it difficult to understand how Dadasaheb could abuse the Communists from public platforms and then go to Annasaheb's house for dinner.

Slowly the Communist movement began to fade from the area. Because of decentralization, Maratha society began to move closer to the ruling class. The zilla parishad and the sugar mills became like the weapons in the hands of an eight-armed goddess. Some give the credit for this to Yashwantrao Chavan.* Whatever may be the truth of that, it is true that the political colour of our area underwent a

---

*Yashwantrao Balwantrao Chavan (1913-1984) was a doughty Congress politician, the first chief minister of Maharashtra after the division of the Bombay State, defence minister under Nehru, and one of the ministers who supported Indira Gandhi's emergency.

radical change. I could never understand how a village that had had all the markings of Communism could become supporters of the Congress Party, almost overnight.

Many prestigious people went over to the Congress. No one could figure out how Datta Deshmukh got left behind. However, when Dr Ambedkar issued an order, they would still swarm out as bees from a hive, seeking their own advantage.

At that time the Left-leaning parties were not aware of the issues that Untouchables faced. The bahujan, the majority, were, at one point, Communists. At the same time, they might have been part of the Satyashodhak Samaj or a similar movement. But they had never asked themselves what changes they wanted in their own culture. If the zilla parishads, the sugar factories and the political power centres of Maharashtra had fallen into their hands, then, even if unconsciously, they would still have aspired to Brahminical culture.

Marriages had to be conducted by Brahmins; so also funeral rites. The celebration of local festivals, the Satyanarayan Pooja, the Parayana—recitation of religious stories—in the month of Shravan, were all conducted in the orthodox manner. Whether the rich called themselves Communists or Socialists, they were all united in their way of looking at the question of baluta. If the Mahars of a village refused to do the demeaning traditional work demanded of them, they were ostracized in the old fashion. Severe and immediate boycotts were imposed if they did not play music at the village fair, if they did not carry the ceremonially decorated bull to the temple. Left-wing parties did not protest these things with morchas. At least, not in my experience.

On the one hand, the Mahars were in the process of abandoning their old ways, refusing to accept the old religious order, but they had no share in the village's productive operations. They could no longer claim baluta, or yeskarpali, both of which were dependent on them doing unpaid labour. Whatever tiny bits of land they had once had—their boneyards—were now pawned to the rich farmers of the area. The Mahars now went to the city to earn their bread or to the sugar factories as cheap labour. And so the Maharwadas began to empty.

I remember a debate that raged at that time. The Mahars' traditional land had been pawned to the rich sugar mill owners for a period of ninety-nine years at some nominal amount. Dadasaheb, Ram Pawar and others began a movement to get this land back for the Mahars. The rich farmers wondered whether the Mahars would be able to look after the land, were it to be returned to them. After all, they said, who had ever seen a Mahar till the soil? It is difficult to say why this movement did not spread as water seeps into sand.

As long as Babasaheb was alive, he was a vital force in politics. Like a volcano, he kept shaking up society. The movement to refuse to pay tax for traditionally owned land was spreading from village to village. 'Mahaarki mhanje gulaamgiri, aamhi he kaam karnaar naahi,' ('Maharki is slavery. We won't do this work') was the slogan of self-respect that resounded in our world. We now had the power and the courage to bring down mountains. But then Babasaheb achieved nirvana. Just as a tent supported by a single pole cannot withstand a storm, the movement began to head towards tragedy. 'Don't covet their palaces; fortify your shacks'—Babasaheb's order blew in the wind. Just as bees are attracted to jaggery, people began to be drawn to power. The Republican Party of India's tie-up with the Congress killed the movement, poisoning it slowly.

I had seen Babasaheb when I was too young to remember much. Once when I was in the hostel, we heard that he was going to address a public meeting in Nasik. The news filled me with delight. I had always wanted to hear him speak at least once in my life. Many students left for Nasik on bicycles and so I hired a bicycle too. I was used to cycling long distances. We managed to cover forty to fifty miles by afternoon. The question was where to stop at night. We went hesitantly to the girls' hostel that Dadasaheb Gaekwad, who would later be a member of the Lok Sabha and the Rajya Sabha, ran at Kismat Bagh. We had never seen Gaekwad before. There he was, blue topi on his head, dhotar, Kolhapuri slippers, tough old black coat. He had just cycled up too. That we too were boarders in another hostel counted in our favour. He invited us to a meal. The girls of the hostel kept peeking at us. I will never forget the sight of Dadasaheb Gaekwad at work. He swept the floors, he spread out the bed rolls for us to sit, he helped the girls serve the food. It was a pleasant surprise to have such an important leader treating us so well.

That night Babasaheb did come to Nasik but he did not address the meeting. The venue was swarming with people, thick as ants. On the stage, important leaders. Shantabai Dani announces: 'Babasaheb has suddenly taken ill. He will not be able to attend this meeting.' She also tells us where he is staying.

We were very disappointed. We had cycled for miles to fill our ears with Babasaheb's voice, the voice that had led so many people to freedom. We had come to store in our hearts his intense and fiery words. Now, we were already dissolving into a swamp as water does. Since we had come that far, we decided, we should try and see him in the morning. We returned to the girls' hostel and spent a night under the eaves. The next morning, we went and hung about the bungalow where Babasaheb was staying. There, one of us spotted him, sitting on a chair on the lawn, in the mild warmth of the morning sun. I could scarce believe that someone born a Mahar could have achieved so much. He was dressed in a full suit that complemented his powerful presence. He had positioned himself there so that at least some of those who had come to see him would not return disappointed. But his illness had worn him down. His face showed it. He had some trouble with his legs. He needed help to walk.

I did see him again, this time in Colaba. He was

descending a staircase slowly, leaning on a stick, Maisaheb at his side. For us children, seeing him was nothing short of seeing a marvel. At this time, Chander went with party workers to his residence. Someone in Kamathipura had started a bogus film company called Bhegubhai & Co. The youth had lined up to pay to audition for the roles of hero and side-hero. This company had been located in the party office. Later, all those concerned with it vanished. The money vanished with them. A party worker took these people's complaints to Babasaheb's home. He even had photographs of people paying their money at the party office. Chander told us that Babasaheb was furious. He tore into the party workers. He also asked to see the worker's file. The man was from Marathwada. 'Arré, what are you doing in the city? If you want to work for the party, go work in Marathwada. Do you know how much our people are suffering there? What good is your intelligence here?' Babasaheb would always say with tears in his eyes: 'I may have managed to achieve something for the Mahars in the city but in the villages, my people are still living under brutal oppression.'

The last time I saw Babasaheb was when he achieved nirvana. I was leaving for work in the morning when I read the news on the front page of the newspaper. I felt as if the earth had split open. It was as if someone close, someone from my family, had passed away. I wept, leaning on the door. Aai and Saee had no idea why I was crying. But as soon as I told the family, they all began to cry too. When I came out, I saw people standing in groups, talking earnestly. Babasaheb had died in Delhi. His body was to return by air that evening. I had been working for just two or three months. I went to the veterinary college to take leave. When he saw the reason on my leave request form, my boss got angry. He said, 'How can you write this as a reason? Ambedkar was a national leader and you're a government servant. Write "Personal reasons".'

Generally, I am a peaceful person by nature. But that day I was certain: I was not going to change what I had written on my leave application. Instead, I said: 'Sahib, he was a member of my family. How can you even begin to imagine the dark cave from which he led us?' And then without bothering whether he granted me leave or not, whether he dismissed me or not, I rushed off to Raj Bhavan. I didn't even bother to buy my return ticket.

People were streaming on to the maidan. I did not go home that night. I dropped down on the grass in front of the Governor's House. In the morning, the stream had turned into a flood. A serpentine queue formed to get a last glimpse of his body. After one or two hours, it was my turn to look upon him. He seemed asleep, at peace. His nose had been stuffed with cotton balls. People were laying flowers and garlands at his feet.

In the afternoon, the funeral procession began. The sun spewed fire down on us as we moved, at a snail's pace, heavy hearts making for heavy steps. I got up onto a bridge to get an estimate of the crowd. It was as if an anthill had broken open. My vision could not encompass the mourners. They say that only Lokmanya Tilak's funeral procession brought so many people out. But what I saw of the raw grief of the people that day, I will never forget. Many men and women were beating their breasts; others were weeping as if they could not stop.

—

It was in 1956, at Nagpur, that Babasaheb converted lakhs of his followers to Buddhism. I could not attend this historic event. But this revolutionary change reached every Mahar home and dwelling. Many families broke the images of the gods and goddesses that had been on their walls, scattering like marbles or cowries the gods of their puja ghars. They turned their backs on pilgrimages, fairs and the old gods: Mari-Aai, Mhasoba, Khandoba and the like. They stopped sacrificing goats and hens. We had a nominal home temple. Aai had had coins of Khandoba and Bahiroba cast in silver. Because they were made of precious metal, she wrapped them up in rags and hid them away. From time to time, when I am looking through the detritus of personal belongings, I find them. I don't know what to do with these images. No one worships them, no one bathes them. When we converted to Buddhism, we promised: 'I will not worship the Hindu religion's Brahma, Vishnu, Mahesh, nor any of the thirty-three crore gods associated with it.'

This oath became part of our blood. In Mumbai, women were asked to wear a white sari at the time of taking diksha.

Shopkeepers had a great old time of it. Men's white dhotars were sold as saris. I remember buying Aai and Saee white saris at twice the ordinary rate on credit.

This reminds me of how religion can degenerate into ritual. I had gone to an engagement ceremony, a sakharpuda in Colaba. The girl was a Konkanastha, a resident of the Konkan by birth; the boy a Deshasta, or one whose family had its roots in the leeward side of the Sahyadris. The Konkanasthas call the engagement a bolgada. The Konkanastha panchayat is a strong prestigious organization. No one could marry but with their permission. This meant that the panchayat had to be bribed. They had to be served alcohol as well. So Deshastha-Konkanastha marriages rarely happened. A Deshastha boy or girl had to become a member of the Konkanastha panchayat. Deshastha Brahmin priests were not allowed to marry Buddhists. It had to be a Bouddhacharya, a Buddhist priest. Permission had to be sought from both sides. To complicate matters, the Deshastha side had bought an expensive sari for the girl. The problem? It was coloured. That was it! Seeing the sari, the Konkanastha side gets angry. They are ready to call the whole thing off. I try to calm things down. In a lighter vein, I tell them the true story of how a wedding had been stalled because the groom was wearing black shoes. 'In other words, all extremes are bad,' I conclude. No one is in the mood to listen to me. This reminds me of the Thakars and their insistence on four annas even when offered a rupee.

It is night now. Everyone goes on a treasure hunt in the neighbouring shops. No white saris are to be found. Finally, dhotars are bought. The girl is dressed in a dhotar and brought to the ceremony.

I did not know whether to laugh or cry.

But then I witnessed another wedding which outdid this one. The boy, this time, had a Gandhi topi on his head.

'Take that Gandhi topi off,' said the organizer.

'Why?' the boy demanded. 'It's white, isn't it?'

'It may be white but it's a Congress white. Remove it immediately.'

Eventually the boy was forced to obey.

Office-going Mahar girls began wearing white saris to work. When it was discovered that these girls in white saris were the Mahars of old and the Bouddhas of today, upper-caste girls stopped wearing white. This amused me. Notions of caste are tenacious; they cling to us, leech-like.

'You may have abandoned Hinduism and become Bouddha but you're still within the fold,' said Savarkar, and many caste Hindus would agree. 'You may have become Buddhist but in the end you're still Mahar.' In order to identify those who were once Mahars a new term was coined: neo-Buddhists. When a Hindu converts to Islam or Christianity, how come we don't hear terms like neo-Christian or neo-Muslim?

Babasaheb wrote an open letter to the nation. He mooted the idea that there should be just one single opposition party to the ruling class. He decided to dismantle the Scheduled

Castes Federation and create the Republican Party of India, RPI, on democratic principles. He established the Presidium in order to carry out the responsibility of forming the party. But the leaders of the Presidium soon began to fight with each other. The promises they made while touching Babasaheb's feet were forgotten. Factions began to be formed around whether there should be changes made or not.

The party's constitution was to be written by 3 October 1957, but who it should be ascribed to became the sticking point that prevented it from being written. The Pro-Changers were all lawyers. The leader of the No-Change faction was Dadasaheb Gaekwad. It seemed to be a straight case of the trousers versus the dhotars. 'Who cares for all this paper?' asked Dadasaheb Gaekwad, mocking the writers of the party's constitution. But then the Dadasaheb of my district decided to make it his battle. And the fight began to fascinate me, as one in a tamasha would.

Dadasaheb was from my zilla. This meant I began to work for the Pro-Change faction. Almost every village had its own faction, formed according to the power groups in the village. The struggle began to acquire an unwarranted importance in political life. Western Maharashtra was carved up according to districts; Vidarbha, on the other hand, had its own sub-groups and the factions were decided according to these. The Baavanes, the Laadvans and the Kosres were the subcastes of the Mahars of the Vidarbha while Western Maharashtra had only the Somvanshis.

Awale Babuji was a mainstay of the Pro-Change faction. The people from his sub-caste in the Vidarbha were all ranged on his side. As against this, Khobragade's sub-caste was more numerous and so his strength was greater. Besides the Mahars, the Republican Party could not attract any of the other landless labourers. In other words, nothing had changed except for the names. And to add to everything, the party split.

It was not the time to sort wrong from right. I went with the flow; my chief occupation was to put what the leaders said into poetry. Shakespeare put the lines, 'Look here, upon this picture and upon this,' into Hamlet's mouth. In much the same way as the Prince compares the Usurper with his Father, I magnified the achievements of the Pro-Changers and reviled the No-Changers. The Party also had a newspaper for which I churned out many poems of this kind, all meant to strengthen the position of the Pro-Changers.

Seeing the RPI leaders in action did not leave me very impressed. Many of them would try and imitate Babasaheb. Since he had a dog, they would keep dogs. Since he used an expensive pen, so would they. Wearing a suit became the done thing. When these leaders began to turn up at condolence meetings or funeral processions in suits, I began to feel a terrible disgust. I found it difficult to see that while the villagers who had come to the city ate lhapsi on leaf plates seasoned by the dirt of the streets, their leaders ate chicken and drank alcohol in their homes. They pampered themselves on the members' contributions.

Once, I went to a No-Change leader's meeting. He finished his speech and asked for questions. My suppressed mischievous instincts came to the fore and I asked: 'People are saying that the statue of Babasaheb Ambedkar in the Fort area looks like you.' He should have been able to see the mockery in the question. He got angry instead: 'My nose looks like Babasaheb's; should I cut it off? If I am the same height as he was, should I lose a few inches?' There was much amusement at his reply.

One of the leaders of the Pro-Change group was billed as The Constitution-Maker. All the other leaders of the Pro-Change Party were loud in their praise of him. 'India's Kennedy' was the sobriquet often applied to him. This was the time of the Samyukta Maharashtra Movement. Such was the mood that if a stone had been anointed and entered into the lists, it would have won. When he was duly elected, his pride began to swell. In those days, we would meet in the evenings at Bhatia Baug. One day there was a mad scramble to get pictures taken with 'Sahib'. He reluctantly got ready to be photographed and we all went to a photo studio in Fort. 'Sahib' suddenly lost his temper as if he had been attacked by a million ants. He yelled, 'Either you walk ahead or let me.'

The followers were disappointed. Was he disturbed because they were in tattered clothes?

Sahib was stern, sometimes terse to the point of rudeness. If, by mistake, party workers turned up at his house, he would drive them from his door. If the person managed to get in, he would have to face the equivalent of a legal cross-examination.

Recently, I went to this Sahib's house. With me was a prominent Dalit writer. Since I had gone with him, 'Sahib' asked which zilla I came from. In other words, he wanted to know which faction I belonged to. While we were talking, the author happened to mention the word 'society'. After a pause, Sahib asked us, 'Tell me how you would define society.' The writer said: 'There are many possible ways. The engineer and the doctor define it one way; politicians in another; authors in yet another.' This angered 'Sahib'. He said, 'You're the first person I've met to suggest that there can be many ways to define society.' That was Sahib.

He knew nothing of Communist thought. When it suited him, he would critique Communism but when the elections approached, he would sign up where he saw his own benefit, whether with the Muslim League or the Communists.

But he was the only ideologue of the Pro-Change faction. His theme song was 'Parliamentary Democracy'. Since he had heard that when the British people presented themselves as a delegation to Parliament, they called it a petition, he would say, 'Don't call it a morcha, call it a "petition".'

The Communists were a force in the Samyukta Maharashtra Movement but the Bouddhas withdrew from the committee because they felt that if they remained, it would spread their Communist ideology. They took an aggressive stand. 'Let us uproot the seedlings of Communism from every country,' said Sahib, and his words made headlines. At this time, Dadasaheb Gaekwad announced publicly, 'I am a Communist to my bones.' He also added that he would use the tactics of Kacha—who burst out of the stomach of his preceptor Shukracharya—with the Communist Party. Dalits and Buddhists would argue vehemently in the political arena over this remark. Until recently, they would still brand Dadasaheb a Communist, based on this one statement.

When Dadasaheb was leading the nationwide satyagraha of landless labourers, the Pro-Change faction mocked him, and I appreciated their stand. But slowly this non-violent protest achieved unprecedented success.

Suddenly we understood what a 'jail-bharo andolan' meant. It was not only the Bouddhas who took part in this agitation but all the grassroots-level landless labourers who came together on the land issue. It defeated the Pro-Change critique. In spite of the dispute among the leaders, Dadasaheb participated in the satyagraha at the Nagar zilla. A group of satyagrahis from Sholapur took possession of the Collector's house. One of the workers fulfilled his long-standing ambition of sleeping in the Collector's bed. Later, he accepted his punishment with every indication of happiness.

The Pro-Change faction knew how to fashion rousing slogans. One of them was: 'Bring back the elephant as our election symbol'. Another was, 'All the Buddhist caves and stupas should be transferred to us'. And, 'Make India Buddhist'. They would enthuse gatherings with these words. Every 6 December, they would demand that the government release the confidential report on the death of Dr Ambedkar.

They began a whispering campaign that his death had occurred under suspicious circumstances and that one of the No-Changers and his Brahmin wife had been involved. This spread disaffection. At public meetings, they would demand a proper memorial that would befit his stature, a university such as the Aligarh Muslim University or the Hindu University or even a research centre that would bear his name. They asked that people should go to the bank and deposit money for this and people responded with delight. Their experience had shown that all the the money given to leaders directly, in the form of cash, ended up being misused. So this idea of depositing their contributions in a bank seemed like a solution. In seven or eight days, the figure rose to sixty-two thousand rupees. The leaders could not believe these figures. And so what happens to other funds also happened to this one. The leaders began to fight over it. The accounts were frozen. The No-Change faction popularized the idea of having a marble dome over the Chaityabhoomi stupa—the place where Babasaheb was cremated. They say it rained money but up to now, no marble has materialized. The money evaporated like mercury. The public did not get any accounts. The grassroots-level workers from all over Maharashtra had sent money orders. That money, all from Mahars who could scarce afford it, is rotting in the bank. It could not be used for any constructive social work, either.

Slowly, a sadness came over the community. The movement began to cool down, a fireplace without fuel. The shadow of politics began to fall on the cultural, social and educational institutions of the community.

That wasn't all. The effect began to be seen at wedding ceremonies, at funeral processions. Even if it were some ordinary person who had died, his attributes now had to be extolled. To speak at such ceremonies was seen as an honour by party workers. It was of course only party workers from the faction to which the dead man belonged who were so honoured; the other faction would be ignored.

'We'll take our revenge when one of our members dies,' the rival faction would say as they went home.

I remember going to one such programme in the zilla. The public meeting was held in the evening. In the afternoon, the leaders had a meeting with the workers. In a hall, the leaders were discussing political matters. I was listening with blind faith to the discussions. Just as we were to be served lunch, the announcer said in my ear, 'A respected leader is coming from Mumbai by ST bus. Will you go and meet him?' I was confused. This was a job that should have devolved on one of the local workers. It wasn't as if only I would recognize the leader; his was a well-known face. But I did leave the hall. I began to suspect that the man just didn't want me to eat with them. My mind was like a wounded bird. I did not go to the ST stand. All day, I wandered in the village. At night, without attending the meeting, I caught the bus back to Mumbai. These leaders seem to be like any other aristocrats. They have no qualms about treating their followers as slaves.

Gradually I began to learn some home truths about these leaders: men I had seen as giants were midgets. If we did not set the limits, they certainly would not. I began to hear many odd tales about these leaders. One of them went to London and returned a barrister. When he went to a village now, he felt embarrassed to bathe in the open. England had taught him to perform his ablutions behind closed doors. People would say: 'When sahib has a bath, four workers have to stand guard, holding out four dhotars as cloth walls around him.' This was how he would recreate his English bathroom. Later, this barrister ran away with a woman who was running an eatery, or so it was rumoured. He was sacked from the party.

Another RPI member, one who went everywhere in a full suit, was invited to the Ambedkar Jayanti celebration in a village. He stuffed his face with chicken; then he made a fuss about sleeping in the open. Finally, arrangements were made for a room. Right next to the room was the kitchen. The wife of the party worker whose house it was had cooked up a delicious mutton curry. She was curled up near the fireplace. In the night, this sahib's lust was aroused. In the dark, he began to make his moves on the woman. The poor lady was fast asleep. When she realized that the sahib who was sleeping in their home had suddenly begun making amorous advances, she was terrified. She began to scream the house down. The men who were sleeping outside woke up. They began to abuse the leader. But the man was too quick for them. He grabbed his suit to his chest and began to run. The workers gave chase but lost him. The next day they came to the city to seek him out. They went to the house of the person who had recommended him for the event. 'A fine fellow you sent us who comes with the intention of fondling our wives and sisters,' they say. And yet this man still wanders around, his head held high. He has even been elected to office. Who will guard us against our guards? the common man might well ask.

Dadasaheb was neither a drinker nor a womanizer. Even as children, we knew him to be free of these vices. At that time someone whose nom de guerre was Milind had written a pamphlet that became very famous. It was called 'Who Saved the Republican Party of India from the Communists?' The cover illustration was of party workers yoked to a cart with a driver wielding a whip. There was a man depicted as being dragged behind it: Dadasaheb. The man on the cart, the driver, was the man they called India's Kennedy, the man who was praised as the Constitutional Expert. The workers spoke openly about their feelings about 'Kennedy'. 'That one? He'll piss in your plate and then coo in your ear. He bites the hand that feeds him,' they said. Whatever the constructive programme, Kennedy would be there. He would talk endlessly about parliamentary democracy but he had no real belief in internal democracy. The workers believed that Milind was Dadasaheb but the pamphlet quoted Voltaire and Abraham Lincoln as Kennedy often did. And which 'Milind' could have written such a fine work? the workers wondered.

One result of this was that a split in the No-Change faction became inevitable. Angered, Dadasaheb took up government service.

—

This social work and its madness meant I paid very little attention to the home front. Saee was illiterate and found all this repugnant. She did not like to be parted from me even for a moment. Sometimes I would throw her a line I had read in Savarkar's *Kaale Paani*: 'My dear, what does the world mean? Don't the crows build their world, stick by stick? That's our world too. The grass is always greener on the other side.' These sentiments which seemed to belong in a public forum would leave her embarrassed at her illiteracy.

In the first two years, Saee failed to get pregnant. She desperately wanted to have a son. From time to time she would go to her uncle's home. This was near Golpitha in the Bombay Port Trust chawls of Siddharth Nagar. The area was not very nice. All day eunuchs and prostitutes stood around and made bawdy, raucous conversation. I wished she wouldn't go there.

Once she came back with some sacred ash from a bhagat who promised children. Generally, I did not get angry with her but this time I was furious. I threw her out of the house and did not let her back in until she had enacted one of those 'forgive-me-I'll-never-ever-do-it-again' scenes so common in plays.

Finally, she did get pregnant. I was like the poet Diwakar in Rajkamal Pictures' *Navrang*. Saee wanted a boy; I a girl. Aai was on Saee's side. She wanted a grandson to carry on the family line.

And what is one supposed to feel when one's wife and

mother-in-law are both in the family way? This mother-in-law that I'm referring to was my father-in-law's mistress of many years, a Deshmukh, a Maratha by caste. As a Deshmukh widow—her husband had died young—she was not allowed to marry again. I could not figure out what she saw in Saee's father. He was black as tar while she was very pretty; her skin fair, her body bright. When she began to show, my father-in-law brought her to the city to stay with me, his son-in-law. The woman looked pale. She was terribly embarrassed about the pregnancy and kept her gaze lowered at all times. Women in her condition—and she was in an advanced state now—generally went to Pandharpur but my father-in-law had taken it upon himself to bring her to Mumbai.

Both his mistress and his daughter delivered at the same clinic. We had a girl; she had her mother's face and dark blue eyes; her skin was pink, her body so cottonwool-soft, it seemed as if she might dissolve through one's grasp. She reminded me of a girl I had known in school. We named her Bakula. Then, to my embarrassment, my 'mother-in-law' delivered a fair-skinned boy. But when she came home, there was no child in her arms. The women of Kawakhana began to whisper among themselves. The municipal clinic had a cradle for orphaned or unwanted babies. She had put her baby there. With her head held high, she returned to the village. My father-in-law went with her. This disturbed me for a long time. That boy she abandoned, what eventually became of him?

—

I give you fair warning: I am now going to talk about private family matters. Up to this point, I have taken pleasure in describing the lives of others and their problems but I have shied away from the personal. In other words, I was simply following the Great Indian Ethic. If a man does it, it doesn't matter. But if the slightest shadow of doubt is cast upon a woman, you know the kind of Ramayana that can develop.

In all that follows how much was Saee's fault and how much our circumstances were to blame, I still cannot tell. What transpired seemed to follow the script of some suspense film, in which several strands are knotted in confusion.

It all began when our chawl was to be demolished. The owner wanted to build a multi-storey tower there. The tenants, who had lived there for generations, came together and decided that we would have to be given alternative accommodation. I had never seen the actual owner but we all knew the rent collector, Mehta, a burly fellow in a velvet sadra and dhotar. He was dark-skinned and hefty. He adopted a policy of divide and defeat. He said he was ready to provide new houses but asked who he should assign them to. We had no rent receipts in our names and Kaku, my aunt, certainly did not want us living in her new room. Just as Kaku did not want us, the cousins did not want her, their late brother's widow, to stay with them. Nor did she want them with her. Finally everyone was given different written agreements on stamped paper. Mehta would meet the tenants in different lots in order to con them. Finally we were asked to leave until the new building came up.

Everyone else spread out and made shift in other places. Aai, Saee, Bakula and I went to stay with Chander in a neighbouring building. We were all living on the dream that we would soon have homes in a fine new building. Many might find this strange, how so many of us had managed in one ten-by-ten-foot room. But in our new home, we had even less space. There were three families living here, including Chander's. At night, it was divided up by temporary cloth walls. Even today, thinking about it makes my hair stand.

For two or three months we lived here as sub-tenants, and around this time, the rumours about Saee began.

I was to blame for this too. In one corner of the building, there was a cycle shop. A Muslim youth by the name of Mehboob worked there. He was a little shorter than I, fair-skinned. He was a manual labourer at the cycle shop and so his body looked muscular. He was a sweet-natured fellow with a large stock of shaayri, Urdu couplets that he knew by heart. I liked him very much and often spent a lot of time with him. We would go out to a restaurant and have a cup of tea together. Once or twice, I specially invited him over for puran poli. One day he was feeling terribly ill so I took him to the municipal clinic. When we got home, I put Saee in charge of his medicine as he had no one in the city to make sure he took it on time. He began to sleep on a string cot in our balcony. This was when whispers started but I dismissed them as malicious nonsense. I saw them as the fevered imaginings of someone who felt that Saee, my mother and I were staying on in Kawakhana to ensure we got a home in the new building. These rumours, I thought, were intended to drive us out. As a result, I sought out Mehboob all the more. We began to spend hours in restaurants. Aai tried to warn me that Saee might be stepping off the straight and narrow but I got angry with her. 'Give me proof,' I demanded. What proof could she offer? She shut her mouth and went off to her daughter in the village. Now the trickle of talk became a flood. At the time I was writing *Buddhayana*; probably inspired by G.D. Madgulkar's *Geet Ramayana*. I had composed some ten to fifteen songs. I showed these to a college friend. He read some and said while looking at me strangely, 'What are you writing Buddhayana for? Write the Fuckayana.' (He used the word Bhogayana).

He had the same look in his eyes as my college friends now have when I walk around in Kawakhana. I reminded myself that I could have no room in my mind for doubts about Saee. I reminded myself how she had complained about my friend's advances.

How could I punish her on the basis of these vague suggestions? Her love had not dimmed after marriage. No, there could be no doubts.

But then one day I come home from work, and I shout 'Bakula' at the top of my voice, as I usually do, for I adore my little girl. The chawl is dark. Saee is not at home. Hearing my voice, she appears from the general direction of the toilet. In her hand, she has a brass vessel full of ash. I peer curiously in the direction of the toilet. Mehboob is washing his clothes there, at the tap. And finally a storm of doubts begins to whirl in my head. That night I do not sleep. I interrogate Saee relentlessly. She starts to cry, swears her innocence on her child's head. I don't know what to do. My head aches from trying to sort it all out.

The next day is Sunday. I don't have to rush to work. Where do they go to meet, these two? I tell Saee I'm going to a political meeting and slip out. Every day Saee goes shopping at the Haagri Bazaar in Kamathipura. I go there and conceal myself in a corner. If she's dressed up, I tell myself, I will know she's out to meet her lover. For getting decked up is not something Saee bothers about. She's remains unkempt and careless of her appearance. If I ask her, 'Why so slovenly?' she replies, 'Why should I dress up?' Today too she comes to the market in her usual way. But even that sweet disorder in her dress cannot conceal her beauty. I begin to regret doubting this pure and innocent face.

When she returns from the bazaar, there he is: Mehboob, standing at a corner, talking to her. I want the earth to split open and swallow me up. I walk up to them. Saee sees me and panics. I tell her to go home. I take Mehboob to an Irani restaurant. He begins to weep. 'I swear on the Quran, she is my sister…' he mumbles. I don't know what to do but I tell him he must leave Mumbai immediately.

When I return, he's packing to go back to his village. I never see him again.

A devil has awoken in me. I torment Saee through several nights, demanding the truth. She says nothing. I had read

Russell's *Marriage and Morals* but books are of no help now. I spend the next ten or fifteen days in intense internal debate. I lose weight. Now I'm reduced to a ninety-pound weakling. I often think I will die thinking my way through this. Fireflies flash and dance in front of my eyes.

One week later, it was Diwali. I bought new clothes for Saee and Bakula. I decided to take Saee and leave her at her mother's house. Saee had no idea she was to be abandoned there. When I was leaving, I told her family I had tuberculosis: 'Keep her here for a while.'

I returned to Kawakhana which seemed to mock me with memories. My restlessness increased. I began to feel I had been cuckolded. I spoke politely to no one. As night fell, the tears fell too. My heartbreak was a physical thing, an actual ache. I would fumble my way through the work day. When Kawakhana became too much for me, I would go to Sewree to my sister. She lived there with her husband.

The village began to say that I had gone mad. I found it was possible to feel love and hate at the same time. I would tear paper on the streets, throw stones, they said. Aai was shattered. She was sure Saee had used black magic against me. Once she brought a Konkani bhagat home. He sacrificed a cockerel and threw various antidotes at me. I watched, numb. I was too weak to oppose this mumbo-jumbo. Once or twice Saee came back, bringing the child with her. I would buy her a sari and blouse and give her the money to go home again. She hoped I would take her home one day. She did not know I was playing a double role.

A year passed, more, but I did not seem to be able to recover my zest for life. I seemed to have fallen, crumbled. One of my friends, Sable, was a source of strength in those days. He began to wonder how I could have managed to live without a woman for so long. In truth, he was a man of good character who did not even touch alcohol. (Nor did I feel, however shattered by all this, that I should drown my sorrows in drink.) Sable would take me each night to Foras Road, to Pawan Pul and other red-light areas. But the women repelled me.

My body was not stirred. I would wonder: 'Damn it, am I a eunuch now?'

There was a girls' hostel in the taluka. I went there once for the annual trustees' meeting, but only as an activist. The students and the cook were always fighting. The trustees asked me to resolve these quarrels before I returned to Mumbai. One of the students there had the eyes of a cat. She was fair but short. She really liked me. One of my relatives told her about my tragedy. He also added that I was very poor.

'I'll live with him in a hut,' she said.

But I was now frightened of women with light eyes. I sent no reply.

Around this time, a friend arranged a woman for me, one he had found wandering alone on Chowpatty. She was dark but good-looking. She took us to Navalkar Road. My friend waited outside the room-by-the-hour place. The woman was a prostitute who would solicit men and bring them back to her room.

'So who did you snare this time?' the others asked, laughing at me.

I was terrified. I thought I'd never be able to trust anyone ever again. When she stood nude in front of me, I felt nothing. No desire at all. With cold eyes, I looked at her. Perhaps she was surprised by the novelty of this. I still remember our conversation.

'Are you married?' I asked.

'I marry every day,' she replied despondently.

When I left without doing anything, my friend asked her what happened.

'Your friend is good for nothing,' she said.

My friend looked at me as if I were weird. This was my first and last experience of prostitution.

No, that's a lie, a small lie. I had earlier gone with a rich friend to a kotha to listen to the women sing. In front of us, four or five young women, gajras tied to their wrists, were clapping and singing.

I saw a child's slate and school bag. I saw children sleeping in the back room. All this made me uncomfortable. I could not enjoy the music.

One of the dancers reminded me of my daughter. The same blue eyes, small face, fair complexion. While she was dancing, it became apparent that she was pregnant. I felt my mind glow red-hot, a furnace about to explode.

Did my friend sense this? Who can tell? All I know is that he stopped her dancing.

—

If there was any respite during this time, it was out of an unfortunate incident that happened to someone else. The human mind is truly strange. Yes, we say, 'I wouldn't wish it on an enemy,' but when someone else suffers as we suffer perhaps there's a sneaky satisfaction in it. When I heard this story, I saw my own personal trauma as nothing.

No one in the office knew what was happening in my personal life. At the next table in the office sat an upper-caste married man. He was of unimpeachable character and a good sportsman. He was well-educated, had finished his BSc. Then suddenly he collapsed into a morass of anxiety that darkened his face. Since we sat next to each other, one day he confided in me. I could not believe what had happened to him.

He had recently left his wife. He was now fighting a court case to get custody of his children. According to what he said, his wife had committed incest with her brother. I had never heard the like. When I showed disbelief, he showed me some letters that the brother and sister had exchanged. One letter the brother had written to the sister had 'By the blessings of Sai Baba' written on the top. One of the sentences in it was telling: 'I don't see why we should stop what we've been up to even after your marriage. I'm sure you know what I mean.' I was looking at a truly twisted side of life. How could this letter be anything other than the truth? My colleague said: 'I was often on tour. And what force in the world could be greater than that with which a brother would protect his sister?' He had even photographed the letters to present them as proof. For some reason a story Javji Buwa had told me in my youth came to mind.

'There was once a Brahmin. When he laughed, pearls and coral fell from his lips. The king heard about this. He wanted this miracle worker to adorn his court so he sent his soldiers to bring the Brahmin to him. After walking about a furlong, the Brahmin remembers that he has left his almanac at home. When he gets home, he finds his wife frolicking with another man. He goes back to the court, but does not smile. Farces are presented, jokes are cracked but the Brahmin is stone faced.

'Finally, the king consigns the Brahmin to a dungeon. One night, by the light of the full moon, the Brahmin sees the King's favourite queen carrying a panchaarti, a tray with five lamps on it. She is performing the worshipful ceremony that is due to her lord and master to the stable lad. Then he demands that she get down on all fours and sits upon her back. He begins to encourage her to gallop, shouting, "Eeeya. Eeyaa". The Brahmin begins to laugh and laugh. In the morning, the jail is found to be flooded with coral and pearls.'

I now felt that there was a truth hidden somewhere in this story.

—

It was now impossible to stay in Kawakhana. The building in which we were supposed to get new homes began to rise, floor upon floor, but we choked on the dust. The owner never mentioned our homes again. Finally, Mehta dealt only with those of our relatives whose names were on the receipts. He gave them a few thousands and sent them off. Since we had no paperwork to back up our claims, we could not even go to court. To this man, the owner of the new building, who was going to sell each flat for fifty or sixty thousand rupees, we were expendable. At the end all our relatives left Kawakhana. My own mental state was precarious. I felt that my world had been destroyed, crushed by the rise of the building. Staying there meant being reminded again and again of the past.

Aai and I left Kawakhana. Aai was deeply concerned about me. Her only son's world lay in ruins about him. When Saee was around, she could not stop singing her daughter's praises, generally in such a manner as to put Saee down. Now that Saee was gone, she was snapping at the same daughter. She began to be protective of me. I found this interesting. We had no place to go in Mumbai, no place to rest our heads. We went to live with my sister at Sewree.

You have probably seen a tree growing from the fork where two older trees have taken root close together. They say that a bird drops seeds in the fork created by the two older trees and a third tree takes root there. When we went to live in Sewree, my splintered mind began to sprout new growth. I began to feel curiosity again. But before that you must understand the geographical and social environment of Sewree.

If you leave Sewree station and walk a few steps towards Wadala, a huge slum that almost touches the railway line appears. The houses, all made of tin, lean against each other. A narrow path runs in front of them. Step off the path and you find yourself in a chakravyuha. In the first week, two things made life difficult. One was Sewree's life-threatening stench. There were storehouses of dried fish in the area. You had to hold a handkerchief to your nose as you entered. But slowly you got used to it. It became a habit and you stopped smelling it at all.

The smell brings back another memory. Once, I got into the first-class compartment of a train carrying a bundle of dry Bombay duck. All the passengers began to ask each other where the smell was emanating from. They started to sniff around, trying to detect the source of the stink. Embarrassed, I got off at the next station and got into a third-class compartment. No one there seemed to smell my bombils.

The second reason that made life in Sewree difficult in the beginning was how close the local trains ran to the homes built there. As they thundered past, they disturbed one's sleep. The ground beneath one's feet shook as if in an earthquake. But one grew accustomed to that too. I read somewhere that if you have your eyes fixed on a goal and you move towards it with complete focus, you can find the happiness of heaven in the innermost circles of hell.

In this hell, my sister had carved out her life. Her room

in the chawl was ten-by-twelve, bounded by tin walls. You could hear clearly what was being said in the next house. There was a common tap outside. Your feeble attempts at personal cleanliness were vanquished as soon as you stepped out of the house. Outside was a small clearing, a tin roof over it. All around were Muslims, most from the ghats, some from the Konkan. Their dialect was an intriguing mix of Marathi and Hindi. They used phrases like 'Kaawlyaan fadka faadya' when a crow had torn a piece of cloth or 'Mhaisne gobar haagya' when they wanted to say that a buffalo had taken a dump.

Only a couple of households were Mahars. That the Muslims felt the Mahars would pollute them and would not drink or eat in Mahar homes shocked me. This was how deep caste went, how twisted its workings were. In that ten-by-twelve space, my sister, her husband, their son and father-in-law lived. And then there was my brother-in-law's Konkanastha friend Sawant and his amiable wife Champatai.

To add to all this, now Aai and I had arrived to stay. Going to the toilet was a surreal experience. I remember white worms wriggling in the shit. I learned to control myself until I got to the office.

I had moved to Sewree but I had brought my malaise with me. It was hard to erase my memories of Saee and Bakula. I would crouch on a bench in the courtyard for hours, my head between my knees. I did not feel like reading. I did not want to play with my nephew. Aai hovered around, anxious. She did not know what to do.

—

This was my emotional state when I met Salma. Now someone is going to say: Ah, *Salma*. It might occur to that person that since my world had been destroyed by a Muslim, I was seeking out a Muslim girl as revenge. But when I saw Salma for the first time and when she made the first moves to get closer to me, it was either a coincidence or you could say we were doing what comes naturally. For me, it was nothing short of a marvel.

Salma's house was right in front of ours, separated by a distance of ten or twelve feet. She would go to the common tap to fetch water, passing by our door. Whenever I sat in front of the house or in the courtyard, I could see her home.

She was a slim girl, dark-skinned, with deep black almond-shaped eyes. She must have been about sixteen or seventeen years old. She wore kurta-pyjama with a slithery dupatta. A long plait flowed down her back. She was truly attractive; the boys of the area called her Nargis, after the film star. Her body was beautifully shaped.

One day she asked, 'What is the matter with you? You sit there looking so sad.' I laughed sadly at this. She was friends with my sister and Champatai. Sometimes she would come dancing into the house on her way home. She had some idea about what had happened to me and would say, 'If your wife comes here, I'll beat her with a stick.' Who knows what she saw in me? I frightened myself in the mirror: my cheeks sagged, my eyes were sunken and had dark circles around them, the result of too much weeping.

Once she splashed water at me deliberately. I felt nothing other than a mild irritation that this chit of a girl should be harassing me. I would often feel that she was toying with me as a cat toys with a mouse. After what I had been through, this only seemed amusing. Although I didn't realize it at the time, even feeling this much meant she was breaking through.

Salma's father was a well-known gang-leader in the area. I had seen him coming and going a few times. His sharp gaze frightened me. He didn't pay much attention to Salma's mother. He had married a second time, a much younger woman with whom he had set up another home. But his writ still ran in the house. He would drop in whenever he felt like it.

Salma was unwilling to stop pursuing me. Talking to her openly was impossible. She was kept in seclusion in the zenana. She was required to wear a burkha when she left the home. But she was smart. She had only studied up to the fourth standard in an Urdu-medium school but she knew how the world worked.

We began to communicate in code. When she woke up in the morning she would sing a line from some mournful Hindi film song: 'Abhi na jaao chhod kar ki dil abhi bhara nahin' ('Do not go just yet for my heart has not had its fill') or 'Hum bekhudi mein tum ko pukare chale gaye' ('Out of the depths of distraction, I call out to you'). I would get up just as she began humming the opening bars of one of the songs of her morning repertoire. As a child might, I would once again realize: 'Oh, she's speaking to me.' She would tell me to come home early, for instance, making out as if she were speaking to her younger siblings. I was supposed to decode all this as best as I could.

I began to see a change in myself. Until a few days before that, I would have been thinking of Saee. But now Salma's dark eyes began to flash out of the files I was looking at in the office. Where I had been coming home late at night, I now hurried back as soon as I could. As I came into the chawl, I knew Salma would be waiting for me, all dressed up. She would greet me with a surreptitious salaam. I felt I had arrived at the court of a king.

It didn't take long for the Muslim women to start gossiping. They began to look at me suspiciously. If I went to the tap, they would say: 'Hey Roshan, can't you see? Your son-in-law is here.' This would embarrass me greatly. At home, my mother would beg me to cease and desist. 'Boy,' she'd say, 'that man is a monster. He'll chop you up into bits.' I would reply: 'Why? What have I done? I've stayed within the bounds of propriety.'

Aai trusted me completely. But she knew one thing: Salma had brought her son to his senses; he was now talking and laughing as he used to. Aai could feel no anger at Salma. She had started me on a diet of dried coconut and dates. When Salma came over, Aai would offer her some as well.

At that time I noticed something interesting. Even if the Muslim women had noticed something, they seemed to have never spoken of it to their menfolk. Perhaps they knew that if our flirtation came to the notice of the men, blood would be shed. That some low-caste boy should be after one of their girls would have been enough provocation.

I began to rise with the sun and exercise. I began to dress well. Someone could love me, this itself felt good. A physical relationship with Salma was out of the question. She had many watchdogs guarding her. And anyway, I had satiated myself with sex. I felt no lust for her. And yet, at times, I would flame with desire for her. It was a rebirth; a sea-change that had taken place in five or six months. People who had seen me earlier could not recognize me now. One woman had destroyed me and another had given me my life back. The power women wield was made apparent to me.

Salma's way of showing her love was tantalizing, a kind of poetry. If I said to her, 'Don't cover your hair with that dupatta,' she would pay no attention and it would stay stubbornly over her head. But the next time she appeared, it would be around her shoulders.

A trifling incident revealed to me the depth of our relationship. The festival of Id was celebrated with great enthusiasm. Through the days of fasting, a fakir would wake everyone up, singing and playing on his daf. Salma was dressed to the nines for Id. Her hands were hennaed, her eyes dark with kohl, the parting of her hair dusted with powdered pearls, her clothes festive and floral. I could not take my eyes off her. Everyone cooked sheerkurma on Id, a delicacy made of vermicelli and milk. Tradition demanded that you serve this to your guests. Salma appeared suddenly with sheerkurma for me. She put the glass bowl into my sister's hands and said, 'This is for *him*,' and she tried to make good her escape. I was halfway through a glass of tea at the time. A viciousness awoke in me. These people, I thought, avoid our homes, see us as unclean. This had been riling me for a while now. I stopped Salma and asked her quietly in Hindi, 'Do you really love me?'

To which she said, 'How would you know? Only god knows.'

I set a trap for her: 'Will you drink this tea that has touched my lips?'

To which she said, 'Tea? I'll drink poison if you give it to me.'

And she swigged the tea that had touched my mouth.

All day, pleasure tingled through my body.

Sometimes we would have pretend fights. Around this time, people would be coming to see her, to examine whether she would make a good daughter-in-law. One day, I heard that another family was coming. Whether for this boy or otherwise, she was exceptionally well-dressed that day. Her anklets were tinkling. Her hair was woven with an expensive gajra of mogras: it must have cost two or three rupees at least. She came to the door of her house dressed this way and struck a rather attractive pose. She reminded me of the Ajanta mural of the Black Queen looking at herself in a mirror. I pretended to be immersed in the book I was reading.

Finally, she could stand it no longer.

'How do I look today?' she asked.

I lost my temper. I snapped: 'I know why you've gone to all this trouble.'

That was it. Salma flew into a rage. She snatched the gajra from her hair, tore it into bits and threw them at me. I looked at her, stunned. She stomped off into the house.

When she appeared again, she was wearing crumpled old clothes. Her face bore marks of recent tears. This frightened me. I had been enjoying a mild flirtation. Had she really fallen in love with me?

What a coward I am became clear to me. Salma once sent me a letter, delivered by a child. It was written in Urdu. How was I to read it? Finally, I stationed myself near an Urdu school and got a Muslim boy to read it to me. 'Mere shehezaade,' it began. My prince? I was done for. When I heard more, I began to sweat. She suggested that we elope. Where could we go? I had never looked at her in this way. And even if we did elope, her father would have dug us out of wherever we chose to go to earth. I did not know what to do.

In Nagpada, a Mahar boy had fallen in love with a Muslim girl. Rumours were rife and so the Muslim boys of the area collared him and dragged him off to a mosque to be circumcised. For the next fortnight, he walked about with his lungi loosely tied about his waist, as if he were suffering from a disease down there.

What if that happened to me?

I realized what a high wall, a wall of religion, separated Salma and me. I began to avoid her eyes. She would mock me, calling me a coward as I came and went. Once again, I had lost a battle.

The day I had not wanted, dawned. Bedecked in flowers, Salma's groom awaited her outside the door. He had ridden up on a white horse. When he got off it, several people fell to fanning him industriously. Inside Salma's home, women began to play a dholak and sing. That day I saw no sign of her. I was distraught but not shattered, as I had been by what happened with Saee. Perhaps I had grown accustomed to these blows. But I did send Salma a nice wedding gift.

Salma's husband was a fitter and her new home was in Bhendi Bazaar. After work, my feet would turn in the direction of her new home. This was a kind of madness, I suppose, for I had no idea what her exact address was. Once I went to a mosque because someone had told me you could see the windows of her home from it, my only clue. The Muslims who were washing their hands and feet, performing the ritual ablutions of vazu looked at me with puzzled eyes. What was a kafir doing in their midst, they seemed to be wondering.

One day, as I was wandering around the area, Salma saw me from the second-floor gallery of a building. She called out my name in a voice I could not fail to hear. I was now in a quandary. What could I say if I went up? What would her in-laws think? Would they suspect? I went back home. But Salma's courage in calling out to me was a surprise.

Later, when she came to her mother's home for a visit, she took me to task. 'Why didn't you come home?' she demanded. I didn't know. What had she told her in-laws about me? Even the idea that a Hindu boy could look at a Muslim girl with eyes of love would have seemed impossible.

Whenever Salma came home she would urge me to get married. My aimless life, adrift like a kite cut loose, must have worried her.

Once I did muster up the courage to visit. It was afternoon, and her husband was at work. Her old mother-in-law was at home. Salma was delighted to see me but she was also flustered and fluttered about trying to get the hospitality right. She sent her mother-in-law downstairs to get me cold lemonade. All the while, I was studying Salma intently. She was pregnant. I don't know why I should have felt happy about this but I did. I pointed at her swollen belly and said, 'Did I have a hand in this?'

'Wash your mouth out,' she said.

That was Salma.

She had once given me a photograph. It's still at the bottom of a trunk somewhere. After all these years, I haven't been able to tear it up. She also gave me another keepsake.

She loved knitting. She knitted me a white cotton undervest that I had kept for years. When I put it on, I felt I had on a coat of armour. Later, when I married a well-educated woman, I did not hide my past from her. What was her response? She took the banian and used it to wash the floors. She did not throw it away for a long time. She would wash it clean and use it again. When it was filthy, she would dangle it as one might a dead rat and would say: 'Look, the symbol of your love!'

—

Soon after Salma got married, we left Sewree. But Salma's marriage was not why we left; it was for another reason altogether. When my sister got married, her husband had been in the last year of his school education. It was assumed that he would pass his SSC and get a job in an office. But what happened to me, happened to him. He passed quite a few subjects but failed in English. At around the same time, his mother died of cancer. His father showed no concern for the family. In his old age, he immersed himself in wine and women. I took pity on the young man's plight and got him a job as a peon in my office. So there we were: me, the boss; my brother-in-law, the peon. I did not reveal our relationship to anyone. But my brother-in-law did not particularly care for being a peon. He sat on a stool all day, reading novels. His clothes were an immaculate white, as if rinsed in Tinopal.

Everyone in the office called him 'Chhote Saab' or 'Little Boss'. He had none of my timidity. He was a peon but adopted the airs of a millionaire. He didn't seem overawed by the bosses and chatted to them as equals. Sometimes they would take him along when they went on field trips. He had heard that it was the tradition that the peons did all the cooking on tour. So on the first day, he put so much chilli powder into the food that he was never asked to cook again. Thus he sat at his ease while the bosses did the cooking. He would come back from these trips with lots of interesting stories. But he really did not like being a peon and finally he decided to go back to the village.

In the early days, he did take a beating. He opened a cycle shop but it failed. Once, he took a job as a worker in a cycle shop in the area. Things were hard; my sister had to work as a labourer. My heart bled for them at this time.

But then he set a Gandhi topi on his head and got into politics. At first it seemed to be more of his big talk but after a few years he had dug a well, planted grapes and sugarcane and had me stumped. All this because he took a basketful of government loans. I find it difficult to sleep peacefully if I owe someone ten rupees. How did he find the nerve?

Aai and I were now living with a relative. It was at this time that she fell ill. Working in the hostel kitchen had left her covered with blisters. She found it difficult to walk. She had problems with her blood pressure as well. She refused to go to a doctor; clinics terrified her. She believed that those who went to hospitals did not return. When I finally managed to force her to go, we were told that she had a growth in her stomach. She would need an operation. We got her up to the operation theatre but there she baulked. The gleaming instruments, the huge machines, the smooth tables were all too much for her. She sat up and said: 'Take me to my daughter's village. I want to die there.' Finally, I did leave her at my sister's house.

I get a telegram saying she's ill. I know what is going to happen. When I get to my sister's village, it seems like Aai is at death's door. I am deeply depressed; I have not had any real success for her to witness. She makes me sit by her side and says: 'Boy, get married. Take a bhangi girl as a wife if you must, but don't remain alone like this.'

The night she died, I had gone to Sangamner. I was to return the next evening. But when night fell, a strange melancholia took me in its grip. My brother-in-law was with me. 'Let's go back home,' he said. It was a distance of ten or twelve miles. Pitch-dark. Lonely road. Cricket song. We had to cross a river that rose up to our waists.

We arrive and Aai is drawing her last breaths. I watch her die, nursing her head in my lap. I feed her drops of milk with a spoon. My sister is close at hand, her face blotchy with tears.

It is difficult to say when she died. Death came on little cat feet. The neighbours knew but to spare my feelings, one of them said: 'Hold a thread in front of her nose.' She had given no sign of leaving. She seemed to be asleep. I had never seen so peaceful a death. My father had not gone gentle into the good night.

Why such a difference, I wondered for many years.

Aai was cremated on the banks of the river. I watched as the growth in her stomach burst into flames. And I thought: I couldn't save her, not from this, not once, not ever.

I did not weep. I performed the last rites with commendable composure. But even in this state, I did not let them shave my head. I left her remains for a long time with my brother-in-law. Whenever I went over they would say, 'Arey, take these ashes and immerse them in the sea in Mumbai, why don't you?' I thought this was foolish. I could see no difference between her ashes and any clod of earth. Eventually, I think my brother-in-law immersed them in the Godavari at Nasik.

—

Now came the desert years. My life seemed hollowed out without Aai. She had moved mountains for me. And what had I been able to offer her in return? One of the last links had been snapped. And it was all my fault. When I am alone now, a recurrent regret: Bakula. I remember a poem:

> Deep in a dark cave,
> A thread of light trembles.
> Hands seeking maternal love
> Struggle to break free.

Whose hands am I referring to? I can no longer tell. Perhaps I mean Bakula's hands. I am still concerned about her. I did want to rescue her from the Pit; the urge came back again and again. I did try two or three times. I went with Sadashiv and Sable but each time I reached the village, Saee would take Bakula to another village. She was bitter. She would say, 'Fancies himself a leader now, does he? Wait till she grows up. I'm going to offer Bakula to Lord Khandoba as a murali. I'll make her dance for him.'

When I heard this, something inside me broke.

Saee got married to an old man; he could have been my father. They say he had children my age. Why had she committed hara kiri in this way? Once or twice, I saw her in passing at the Sangamner market. She was dressed in rags. On her head, a bundle of fodder. On her back, a young child strapped to her with a dhotar. I did not dare to catch her eye. I felt responsible for her condition.

EPILOGUE

LOOK, I'VE TALKED too much. If I were a pot, my mouth would have broken. They say talking eases the mind. I don't feel much better. In fact, telling you all this has brought back some of the pain. My nerves feel slack.

I have lived my life in fear. The causes may be personal or they may lie in the deprivation into which I was born. Since we're talking about it, remember how scared I was during the Emergency? A grassroots worker who had gone underground once sent me a packet of Nirodh condoms. What had he written on it? 'Some prophylactics, because a coward like you should never have offspring.' But he too was a coward. The note was anonymous.

Not even thirty years after national Independence came the Emergency. When we regained our democracy, we began to call it the Second Independence. I was as confused and as terrified as I had been for the thirty years that followed the first. The grassroots workers who sent me the condoms must be thriving. As for me, I don't think anything has changed— same shop, same business, different signboard. I am still in the same precarious condition. At any moment, this system might spit me out onto the streets. That doesn't matter; I'm nearing the end. What this country has in store for my children is still a mystery.

It is in this state of anxiety that I keep bumping into you. People don't like it when you tell them what you really feel. But there's always an abiding fear of loneliness.

And it isn't as if I always listen to you either. Do you remember that time during the Emergency when a national organization of writers invited me to Delhi? They bought me an air ticket and booked me into a five-star hotel. Prime Minister Indira Gandhi was to be present at the conference. You kept telling me not to let this chance slip. But inside me uncertainty bubbled, as alcohol froths in a still. I refused the invitation. Once again, I lost the chance to look down at the earth from an airplane. But I did not regret it at all.

I think this restlessness is my permanent state. When it ends, I will feel as if I am bearing my own corpse and I shall feel profound grief.

Dagdu Pawar is now walking away, his shoulders slumped. Like Christ he carries a heavy cross, and it seems to have deformed him. Unlike Christ, he does not have a halo around his head; his welts have begun to fade.

Slowly, he gets lost in the crowd.

ACKNOWLEDGEMENTS

I MUST FIRST thank the Pawar family: Daya Pawar for writing this book and Pradnya Daya Pawar for trusting me with it. Pradnya was unstinting in her help, especially with the footnotes.

And my thanks also to:

Shanta Gokhale, for being my translation guru. When I said, 'Do you think I could translate *Baluta*?' she said, 'Of course,' and just as Daya Pawar's teacher turned him into a poet, her faith made me a translator.

Neela Bhagwat, my Marathi teacher, and my first filter for each work of translation that I do.

Andrea Pinto, who brought me the books I needed to contextualise my translation and located Alexander Robertson for me in the Jawaharlal Nehru Library at the University of Mumbai; and to all the other staff at JNL, including Mr Shankar Kharat, who took an encouraging interest in the project.

My personal assistant, Santosh Thorat, who discovered the first volume of a Dalit Marathi dictionary that explained many things, and to his mother, who also volunteered much local information.

Ravi Singh, who has been a constant source of encouragement and whose ability to see the book as it should be done never gets in the way of the book as the writer/translator wants to do it.

JP